Private No More

New Perspectives on the Civil War Era

SERIES EDITORS
Judkin Browning, Appalachian State University
Susanna Lee, North Carolina State University

SERIES ADVISORY BOARD
Stephen Berry, University of Georgia
Jane Turner Censer, George Mason University
Paul Escott, Wake Forest University
Lorien Foote, Texas A&M University
Anne Marshall, Mississippi State University
Barton Myers, Washington & Lee University
Michael Thomas Smith, McNeese State University
Susannah Ural, University of Southern Mississippi
Heather Andrea Williams, University of Pennsylvania
Kidada Williams, Wayne State University

Private No More

The Civil War Letters of John Lovejoy Murray,
102nd United States Colored Infantry

edited by
Sharon A. Roger Hepburn

The University of Georgia Press
ATHENS

© 2023 by the University of Georgia Press
Athens, Georgia 30602
www.ugapress.org
All rights reserved

Set in 9.75/13.5 Baskerville 10 Pro by Kaelin Chappell Broaddus

Most University of Georgia Press titles are
available from popular e-book vendors.

Printed digitally

Library of Congress Cataloging-in-Publication Data

Names: Murray, John Lovejoy, approximately 1830–1865,
author | Hepburn, Sharon A. Roger, 1966– editor.
Title: Private no more : the Civil War letters of John Lovejoy Murray, 102nd
United States Colored Infantry / edited by Sharon A. Roger Hepburn.
Description: Athens : The University of Georgia Press, 2023. | Series: New perspectives
on the Civil War era | Includes bibliographical references and index.
Identifiers: LCCN 2022031525 | ISBN 9780820363448 (hardback) | ISBN 9780820363455
(paperback) | ISBN 9780820363462 (epub) | ISBN 9780820363561 (pdf)
Subjects: LCSH: Murray, John Lovejoy, approximately 1830–1865—Correspondence. |
United States. Army. Colored Infantry Regiment, 102nd (1863–1865)—Biography. | African
American soldiers—United States—Correspondence. | Free Black people—New York (State)—
Lockport—Biography. | United States—History—Civil War, 1861–1865—Regimental histories.
Classification: LCC E514.5 102nd .M87 2023 | DDC 973.7/3092 [B]—dc23/eng/20220712
LC record available at https://lccn.loc.gov/2022031525

Contents

Acknowledgments   vii

Introduction   1
Editorial Note   37
Chapter 1. January–June 1864   41
Chapter 2. July–August 1864   62
Chapter 3. September–October 1864   79
Chapter 4. November–December 1864   96
Chapter 5. January–March 1865   118

Bibliography   135
Index   143

Acknowledgments

MANY PEOPLE AND INSTITUTIONS WERE INVOLVED IN BRINGING this project to completion. Most important among them are the researchers at American Civil War Ancestor, whose services in digitizing archival material provided the raw material on which this collection is based. Without their work, John Lovejoy Murray's letters would have languished unread in the archives. During various stages of research, I spent time in the National Archives and Records Administration in Washington, D.C., and found both the staff and their collections of great assistance. I had the great fortune to work in archives and museums in Michigan, including the Archives of Michigan, the Underground Railroad Society of Cass County, and Michigan's Grand Army of the Republic Memorial Hall and Museum, among others. Bruce Frail, with American Civil War Ancestor, provided invaluable assistance in these archives throughout this entire project. In March 2020, I was conducting research at the Archives of Michigan when I had to cut my trip short. After a two-year interruption, I returned to the Archives of Michigan and the State Library of Michigan in March 2022. There, I was able to view the original flags of the First Michigan Colored Infantry Regiment thanks to Matt Van Acker and Maurice Imhoff, who work tirelessly with the Save the Flags program to preserve, research, and display Michigan's battle flags. Matt and Maurice even allowed me to hold one of the staffs from which those flags proudly waved almost one hundred and sixty years ago.

Many others helped shape the final product. My sincere gratitude goes to Susanna Lee, Judkin Browning, and Mick Gusinde-Duffy, at the University of Georgia Press, for their help and advice through every stage of the publication process. Their patience as I worked through revisions while juggling academic and personal duties was much appreciated. Their careful editing, and that of Zubin Meer, made this book a more polished narrative. If any mistakes remain, they are entirely my own. I would also like to acknowledge those readers who reviewed different versions of the manuscript and offered their suggestions, challenging or gently prodding me to broaden my focus and approach. This book is more firmly grounded thanks to their insights. Among those readers to whom I owe a great debt are three groups of students in my American Civil War and African American History classes at Radford University, in Radford, Virginia. These students provided thoughtful suggestions from their perspective as young scholars. The annotations accompanying the correspondence in this book were shaped by their questions and comments. My hope is that this book will be a tool for learning and teaching, and if I have been successful in that endeavor, it is my students who made it possible.

I am grateful to Radford University for supporting my work, both financially and in terms of time off. My personal appreciation goes out to Kate Hawkins, former dean of the College of Humanities and Behavioral Sciences at Radford University, for providing generous research grants to digitize pension records from the archives. Without this funding, I could not have acquired all the pension files for the 102nd United States Colored Infantry Regiment and may never have seen Private Murray's file and letters. Both Kate and Matthew Smith, current dean of the College of Humanities and Behavioral Sciences, supported this project with course-release time for me to pursue my research and writing. The final stages of this manuscript were completed during a semester of Faculty Professional Development Leave, granted by Radford University. Without this time, my duties as department chair in particular would have prolonged the completion of this manuscript by several years.

I dedicate this book to my family: my parents, Armand and Meg Roger—see Dad, I do work; my sons, Ryan and Casey, who have had to share me with John Lovejoy Murray for years—maybe they will actually read this book; and my sister Marcia, who was always there to drag me on a hike up a mountain when I needed to relieve stress and never pushed me over the edge. She even picked me up a few times and never once stopped to take a picture first. She certainly did laugh though.

Private No More

Introduction

*"I came Down here to fight . . . we have Pledge
our self to Stick By one other till the last"*

PRIVATE JOHN LOVEJOY MURRAY, COMPANY E, 102ND UNITED STATES Colored Regiment, expressed the above sentiment in a letter he wrote to his mother from Baldwin, Florida, in August 1864.[1] During a skirmish with Confederate pickets earlier that day, a rebel minié ball split the wood in Murray's gun and cut the pack over his shoulder, dropping his tent to the ground.[2] Murray never returned home to reunite with his family and friends. He was one of almost forty thousand African American Union soldiers who perished during the American Civil War. An enemy bullet did not strike him down. Nor did he languish in a prisoner of war camp. Private Murray died in a hospital in Charleston, South Carolina, the victim of a ravaging fever, on April 12, 1865, three days after General Robert E. Lee's surrender at Appomattox and three days before President Abraham Lincoln's assassination.

During his service in the Union army, Murray wrote home often to his mother and other family members and friends in Lockport, New York. Never having married, John Murray left no widow or children. After his death, John's mother, Sarah Wells, applied for a federal pension based on her late son's military service. This pension file, retained at the National Archives and Records Administration (NARA) in Washington, D.C., contains fifty-six letters penned by Murray to his family and friends. Also in the file are four letters written from Sarah to her son late in the war. Sarah gave all these letters to T. D. Yeager, a special examiner for the U.S. Pension Bureau, as evidence in support of her claim.[3]

---

1. The regiment, originally organized and mustered as the First Michigan Colored Infantry, was later redesignated the 102nd United States Colored Troops (hereafter cited as 102nd USCT). Both designations were used interchangeably throughout its service.

2. John Murray to Dear Mother, Balding Station, Florida, August 18, 1864, Civil War Pension Files, RG 15, National Archives and Records Administration, Washington, D.C. (hereafter cited as CWPF).

3. Among the valuable sources housed within the depths of the National Archives with

Union veterans of the Civil War were beneficiaries of financial assistance from the federal government, most important of which was military pensions. Pension records reveal a mixed record for African American veterans. The federal government recognized their status as veterans and rewarded their service with access to military pensions for themselves and their dependents: widows, minor children, and fathers and mothers. There was nothing in the application process that required applicants to be White. The process of submitting and approving pension claims, however, was not color-blind. Various obstacles hampered African American efforts to obtain the pensions due them. Race and class discriminations embedded in a system built primarily for elite and middle-class White families intensified the difficulties Black veterans encountered. Black veterans and their dependents often had difficulty establishing their ages, the dates and legality of their marriages or proof of death of prior spouses, their legal parentage, and the birth dates of themselves and their children. White veterans and their dependents also confronted such impediments, but they were not as prevalent as they were among the Black community, nor were they as difficult to resolve. These challenges did not necessarily prevent African Americans from receiving pensions, but they certainly made the process more complicated and lengthier. Regardless of whether such delays or outright rejections were due explicitly to racial discrimination, they nonetheless posed a hardship to African American veterans and their families.[4]

Although Sarah Wells encountered challenges in her quest for a pension, race does not appear to have been at issue, at least not in any overt way. Rather, the Pension Bureau initiated an investigation after another

---

the potential to contribute significantly to scholarship are the vast pension collections of Civil War soldiers and their dependents. While scholars continue to explore the Archives' records, the pension files and the rich documents contained within them remain underused.

4. Logue and Blanck, "'Benefit of Doubt'"; Sven E. Wilson, "Prejudice and Policy"; Shaffer, *After the Glory*.

The 102nd USCT serves as an example of the experiences of Black veterans within the pension system. Of the 695 102nd USCT veterans to apply for invalid pensions, 607 were successful in their efforts (87.3 percent); 324 of the 437 widows who applied for a pension received one (74.1 percent), as did 36 of the 68 minors who submitted claims (53 percent); 31 of 51 dependent parents who sought a pension were approved (61 percent). Organization Index to Pension Files of Veterans Who Served between 1861 and 1900, T289, NARA.

woman submitted a conflicting application.[5] There were two John Murrays enrolled in the 102nd USCT. John Lovejoy Murray, Company E, was the son of Sarah Wells. John Murray, Company K, who deserted less than two months after his enlistment, was the son of Catharine Murray who lived in Detroit. When Catharine learned that a John L. Murray died in Charleston during the war, she became convinced that her son was dead and that she deserved a mother's pension. Catharine's filing for a pension triggered the special examination into the validity of Sarah's request. Sarah furnished wartime letters in her possession to the special examiner in her case to prove that John was her son and that her claim for a mother's pension was legitimate. After his investigation, Special Examiner Yeager concluded "beyond a doubt that Sarah Wells was the mother of the soldier and the correspondence between the claimant and soldier confirm that fact." Sarah subsequently received a pension of eight dollars per month.[6]

Despite Yeager's promise to Sarah that the letters "should be returned to her as soon as possible," they never were.[7] At the expense of John Murray's family and friends, who parted with these precious pages from their loved one, readers today are able to experience the war through the eyes of a literate northern free Black solider. The documents submitted to the Pension Office are not just a few scattered epistles. This collection composes a significant intact body of communication. Its sheer quantity is in itself remarkable. The Murray collection is the largest known to exist from the 102nd USCT.[8] The letters printed

---

5. If an application for pension was suspect for any reason, the Pension Bureau assigned a special examiner to personally obtain additional testimony from the claimant and witnesses, judge for himself the validity of the claim, and make a recommendation as to whether it should be granted, denied, or subjected to further examination.

6. John Murray, CWPF.

7. T. D. Yeager to Mr. Moore, Chief Widow's Division, Pension Office, September 9, 1873, John Murray, CWPF. The Pension Bureau often failed to return to their owners many of the items provided during investigations. Letters, marriage certificates, and photographs, among other items, submitted as evidence in a pension application often became part of the permanent pension files. Several pension files of veterans of the 102nd USCT include correspondence penned during the war. Others contain photographs of soldiers taken during or after the war, and marriage certificates are commonly found.

8. Besides the Murray collection, the available pension files associated with the 102nd USCT contain only a few letters written during the war. Substantially smaller than the Murray collection is a cache of letters written by or for Private Alonzo Reed, Company E, located in the Rubenstein Rare Book & Manuscript Library at Duke University. Other

Special Agent Yeager, September 9, 1873.
Civil War Pension File, NARA; photo by American Civil War Ancestor.

within this volume represent the entirety of extant correspondence received by Murray's family and friends. How many letters, painstakingly scribed by John, were lost or destroyed in transit is unknown.[9]

Mail was a treasured link between Civil War camps and battlefields and home. Writing and receiving letters helped morale. It maintained the connection between soldiers and civilians: husbands and wives, brothers and sisters, sons and mothers. By 1860, the federal postal service was the nation's largest bureaucracy and during the war was an ef-

---

record groups in the National Archives contain a small number of communications authored by 102nd USCT soldiers. There are undoubtedly some letters scattered in local historical archives and still others held in private collections.

9. Excerpts contained in Special Examiner Yeager's report suggest that there were letters written by Murray to friends that the Pension Bureau did not retain in the file. Presumably they were shown but not given to Yeager.

fective communication system. It was this relatively reliable and cheap postal system that encouraged a regular exchange of letters between soldiers and their family and friends; between the battlefront and the home front. Although precise numbers are not, and never will be, available, letters "carried to and from the armies numbered in the tens of millions over the course of four years."[10] Millions of personal stories were thus recorded and preserved for posterity. Letters such as those featured in this work are a means of recovering the human dimensions of war, providing valuable insights into what it was like to serve during America's most deadly conflict. Along with diaries and journals, letters from soldiers like Murray afford readers today the closest contact possible with actual Civil War soldiers, allowing us to eavesdrop on their innermost thoughts and feelings.

Wartime created difficulties for postal delivery. Correspondents had to wait for weeks, even months, to receive mail. While it was relatively easy for the army post to find soldiers when they remained encamped for several weeks or more, armies were often in motion. This continual shifting of location made delivering the mail a challenge. Friends and family at home had to rely on information from a soldier's last letter regarding his whereabouts, but there was no guarantee that the soldier was still stationed at that camp and with his regiment. Murray closed most of his correspondence with instructions as to where exactly to send letters to him. In several letters in December 1864 and January 1865, he specifically mentioned that the mail was disrupted because of fighting in the area. In others he informed his family that his regiment was temporarily moving, but he encouraged them to continue writing, assuring them that the letters would find him. Other inevitable wartime disturbances interrupted postal services. It is clear from both John's letters home and those written to him that the intended recipients did not receive all their correspondence. However, it seems that most letters were received.

John Lovejoy Murray was born free in Edinburgh, Saratoga County, New York, located north of Albany.[11] Without a birth certificate, family Bible record, or other documentation, the exact year of his birth is unknown. When he enlisted at the end of 1863, he gave his age as thirty-

---

10. Bonner, *Soldier's Pen*, 9. See also Barton and Hall, *Letter Writing*.

11. Named after the city of Edinburgh in Scotland, the town of Edinburgh, New York, lies on the shores of Great Sacandaga Lake.

four. State and federal census enumerations show his age as nineteen in 1850, twenty-five in 1855, and thirty in 1860. While none of these records constitutes definitive proof, taken together they indicate a birth date of between 1829 and 1831. There is no indication that either of his parents were ever enslaved persons, though they could have been. In 1799, New York passed an act for the gradual abolition of slavery. A subsequent law passed in 1817 set July 4, 1827, as the date of final emancipation within the state. Sarah was born in Niagara County, New York. The birthplace of John's birth father, Alonzo Murray, is unknown. Alonzo died near Rochester, New York, around 1840, while John was still a child. John's widowed mother married Asher Wells on February 15, 1841, in Lockport. John did not take his stepfather's name, but he consistently referred to him in his letters as "father," suggesting a close relationship between the two. No evidence suggests that John had any siblings.[12]

Within a year or two of Alonzo Murray's death, John's mother, probably for financial reasons, sent her son to live with another family. According to family friend Lucinda Crain, John came to live with her stepbrother, Albert Adams, when John was about twelve and remained there until he was twenty-three. He then lived with his mother and stepfather for the next several years. From 1856 to 1859, John resided with Chester F. Shelley, sheriff of Niagara County, for whom he worked. Shelley was part of the Crain family, married to Lucinda's sister, Clarissa. The full extent of the relationship between Murray and the Crain family is ambiguous. At various times before his enlistment, he worked for different members of the extended Crain family. Lucinda and John, and perhaps other members of the Crain family, exchanged letters during Murray's military service. Lucinda was instrumental in proving that Sarah was indeed the mother of John Lovejoy Murray, providing several supporting affidavits on her behalf. What makes the relationship between the Crain family and John Murray less common at the time is that the Crains were White.[13]

---

12. John Murray, CWPF; U.S. Federal Census, 1830–1880; New York State Census, 1845, 1855, 1865; John Murray, Compiled Military Service Record (hereafter cited as CMSR), RG 94, NARA.

13. John Murray, CMSR, CWPF; U.S. Federal Census, 1850, 1860; New York State Census, 1845, 1855, 1865. John Murray appeared twice in the 1860 federal census. On an enumeration dated July 9, 1860, in Niagara County, Murray's name was part of a list of

The 1860 census records John Murray's occupation as a waiter at the Eagle Hotel of Lockport owned by Lyman Spaulding. For at least one season and perhaps more until his enlistment in the Union army, John Murray farmed for shares on Albert Adams's farm. Affidavits in the pension file attest that his share amounted to $200 one year. While off at war, he encouraged his mother to have his crop of wheat harvested, telling her that there was "eleven acre in the field if the wheat is good it will be Just as goad as A Hundred Dollars in your Pocket."[14] John was literate by the time he enlisted. Perhaps his literate mother or a member of the Crain family, likely Lucinda or Adam, taught him. He closed many of his letters with "excuse bad spelling," indicative of an awareness of proper conventions that might suggest a level of formal schooling, though no evidence indicates that John attended school at any age.

In the fall of 1863, John Murray traveled more than two hundred miles from Lockport to Detroit. Information in the pension records suggests that Murray headed to Michigan seeking employment. His mother believed he left New York intending to find work in the lumber business, not to enlist.[15] It was not inconceivable, of course, that John kept his true intentions from his mother to spare her from worry. If his primary objective was to enlist, he need not have gone to Detroit. He could have enlisted in one of several other Black regiments already in existence or in the process of organizing, among them the Fifty-Fourth and Fifty-Fifth Massachusetts Colored Infantry Regiments, the Twenty-Ninth Connecticut Colored Infantry Regiment, and the Twenty-Sixth United States Colored Infantry raised in Murray's home state of New York. At least one associate of his, Elias DeGroff (DeGraw), enlisted in the Twenty-Ninth Connecticut Colored Infantry the same month Murray enlisted in the First Michigan Colored Infantry. Presumably, other Black men from the Lockport area with whom Murray was acquainted joined different regiments.[16] There is no indication of any personal ties to the state of Michigan behind his enlistment.

---

hotel employees. Murray was also a member of Albert Adams's household on the enumeration for Niagara Falls taken on July 19, 1860.

14. U.S. Federal Census, 1860; John Murray to mother and father, Hilton Head, S.C., June 12, 1864, CWPF.

15. John L. Murray, CWPF.

16. Elias DeGroff (DeGraw), CMSR. Elias enlisted in Connecticut on December 19, 1863.

Murray was one of almost three hundred men who volunteered for the First Michigan Colored Infantry in December 1863. The mobilization of free Black communities in the North depended on patriotic appeals and organization aided by governors and others. Most frequent among the reasons noted by Black soldiers for fighting in the Union army were emancipation, saving the Union, and fighting for equality, the last in terms of the right to vote, the opportunity to own land, equal treatment before the law, or full citizenship. There are no clear indications in Murray's letters pointing to any fervent ideological or patriotic impetus for his enlistment. Intensified recruiting efforts in and around Detroit likely helped entice Murray. Perhaps recruiters awakened his patriotism and sense of duty. Perhaps the lure of a soldier's income proved more promising than a laborer's job in Detroit. Contextual evidence throughout his letters suggest that Murray enlisted to receive a substantial bounty. Again, there was no clear indication of why he joined the First Michigan Colored specifically. Other enlistment opportunities with bounties were available. Recruiting agents from Rhode Island were in Detroit during the fall of 1863, and they may have offered a higher bounty. Whatever his motivation may have been, Murray enlisted as a private in the First Michigan Colored Infantry Regiment on December 1, 1863, pledging to serve the U.S. Army for three years. He was subsequently assigned to Company E.[17]

Henry Barnes, a British-born abolitionist, was the force behind the organization of the First Michigan Colored Infantry. Barnes cofounded the *Detroit Tribune* newspaper in 1851, and when the *Tribune* merged with the *Detroit Advertiser*, he became editor of that Republican-affiliated newspaper. In the spring of 1863, Barnes began a campaign to raise a Michigan Black regiment. He first appealed to Governor Austin Blair for approval and assistance, and when Blair, unlike Massachusetts governor John Andrew, proved to be less than enthusiastic, Barnes turned to Secretary of War Edwin Stanton. In July 1863, Secretary Stanton instructed Governor Blair to raise "one Regiment of colored Infantry in the State of Michigan. To these troops no bounty will be paid. They will receive ten dollars per month . . . three dollars of which . . . will be

---

17. *Detroit Free Press*, September 15–17, 1863. According to military service records, 270 men enlisted in the First Michigan Colored Infantry in December 1863. Private Murray was credited to the First Congressional District of Michigan, Lenawee County, Township of Tecumseh. 102nd USCT, CMSR; John Murray, CMSR.

deducted for clothing, these troops will be commanded by White officers."[18] Barnes accepted a commission as colonel and recruitment for the First Michigan Colored officially began in August 1863. When John L. Murray enlisted a few months later, fewer than four hundred men were then in the regiment.[19]

Through the fall and winter of 1863–64, while recruitment for the regiment continued, members of the regiment quartered and trained at Camp Ward, named for the Detroit industrialist and leading Republican Eber B. Ward.[20] The camp was part of the Union army's barracks complex located on the city's east side just a short distance from the Detroit River. There the men endured less than ideal conditions that exacerbated the already poor health of many of the soldiers. Shoddily constructed barracks, initially built for temporary use, exposed the men to the elements. Persistently leaky roofs, a lack of flooring, and crevices in the walls large enough to let snow in provided little protection from a bitterly cold winter.[21] Private John Anderson later recalled that, during the winter at Camp Ward, they "had no blankets for some time nor beds . . . and the weather cold and snow on ground."[22] Similar accounts by other soldiers who suffered for months in the barracks at Camp Ward echo Anderson's statement. The weather took an especially bad turn at the beginning of the new year. Thursday, December 31, hovered around forty degrees, but the temperature plummeted and dropped to well below zero the next day. According to a local newspaper, at least twenty members of the First Michigan awoke New Year's morning frostbitten in their bunks, many of them in seri-

---

18. Asst. Adj. Gen. C. W. Foster to Gov. Austin Blair, July 23, 1863, War Department, Washington, D.C., in Robertson, *Michigan in the War*, 488–89.

19. 102nd USCT, CMSR; Descriptive Book, vol. 1, Book Records of Volunteer Union Organizations, 102nd USCT Infantry, 5 vols., E112–15, RG 94, NARA (hereafter cited as Descriptive Book).

20. Fort Wayne, located on the south side of Detroit, served as a mustering post and training camp for many of Michigan's volunteer infantry and artillery troops during the Civil War. Whether for racial or other reasons, the State of Michigan War Department did not assign the First Michigan Colored Infantry to Fort Wayne, instead ordering the construction of Camp Ward on the campground of the Fifth Michigan cavalry. McRae, *Negroes in Michigan during the Civil War*, 48.

21. Dr. Charles Tripler to Bennett H. Hill, December 19, 1863, Records of the Office of the Quartermaster General, Consolidated Correspondence; *Detroit Free Press*, December 3, 1863, December 28, 1863; Taylor, *Old Slow Town*, 37, 60, 72–74.

22. John Anderson, CWPF.

ous condition.[23] Among them were Ambrose Spence, whose feet froze so badly that he could not stand on them; James Simons, who was "frozen blind"; and John Brown, whose "face froze and the skin was peeled off the left side of [his] face." In consequence of exposure on the parade grounds and in the barracks, at least eight men died that winter at Camp Ward. Scores of others contracted chronic rheumatism and other debilitating diseases that wreaked havoc on their bodies for decades to come.[24] Although there is only one known piece of correspondence between John Murray and his family back in New York to depict John's personal experiences while at Camp Ward, he seemed not to have suffered as badly or fallen ill as so many others did, at least not to the point of hospitalization.

Private John Murray's letters show that his experiences during his seventeen months as a soldier were typical of many African American soldiers. He was with the regiment during its various excursions to Florida, and to Hilton Head, Charleston, Orangeburg, and Beaufort, in South Carolina. He was often on picket or provost duty. He drilled, marched, tore up railroad tracks, built fortifications, skirmished with the enemy, and of course, wrote letters to, and received letters from, home. Sick at the time, he did not participate in the regiment's two significant battles: Honey Hill, South Carolina (November 29, 1864), and Deveaux Neck, South Carolina (December 9, 1864). He died before the regiment began occupation duties at the end of the hostilities in April 1865.

The rediscovery, transcription, and publication of John Murray's correspondence serves in a way to bring Murray back to life and provides a much-needed additional collection of Civil War letters from Black men in blue. Its publication supplements the published collections of soldier correspondence in which Black voices have been underrepresented. When Bell Irvin Wiley wrote the introduction to the second edition of *The Life of Billy Yank: The Common Soldier of the Union* in 1978, he noted "a dearth of letters written by the 200,000 Blacks who donned

---

23. To protect the soldiers from the extreme temperature, the men were removed from their quarters and temporarily moved to different private houses. Whether the men were moved to private homes rather than nearby Fort Wayne because of their race is only supposition, but it does merit consideration. *Detroit Free Press*, January 4, 1864.

24. First Michigan Colored Infantry: Monthly Returns, 1864, Records of the Michigan Military Establishment, RG 59-14, folder 4, oversize box (ovs) 80, Archives of Michigan, Lansing (hereafter cited as Monthly Returns, 1864); Ambrose Spence, James Simons, and John Brown, CMSR, CWPF.

the blue. A careful search has turned up less than a score of these sources."[25] Over a decade later, James McPherson noted in his foreword to Virginia Adams's *On the Altar of Freedom*, "Civil War bookshelves are replete with volumes of letters written by White soldiers. But published letters by Black soldiers are rare."[26] Additional works have been published in the decades since the printing of *On the Altar of Freedom*, but the numbers remain relatively small and even fewer are printed collections of a single soldier. Noah Trudeau's 1996 work, for example, is a collection of letters from the Fifty-Fifth Massachusetts Colored Volunteers.[27] Many works use African American soldiers' letters as sources, to supplement other archival material, but not necessarily as their primary focus. Recent among these publications is Deborah Willis's *The Black Civil War Soldier: A Visual History of Conflict and Citizenship*. In this exploration of the role of photography to recreate the Black Civil War narrative, Willis supplements the photographs with, among other material, letters.[28] Few editions focus exclusively on correspondence of a single soldier. In large part this is because only a small minority of the approximately two hundred thousand African American soldiers in the war were literate. Two-thirds of the Black soldiers in the Union army were newly emancipated enslaved persons, generally men who could not read or write.

Private John Murray was not as eloquent a writer as Corporal James Henry Gooding, the author of the correspondence constituting *On the Altar of Freedom*. Nonetheless, historians' understanding of Black soldiers in the Civil War is richer because of the Murray collection. Most of the published works of African American Civil War writings like *On the Altar of Freedom* and *A Grand Army of Black Men*, the latter edited by Edwin Redkey, are collections of communications written by Black soldiers to African American and abolitionist newspapers. Indeed, the most prolific source of Black testimony about Civil War soldiering are dispatches USCT soldiers sent to northern newspapers. In *A Grand Army of Black Men*, Redkey used the *Christian Recorder*, of Philadelphia, and the *Weekly Anglo-African*, of New York City. As Redkey noted, "The soldiers who wrote to newspapers considered themselves representa-

---

25. Wiley, *Life of Billy Yank*, 16.
26. Adams, *On the Altar of Freedom*, xiii.
27. Trudeau, *Voices of the 55th*.
28. Willis, *Black Civil War Soldier*.

tives of their race and pioneers in the struggle for equal rights. They were acutely conscious of the discrimination they faced, both nationally and in the army."[29] These dispatches provide a window on the public aspects of the war for Black soldiers. But it is in letters like Murray's that we find the more personal accounts of the experiences faced by Black soldiers.

Fortunately for the modern reader, Civil War correspondence was subjected to little scrutiny and monitoring, certainly far less than in later wars where official censors monitored the flow of information. The frankness of John Murray's pen is thus typical of much Civil War correspondence in his open discussion of his experiences, frustrations, and potentially contentious issues. Murray's epistles do not have such a public or apparent social perspective because he was not writing for a public audience, but rather, a private one. At least as private as could be expected at the time. Most Civil War communications were not truly private. Letter writers, including Murray, knew that what they recorded was likely to be read aloud and to an audience. Nonetheless, Murray wrote to and for his family and friends. His correspondence was only shared with a small circle of people in the Lockport, New York, community. As such, the outlook offered to readers is one not generally seen in written communications from Black soldiers to governmental officials or to the press. Indeed, herein lies their value. There is a difference in tone, subject, and style, between letters written for public or political consumption and those addressed to home. Murray's letters were more personal than political in nature. While he related some of the activities of the regiment as a whole, and its role in the larger military objectives, he discussed more his personal activities. His purpose was not to provide readers with a detailed summation of military expeditions and engagements or to extol the virtues of his regiment, but to let friends and family know what he and his comrades were doing on a more intimate level. His correspondence has a much less formal quality to it than letters to the editors appearing in newspapers. Editorials from soldiers philosophized on the social and racial questions of the day whereas Murray spent more time talking about individuals and community happenings. When Murray conversed about inequality of pay, for instance, he typically kept the conversation on a more personal level and did not expound about the greater issues of eman-

---

29. Redkey, *Grand Army of Black Men*, xiv.

cipation, citizenship, and equality at large. While many of the topics and perspectives generally are similar, Murray wrote for personal consumption, not a mass audience. In this respect, Murray illustrates how, within the diversity that prevailed in Civil War America and the armies that it raised, soldiers like Murray maintained their individuality in the face of common hardships and the regimentation of army life.

A comparison can be made between Murray's letters to his mother and those from other members of the 102nd USCT to the editor of the *Detroit Advertiser and Tribune* and published in that paper. While providing news of the regiment's activities, these army correspondence editorials were also intended to exalt the men. Chaplain Waring wrote, "You can tell the ladies of Detroit that the flag they gave us waves over none but brave and determined soldiers." In a letter describing the regiment's action in a recent battle "M" wrote that he "never before saw men exhibit such unyielding bravery in battle... many who were wounded quite severely refused to go to the rear, but kept on fighting while the blood was flowing from their wounds." Meanwhile Murray wrote home that he expected "our Rid Is Cut all to pieces." Following a visit to the hospital after the battle he had a more impassioned description of his wounded comrades, telling his mother that "Some Had there Under Jaw Shoot off. Some Ear and leg an Arm nose. Some Shoot through the neck. It was A Horable Sight to See."[30]

The Murray letters offer a less mediated source for understanding literate Black soldiers from the North than letters published (and edited) by abolitionist journals or newspapers. The letters were placed in John Murray's pension file just as they were written by him in the field and read by family and friends, and they have remained in the pension record since the 1870s. These letters were not passed from one generation to the next as a prized heirloom. They were not stored in a family chest or displayed in a curio cabinet and taken out and read on special occasions or at family gatherings. Indeed, only a handful of people have seen them since the closing of the pension record in the late 1880s.

In addition to the value of John's letters as communication between a soldier and his mother, the letters written to John from his mother Sarah express the hopes and fears of a soldier's mother. Extant correspondence such as these are also rare. Letters sent home by a soldier

---

30. *Detroit Advertiser and Tribune*, December 21, 1864, January 11, 1865; John Murray to Mother, Pocotaliga, S.C., Dec. 7, 1864, John Murray, CWPF.

to his loving family were often cherished and preserved. More difficult to find are those letters sent to a soldier, in Murray's case, sick, hospitalized, and separated from his tent mates. Nevertheless, in this case, they found their way back to the family after his death. This communication from mother to son contains trivial community news, information of family and friends at home and off at war, general comments on family finances and health problems, and the heart-wrenching despair of a mother who fears her only son dead. The Murray collection, more so than letters published in newspapers or elsewhere, illustrates the importance of the connection between soldiers and family. They highlight how Black families and communities attempted to cope with the challenges and dislocations of the war. Mail from home provided comfort to the soldiers while mail from the seat of war provided comfort to those who remained at home.

Sarah, ill herself, repeatedly expressed how concerned she was for the health of her son, both physically and spiritually. Her unvarnished words illustrate how emotionally challenging it was for family members on both the home front and the front lines; desperately wanting to but unable to assist, nurse, or comfort one another except via long distance correspondence. With each of Sarah's letters, the raw emotion of not knowing whether loved ones were still alive tugs at the heart strings. Her words convey her anxiety of not hearing from her son for over a month, the anxiety of the unknown as she imagined him sick, wounded, or taken prisoner. Ultimately, she "made up [her] mind" that her dear son was dead.[31] Sarah voiced an earnest appeal to God to see her son once more, in heaven if not on earth. She encouraged John to commit his heart and soul to God before his time on earth ended and it was too late. These few extant letters are enough to reveal her strong sense of spirituality, something entirely lacking in John's correspondence. None of John's letters mentions God or religion, a fact that likely fueled her angst about his spiritual well-being.

Not unexpectedly, Sarah relayed to her son the family's financial woes. Murray's family, as did so many families of northern Black troops, lived closer to the economic margins than most White families. They suffered economic hardship when a male family member, in this case, a son, was in the army rather than at home helping to support the family. These thoughts undoubtedly weighed heavily on John's mind,

---

31. Sarah Wells to John Murray, Lockport, N.Y., March 25, 1865, John Murray, CWPF.

fueled by a sense of guilt at not being available to help the family more in their time of need and his sense of responsibility to aid and protect his mother. These letters also provide insight into how Black families perceived the war and their role in it. Sarah, like so many other mothers and fathers, was aware of the significance of the war, of the role Black soldiers like her son played, and of the sacrifice he and others were making. "No nation can be free with out sheding blood so if this be true the collerd soldiers will have a name in history I hope if justus is done them."[32] One of Sarah's final letters, written on April 11, 1865, expressed joy and relief at the ending of the war and hope that her son would soon be home. Unbeknownst to her at the time, John never read those words; he had not survived the war.

This collection of letters helps tell the story of Black soldiers as they struggled to freedom. Though Murray's wartime service was not terribly distinguished in the conventional military sense, his reflections on the tedium, discomfort, and danger of garrison life as well as campaigning gives interesting insights into the day-to-day aspects of wartime service and its impact on the troops. His is the story of the soldiers who did not receive accolades for their heroic actions, the ones who spent more time laboring than in battle on the front lines, the ones who died from disease more often than combat. Murray's letters are significant because they are ordinary in some respects yet extraordinary in others. They are significant precisely because his dispatches are replete with mundane everyday matters, and yet they reveal genuine interpretive insights into Black soldiers' Civil War experience. Some of the activities and sentiments portrayed in the letters are hardly distinguishable from those described by White soldiers. Murray exhibits how White and Black soldiers shared the same, decidedly human, concerns in wartime. Murray's communications home are typical of the genre. John opened his letters in much the same way as letter writers of the time did: with a basic statement regarding his own health, good or bad, and the hope those back home were well. A perusal of Civil War–era letters will find, as it will in the Murray correspondence, requests for soldiers and those at home to exchange their "likeness," or photographs. Requests for money or advance warning of money they would soon send home are peppered throughout Civil War mail. Murray's

---

32. Mrs. Asher Wells to John Murray, Lockport, N.Y., April 18, 1865, John Murray, CWPF.

correspondence was no different. Predictably, Private Murray complained about drilling and marching, the weather, his poor health and disease, officers, poor equipment, pay, poor food, and rumors that circulated widely in army camps generally. And like soldiers in wars, John repeatedly urged his mother to write him more often and to send love to family and friends at home.

Black soldiers, as did White soldiers, came from a range of backgrounds and experiences. Some were enslaved persons at the time of their enlistment. Others were freeborn. Some were born enslaved but had either acquired their freedom legally or sought their own freedom by running away. Black soldiers represented both urban and rural America. More Black men who enlisted resided in the South than in the North before the war. Most were unschooled and unlettered. Most were farmers or laborers, but they also represented a wide variety of occupations.[33] Murray identified himself as a farmer. Although many of his experiences may have been typical, John Lovejoy Murray himself, a literate, freeborn, northern Black man, was atypical among Union Black soldiers. This shaped the content of his letters. His unusual background, different from those African American soldiers who were born in slavery or came from the South, often made his viewpoints quite distinct. Having lived his entire life in the free state of New York and never having experienced the life of an enslaved person, Murray likely viewed slavery in a less personal manner. Enslavement would have been more distant and abstract to some degree than say, to Robert Sasser, a comrade of Murray's who had been enslaved until 1864, when he escaped from slavery and enlisted in the Union army. As is clear from his letters, Murray's attitude toward enslaved persons, particularly those who were refugees, was not entirely sympathetic or positive. Indeed, at some points he was downright hostile in his views toward them. Murray's opinion of southerners, Black and White, would have been different had he lived even a part of his life in the South, as did many of his comrades. As readers will observe, Murray's attitude toward southerners was colored by his northern upbringing. In several of his letters John discussed differences in weather, crops, dialect, and even animals

---

33. According to the military service records of the men in the 102nd USCT, over 660 were farmers and approximately 415 were laborers. Close to 250 men described themselves as skilled laborers, including barbers, sailors, masons, blacksmiths, hostlers, shoemakers, waiters and cooks, mechanics, and teachers. 102nd USCT, CMSR.

and insects, between North and South. Positively or negatively, Murray's life experiences colored his view of the South and of southerners, and thus his experiences as a soldier in the Union army stationed primarily in South Carolina.

As expected of soldiers drawn from a largely illiterate population, most of Murray's comrades in the 102nd USCT were unlettered. Only about 25 percent of the regiment's soldiers signed their enlistment papers.[34] The rest of the men signed by mark. This distinction is by no means a definitive indication of a soldier's literacy. Certainly, some of the signatures were not actually those of the volunteers themselves but were those of a recruiter, friend, or relative. Signing one's name to enlistment papers does not necessarily mean the men were literate in the sense of being able to read and write, only that they were able to sign their own name, a substantive distinction.

To modern readers, Murray's spelling, syntax, grammar, and lack of punctuation or standardized capitalization may be jarring. For those unfamiliar with mid-nineteenth-century letters, it may be hard to place Murray's writing more contextually. There is a striking contrast between the quality of Murray's handwriting and the errors of spelling and grammar in his correspondence. His penmanship is quite good, giving the reader a better insight into the soldier's background, perhaps an indication of some schooling. At minimum it required extensive practice. Private Murray, who was sometimes penning three letters a week, perhaps more if he was helping his comrades by writing letters for them, was likely among the more literate of his comrades.[35]

Murray's letters home provide a window into the environmental challenges that plagued soldiers, Black or White, stationed along the coast of South Carolina. What Surgeon Wesley Vincent of the 102nd USCT referred to the "malarious influence in the hot climate of South Carolina."[36] Murray chronicled the ravenous fever that plagued him for

---

34. 102nd USCT, CMSR.

35. During the Civil War, literate soldiers, Black and White, often helped their comrades by penning letters for them. Although Murray himself never explicitly stated that he wrote letters for friends, it seems likely that he did, even if only on occasion.

36. Wesley Vincent, CWPF. The belief that Black people were not as susceptible to malaria as White people was part of the justification for recruiting Black soldiers; so that they could be sent to the highly malarious areas of the South, including the coastal region of South Carolina where the 102nd USCT spent most of its service. Humphreys, *Intensely Human*, 45–46.

months before his hospitalization and ultimate death. Murray regularly reported not just on his health but on the overall condition of the regiment as well. Not only did his ill health prevent him from doing his soldierly duty for weeks on end, but various sicknesses ran unchecked through the regiment, at times seriously detracting from the fighting strength of the unit. The number of men not available for duty due to illness was often substantial. At the end of July, just before the 102nd USCT started out from Beaufort, South Carolina, on an expedition to Florida, there were only 440 enlisted men reported present for duty with the regiment.[37] Sixty-six enlisted men were absent in the hospital and another 146 were sick in their quarters, not fit for duty. During the fall months, from September through November, when the regiment was stationed at Beaufort, no fewer than 173 men each month were reported sick, either in their quarters or hospitalized.[38]

Black soldiers in the Civil War suffered from sickness and disease more intensely than White soldiers and were far more likely than their White comrades to die of disease.[39] Many of them entered the war disadvantaged by a lifetime of malnutrition. Most, like Murray, came from rural areas and were thus more isolated from childhood diseases. They thus had a greater proclivity for, and lowered resistance to, contracting infectious diseases. Albeit difficult to quantify, evidence indicates that inadequate medical care was an important factor in the health issues of Black soldiers. Black regiments rarely had their full complement of medical attendants: one surgeon and two assistant surgeons. The 102nd USCT generally had two, but rarely all three, of their assigned physicians present together.[40] They benefited somewhat by the service of a trained physician who served as a hospital steward, though he also was

---

37. Forty-seven men were on extra or daily duty, and nine were under arrest. Monthly Returns, 1864.

38. Monthly Returns, 1864.

39. About one of every twelve White Union troops died of disease, while among Black Union soldiers the rate approximated one out of five. Berlin et al., *Freedom*, 633. See also Black, "In the Service of the United States."

40. In May and June 1864, both Surgeon Wesley Vincent and Assistant Surgeon Edward Jennings were present with the regiment. A second assistant surgeon, William Spiers, joined the regiment at Beaufort in mid-June 1864. The three physicians were only all reported present with the regiment in July and October 1864. Jennings resigned effective November 5, 1864, and a second assistant surgeon was never assigned to the regiment, leaving Vincent and Spiers in charge of the medical needs of the men. Both Vincent and Spiers suffered debilitating ailments of their own. Monthly Returns, 1864, 1865; Wesley Vincent, Edward Jennings, and William Spiers, CMSR.

absent for several months, first on sick leave and then hospitalized himself.[41] The quality of the medical staff within Black regiments, as established by Margaret Humphreys and others, was often poorer than within White regiments. White physicians, like White officers, were eager for promotion and were willing to transfer to Black regiments to acquire that rank. Wesley Vincent served as an assistant surgeon in the Eleventh Regiment, Michigan Infantry from December 1862 until April 1863, when he resigned to return to civilian life. Shortly after, in August 1863, Vincent requested an appointment as surgeon, specifically stating that "if the good of the service required it, I would be willing to be assigned to a colored regiment."[42] Vincent further specified that he did not want an assistant surgeon's commission. He was subsequently appointed surgeon of the 102nd USCT. Before his service as an assistant surgeon in the 102nd USCT, William Spiers served as a private in Company H, Twenty-Second Indiana Infantry. For at least part of that time, he was on duty as a hospital steward and was detailed in the medical department, but he held no medical rank until mustering in with the 102nd USCT.[43]

Historians of African Americans in the Civil War often point to a dearth of available trained and competent physicians by 1864, which led to lower standards and poorer qualifications exacted for medical personnel and particularly hindered recruitment of qualified physicians for USCT regiments. This is not meant to indict the physicians of the 102nd USCT. In truth, not much is known about the medical care Murray received either by the regiment's physicians or at the hospital.[44] Murray did not often discuss his medical treatment. He did not name

---

41. James B. F. Curtis. Curtis was absent sick from the regiment from the beginning of September 1864 until early February 1865. Even before that, though, he was sick and unable to attend properly to his duty. James B. F. Curtis, CMSR.

42. Wesley Vincent to Gen. W. A. Hammond, Lapeer, Mich., August 17, 1863, and September 1, 1863, CWPF.

43. William W. Spiers, CMSR, CWPF.

44. Vincent was an 1847 graduate of the Willoughby Medical College and practiced in Ohio and Michigan before the war. Federal censuses and draft registration records show Edward [Edwin] Jennings a practicing physician in Midland County, Michigan, yet no indication or record of his medical background has been located. William Spiers enlisted as a private in the Twenty-Second Regiment Indiana Infantry on August 15, 1861. Records show that he served at least part of the time as a hospital steward. The 1860 census records Spiers as a schoolteacher in Indiana. Although he graduated from the University of Michigan Medical School in 1867, it does not appear that he had any medical training or education before the war. Wesley Vincent, Edward Jennings, William Spiers, CMSR,

any of the doctors who treated him. Many soldiers avoided doctors and hospitals, yielding to medical care only when too weak to resist. Murray himself at one point stated, "I Shant go to the Hospital If I can Help my Self," despite then being sick with a fever.[45]

As historian Margaret Humphreys points out, the history of Black soldiers' health and medical issues suffers from a discrepancy in source materials available for White soldiers and for Black soldiers. Much of what is known about White soldiers' experiences comes from diaries, letters, and official reports, which are scarce for Black troops. This book's collection of letters, of a more personal nature, helps to provide context for scholarship on African American health during the Civil War.

These letters bring readers into the everyday camp life of Murray and his comrades. Murray peppered his correspondence with details about the weather, insects, prices of commodities, and conditions of the local crops. He told his mother of eating old flour with worms, mule meat, hardtack, and stewed beef. His mother, when she read of her son soldiering with dirty ragged clothes, no shoes, and no tents, was undoubtedly saddened. She surely passed along the news he shared with her of men from the community who, like her son, were fighting in the Union army. Likewise, she shared information with John about the whereabouts of his friends. Murray's letters described the various duties and activities he and his comrades performed, such as picket and guard duty, drilling in heavy artillery, building forts, marching, and tearing up railroads. Perhaps just as telling are things that Murray did not talk about. He did not regale his home audience with stories of how he and his comrades liberated people from the bonds of enslavement. He did not directly verbalize feelings of patriotism and duty, or manhood and citizenship. Nor did he extol the raison d'être of so many Union White soldiers: of saving the Union, ending slavery, and preserving Republican ideas. Contrary to the idea of war as continual exertion and strife, his letters highlight, for contemporary and present-day readers, just how often the troops were not fighting. He retold his adventures with a Union gunboat stationed in the area and described from his view on the sidelines the aftermath of battle his comrades fought with the enemy at Honey Hill and Deveaux Neck. In a letter written after

---

CWPF; U.S. Federal Census, 1860, 1870, 1880; Civil War Draft Registrations Records, 1863–1865, Ancestry.com.

45. John Murray to Dear Mother, Crew Soil, S.C., November 17, 1864, CWPF.

the regiment returned from an extensive expedition to Florida, Murray told his mother how she would be contacted if he died and that there was no need for her to worry about not hearing from him: "If I get kill our Captain will write to you. He is Bound to write if Enny one get Captured or Kill."[46] This reassurance from a young man to his mother about his possible death is stated so calmly it seems rather shocking to today's reader.

Almost every one of Murray's letters discussed financial concerns of some sort, highlighting the importance of wartime economics. Pay was the most contentious and blatant form of discrimination encountered by African American soldiers during the Civil War. When Black men put on the blue uniform of the Union army, they expected to receive the same financial compensation as White enlisted men, despite the federal government's actions to the contrary. Pay became a symbol of their larger struggle for equality. For most, it was a matter both of necessity and principle. Although few Black men enlisted solely for the money, they and their families often desperately needed the income promised to them by recruiters. Murray's family in New York was no exception. Throughout his writings, John mentioned his intention to send money home, acknowledging his family's need for assistance. His letters often portray a sense of urgency to their financial situation. The extant letters from Sarah to her son further illustrate their financial straits. In one letter, she let her son know that her husband, Asher, had not yet paid his taxes and, she feared, would not be able to. She despaired that the winter was so cold that their hogs froze and Asher was not able to haul wood so the family burned their fence to keep warm.

Throughout most of 1864, Murray provided a running commentary on the differential pay between White troops and enlisted men of the USCT. Murray's correspondence shows an awareness of, and participation in, the widespread protest against unequal wages first provided for by the U.S. government to Black soldiers. While perhaps not contributing any insightful revelations, Murray's numerous comments about unequal pay and treatment by the U.S. Army do confirm and effectively capture the anger, uncertainty, and tensions generated by the inequity.

The subject of unequal pay for the First Michigan Colored Infantry raises an interesting question. Secretary of War Edwin Stanton's instructions to Governor Blair in July 1863 clearly stipulated ten dollars

---

46. J. L. Murray to Mother, Coo Saw, S.C., September 30, 1864, CWPF.

per month as the amount of pay for enlisted men. The organizers of the First Michigan thus knew the regiment's pay would be unequal to that of White privates even before recruitment started.[47] Unless Barnes and other recruiters tried to hide that fact from potential recruits, soldiers like Private Murray signed on knowing what the pay scale was but then later became more aware of the injustice of the inequity. Interestingly, Murray's earliest letters from Detroit did not contain any discussion of pay inequity. Granted, there is no way of knowing how many letters he actually wrote during this time, but in those few extant letters, the subject of pay inequality is conspicuously absent. In fact, he did not mention anything in regard to the controversy until a letter dated April 11, 1864, from Annapolis, Maryland. The regiment arrived in Annapolis on April 1. His letter of the eleventh was only the second written after the regiment left Detroit. This may provide insight as to when Murray and his comrades perceived of their pay as a substantive point of contention, even though they would have known about the inequity during their time at Camp Ward. During the regiment's months of encampment and training in Detroit, however, the First Michigan Colored Infantry was the only Black regiment in the vicinity. Indeed, until the men arrived in Annapolis it is likely that they had not been in proximity to many Black soldiers aside from those in their own regiment. The timing of Murray's initial missive expressing his dissatisfaction indicates that perhaps he and his comrades were not fully cognizant of the injustice of the pay being offered them, at least not to the point of protest, until they were exposed to contentious discussions among other Black soldiers, outside Detroit.

Murray referred specifically to sixteen dollars as the amount he and his comrades demanded. This figure considered that White privates at the time received thirteen dollars per month plus a three-dollar clothing allowance. The pay of Black soldiers was less than clear when Black soldiers were first enlisted. Confusing the matter was the interpretation of the convoluted language of the Militia Act of July 17, 1862, the only law directly addressing Black military personnel. The 1862 Militia Act enabled the president to receive Black men into service for whatever

---

47. In 1862, Secretary of War Stanton authorized equal pay and rations for regiments of Black South Carolinians, and in 1863 Governor John Andrew of Massachusetts raised Black regiments with the promise of equal pay. But these precedents did not apply to all Black soldiers. Recruitment campaigns, especially those aimed at northern free Black men often assumed or implied equal pay. See Belz, "Law, Politics, and Race."

purpose he found them competent. The 1862 Militia Act, primarily concerned with Black men's role as laborers, authorized the pay of laborers at ten dollars per month. On June 4, 1863, the War Department issued a general order that set Black soldiers' pay at ten dollars per month, minus three dollars for clothing.[48]

Black soldiers expressed their disaffection at the unequal pay in a variety of ways. Some penned editorials and petitions to bring attention to their cause and seek redress. Others refused to accept the lower amount. Such protests against the discriminatory pay reached beyond the well-known actions of the Fifty-Fourth Massachusetts Colored Infantry Regiment immortalized in the 1989 movie *Glory*.[49] In mid-November 1863, former enslaved persons in the Third South Carolina Volunteer Infantry Regiment stacked their arms and refused to perform any duty despite warnings from their regimental commander that their action constituted mutiny. Sergeant William Walker was subsequently court-martialed and executed by firing squad in February 1864 for his role in leading this protest. In Texas, a company of the Rhode Island Fourteenth Colored Heavy Artillery refused to accept their pay. Several dozen protesters were court-martialed and sentenced to imprisonment for up to a year at hard labor.[50] Murray often mentioned other Black regiments, including New York, Maryland, and Connecticut units, when he discussed inequality of pay. Pay was something that united Black soldiers. When Murray thought the paymaster was going to pay the regiment in July 1864, he wrote home that "all the Northen Ridgement gointo stack Arms."[51] When it came to refusing to submit to inequality of pay, "the Northern Boys Stick together titer then ticks."[52]

Murray's letters highlight the significance of the dispute over pay to him and his comrades simply by virtue of the time he allotted to dis-

---

48. General Orders 163, War Department, Adjutant General's Office, Washington, D.C., June 4, 1863, in U.S. War Department, *The War of the Rebellion: A Compilation of the Official Records of the Union and Confederate Armies*, 128 vols. (Washington, D.C.: Government Printing Office, 1880–1902), ser. 3, vol. 3, 252 (hereafter cited as *OR*).

49. The Fifty-Fourth and Fifty-Fifth Massachusetts Colored Regiments were at the vanguard of the protest over the pay inequity, most of them refusing to accept unequal pay for well over a year, even refusing the state of Massachusetts's offer to make up the difference in pay. See Trudeau, *Voices of the 55th*; McPherson, *Negro's Civil War*, 201–5.

50. Court-Martial of Sgt. William Walker, 3rd S.C. Vols., file no. MM-1320, Court-Martial Case Files, RG 153, NARA; Berlin et. al., "Writing Freedom's History."

51. J. L. Murray to unnamed, Beaufort, S.C., July 17, 1864, CWPF.

52. J. L. Murray to Mother, Beaufort, S.C., July 22, 1864, CWPF.

cussing the inequality. The first time the regiment was set to get paid, Murray made his stance clear: "last Friday the Pay Muster Come to Pays us off[.] Part of Ridgement took Seve Dollars a month But I would give my time to Uncle Sam Before I would sign the Pay Roll."[53] Noticeably, here and in other places, Murray did not speak harshly of any comrades who did accept their pay. Well aware of the financial stress of many of the men and their families, he did not seem to have any disrespect for them. When the payrolls were first sent to the regiment to be signed, many enlisted men refused to sign the pay musters, despite urging by officers. Captain Wilbur Nelson advised the men of his company to "take what they could get but they appeared set in their determination." He later recorded that many of the men of Company I "wouldn't draw their pay because it is only seven dollars a month." Captain E. J. McKendrie, reported that only nine of the sixty men in Company E received their pay in May 1864. Sergeant George G. Freeman, Company E, helped lead the protest. He "counseled the men of his Co to stack their arms and not do any more duty until it should be known that they were to receive more than seven dollars per month." Freeman was reduced to the ranks September 12, 1864, for disobedience of orders and neglect of duty.[54]

Murray in part equated the lower pay with the unequal status associated with former enslaved persons: "They want to give us Contreband Pay that $10 a month we want $13," referring to the wages paid to Black laborers.[55] Murray perceived the difference in pay being a mark distinguishing laborers from soldiers. He conveyed his sentiment that equal pay was a symbol of manhood or citizenship, writing that he and his comrades demanded that the government "give us our Sixteen Dollars then we will fight like A man But not for less."[56] In short, Mur-

---

53. J. L. Murray to Mother, Hilton Head, S.C., May 2, 1864, CWPF. At this time, there is only Murray's word here that he did not sign the pay muster. The term "pay off" as used by Murray indicates being paid.

54. Special Orders No. 67, Hd Qrs 102nd Regt USCT, near Port Royal Ferry, September 27, 1864, Order Book, vol. 3, Book Records of Volunteer Union Organizations, 102nd USCT Infantry, 5 vols., E112–15, RG 94, NARA (hereafter cited as Order Book); Diary of Capt. Wilbur Nelson, Company I, 102nd USCT, Michigan State University Archives & Historical Collections, April 27, 1864 and April 29, 1864; George G. Freeman, CMSR; Capt. E. J. McKendrie to Brig. Gen. L. Thomas, August 17, 1865, Letters Received, ser. 360, Colored Troops Division, RG 94, NARA.

55. J. L. Murray to unnamed, Annapolis, Md., April 11, 1864, CWPF.

56. J. L. Murray to unnamed, Beaufort, S.C., July 17, 1864, CWPF.

ray substantiates what other Black soldiers express elsewhere. To accept lower pay would be equivalent to acknowledging that the worth of Black soldiers was less than that of their White comrades in arms. Inequity of pay compromised the cause of equality, justice, and republicanism. Men who fought and died for their country had earned the rights of citizenship within it.

Largely due to the pressure exerted by Black protests such as those conducted by Murray and his comrades, Congress passed a military appropriations bill in June 1864 that authorized thirteen dollars per month to Black soldiers who were free on or before April 19, 1861, retroactive to the time of their enlistment. Then, on June 20, 1864, Congress increased the pay of soldiers, Black and White, to sixteen dollars per month. Beginning in late 1864, Black soldiers began to receive their equal wages. Finally, in early September, Murray wrote home that "we was Paid Sixteen Dollars month."[57]

In addition to the rate of monthly pay, the subject of bounty money played a prominent role in Murray's mail. Bounties were a contentious issue among Civil War soldiers, Black and White. Between 1861 and 1865, federal, state, and local governments paid out over $700 million in recruitment bounties as enticement to volunteer enlistees. In July 1861, Congress authorized a hundred-dollar bounty to men enlisting for three years. The Enrollment Act of March 1863, designed to stimulate volunteer enlistment in hopes of lessening the impact of an impending draft, provided $300 to three-year enlistees. Depending on the wealth of the districts, state and local governments sometimes offered bonuses to help meet quotas without having to resort to the draft. The bounty system, imperfect to start, abounded with fraud. Poorer localities saw many of their able-bodied eligible residents enlist in places offering a higher bounty, thus hampering the ability to meet their own quotas. Dishonest men cheated the system by enlisting for the bounty and deserting at the earliest opportunity, pocketing the money. These so-called bounty jumpers then went to a different locality and continued their scheme until caught. The system gave rise to bounty brokers who demanded a fee for their services even though men did not need to

---

57. J. L. Murray to unnamed, Coo Saw Island, S.C., September 2, 1864, CWPF; Appropriations Act of June 15, 1864, *OR*, ser. 3, vol. 4, 448; Circular No. 60, August 1, 1864, *OR*, ser. 3, vol. 4, 490–93. In January 1865, Congress further rectified the inequity in pay by giving all Black troops, irrespective of former status, equal pay retroactive to January 1, 1864.

go through a broker to enlist and receive a bounty. Unscrupulous brokers stimulated bounty jumping by enticing men to enlist, desert, and re-enlist and thereby increasing the fees they pocketed. To discourage bounty jumping, governments and other entities often paid out bounties in installments, typically thirds, rather than one lump sum.[58]

Secretary of War Stanton's authorization of an African American regiment in Michigan distinctly stated that the men who enlisted would not receive any federal bounty money. It is unknown whether Murray knew about this exclusion. Regardless, it is clear from Murray's writings that he believed himself due a federal bounty and more. Stanton's preclusion was only for a federal bounty. Nothing prevented recruits from receiving state and local bounties. The state of Michigan did offer bounties to recruits, including those of the First Michigan Colored. When Murray enlisted in December 1863, an act of March 6, 1863, entitled him to $50 in state bounty money. A substantial number of men who enlisted in the First Michigan Colored Regiment received state and other bounties ranging from $100 to $300, but many of them did not receive what was owed to them until after they mustered out of the service.[59]

In the fall of 1863, some Michigan communities including Detroit, Kalamazoo, and Ypsilanti, began offering bounties to Black recruits in the hopes of filling draft quotas. In November, Cass County approved a $150 bounty to all, including Black recruits, who enlisted from that county. In Detroit, the Wayne County Board of Alderman approved a hundred-dollar bounty to every volunteer, regardless of race, credited to that county's draft quota. To discourage bounty jumping, the county board allocated the bounties in the form of bonds that the soldiers could not cash until their enlistment expired. The system and management of these bounties was fraught with controversy. For financial reasons, many of the men recruited for the First Michigan Colored Infantry were anxious to sell their bonds for a percentage of their value rather than delay compensation. Their families desperately needed the funds. The editors of the *Detroit Free Press*, a newspaper associated with the Democratic Party and consistently opposed to the use of African Americans as soldiers, accused Henry Barnes of defrauding enlistees

---

58. Murdock, "New York's Civil War Bounty Brokers."
59. Michael O. Smith, "Raising a Black Regiment in Michigan"; *Detroit Free Press*, February 11, 1866.

out of their bounties. The allegation was that Barnes coerced recruits to sign their bonds over to him for a lower percentage than they might have received elsewhere, thus procuring substantial sums for himself. Barnes retorted that he was trying to protect recruits from bounty brokers and other unscrupulous men who would defraud the recruits of an even larger part of their bounty. He insisted that the enlistees were aware of his actions and the reasoning behind them.[60]

Whether or not at the prodding of the *Free Press*, several Black enlistees, James Ester and Charles Davis among them, attested that Barnes had indeed induced them to transfer their Wayne County bonds to him for a considerably smaller sum than the hundred-dollar face value. Ester claimed that Barnes gave him twenty-five dollars for his bond. Davis stated that Barnes approached him and many of his enlisted comrades and offered them twenty dollars each for the title to their county bonds. Davis said that he and others sold their bonds to Barnes because Barnes convinced them that if they did not accept his offer they would end up with nothing.[61] Henry Barnes vehemently denied such charges. In a rebuttal editorial printed in the *Detroit Advertiser and Tribune*, Barnes rejoined that "there is not one word of truth, nor a single circumstance or incident to justify any of the aspersions in the article of the Free Press. It is a lie."[62] Captain William T. Bennett, then commanding the regiment at Camp Ward, came to Barnes's defense. Bennett characterized the transactions between Barnes and the enlistees as voluntary and mutually beneficial to protect them from speculators. Even though Private Murray enlisted in Detroit, he was credited to Lenawee County and thus was never directly involved in this particular controversy involving Wayne County bounties. He did at times, however, allude to it as he did when he avowed that Barnes "mad his Brage that he has Mad forty thousand Dollars out of the Black."[63]

---

60. *Detroit Free Press*, August 25, 1863, September 21, 1863, October 24, 1863, October 29, 1863, and November 18, 1863; *Detroit Advertiser and Tribune*, October 30, 1863, and November 20, 1863; *Cass County Republican*, November 19, 1863.

61. *Detroit Free Press*, October 23, 1863. Military records show that Henry Barnes recruited both Ester and Davis and that both were due one hundred dollars in bounty. James Ester and Charles Davis, CMSR.

62. *Detroit Advertiser and Tribune*, October 24, 1863. The *Detroit Free Press* fired back that the affidavits of Ester and Davis were "in due form, and verified before public officers." *Detroit Free Press*, October 25, 1863.

63. *Detroit Advertiser and Tribune*, October 26, 1863; *Detroit Free Press*, October 28, 1863. John Murray to unnamed, Hilton Head, S.C., May 19, 1864, CWPF.

The dispute over bounties became divisive within the regiment. Chaplain William Waring, for one, believed that it was the "operations of bounty speculators" that resulted in "much acrimony" among the recruits at Camp Ward.[64] Murray and others made a correlation between bounties and desertion. John wrote home about his conviction that bounty jumpers were the primary deserters within the regiment: "they have benn a great meny men from Canada Enlisted and get there Bounty Deserted to Winsor."[65] Evidence suggests that Murray's charge was a viable one. William Campbell appeared on a descriptive list of deserters with the remark that "he having enlisted and received his bounty left his camp the following day." Some men deserted so quickly after their enlistment that it seems likely they were bounty jumpers. George Johnson, George Jacobs, and William Jackson mustered in on December 30, 1864. Johnson deserted the next day, Jacobs on January 2, and Jackson on January 4.[66]

Readers will note numerous letters from Private Murray that discuss bounty matters, even more than pay inequality. His letters make it quite obvious that Murray believed someone swindled him of his bounty money. In early May 1864, he lamented that "they Partly Cheated me out of my Bunty."[67] It is unclear how much bounty Murray was promised or was actually due him. Since he enlisted in Detroit, Wayne County, Murray may also have felt that he deserved the Wayne County bounty and was thus deprived of that incentive when he was credited to Lenawee County.[68] His military service record does

---

64. Wm. Waring to Adjutant General, Hilton Head, S.C., June 9, 1864, Letters received by the Adjutant General, Main Series, 1861–1870, M619, roll 0321, RG 94, NARA.

65. John Murray to Mother and Father and Grandmother, Detroit, March 10, 1864, CWPF.

66. Edward Cahill, 1st Lt., Company K, 102nd Reg. USCT to Hon. Chas S. May, Lt. Gov. of Michigan, Camp 102nd Reg. U.S. Colored Troops, Beaufort, S.C., July 13, 1864; Edward Lowe, William Campbell, George Johnson, George Jacobs, William Jackson, CMSR.

67. J. L. Murray to Mother, Hilton Head, S.C., May 2, 1864, CWPF.

68. The pension record details the difficulty Sarah Wells's attorney had in affixing the amount of bounty owed John Murray for his enlistment. One of the problems was that he enlisted in Detroit but was credited to Lenawee County. Volunteer enlistees were sometimes credited to towns and counties other than where they physically enlisted so as to raise the number of enlistees from those localities and thus lessen the effect of the draft. This practice resulted in controversy in regard to the draft quotas in addition to the bounties. John Murray, CWPF.

not shed light on any bounty money either paid to him before his death or owed to him. Murray likely overestimated what was due him, but in his eyes, it was a substantial amount: "My State Bounty is four hundred and fifty Dollars my other if I should Stay will Be three hundred more in all will be $750."[69] Murray's mother was also convinced that her son was due bounty. In one of her letters, she commented on the broken promises of bounty money. Sarah Wells ultimately received a hundred-dollar bounty for her son in August 1866 and another hundred dollars as allowed by a Congressional Act of July 28, 1866.[70]

Murray's thoughts and experiences add depth to understanding race and race relations from the perspective of a northern free Black soldier. A notable dimension to race relations in Murray's worldview is the apparently close relationship he had with part of the White community in Lockport, New York. The family friends to whom Murray sometimes wrote, and to whom he often referred, were members of a well-respected extensive White family in Niagara County, New York. Albert Adams, whom Murray lived with for many years, was the town clerk for Cambria in 1861. Chester Shelley, for whom Murray sometimes labored, was a longtime sheriff. Shelley served as a government storekeeper and superintendent of the gas works after the war. Before her marriage to Asher Wells, Sarah was employed by Squire Spaulding, one-time postmaster of Lockport, living in his household. For many years Asher Wells worked for former New York governor Washington Hunt, even borrowing money from him to buy land. The testimony provided in Sarah's pension claim make it clear that she and her family had close ties to several well-established White families. Murray's contact and relationship with White people were surely different from that experienced by many other, if not most, Black soldiers, particularly those who had been enslaved. He viewed racial matters through a lens distinct from many other soldiers. These experiences and background might have made Murray more likely to form cross-race alliances and relationships while

---

69. J. L. Murray to Mother, Coo Soil, S.C., September 11, 1864, CWPF.

70. In August 1866, Sarah received $272.29 for pay due John Murray for services from July 1, 1864, to his death on April 12, 1865. The check also included $100 bounty allowed Murray by a Congressional Act of July 22, 1861, and $30 arrears of pay minus what he owed for clothing, $7.57. In February 1868, the Treasury Department paid Sarah Wells an additional $1,011 for pay due her son and $100 bounty allowed by the Act of July 28, 1866. Sarah Wells to John Murray, Lockport, N.Y., April 18, 1865; John Murray, CWPF.

a soldier. They may also help explain Murray's oft-expressed animosity towards southern Black people, particularly those formerly enslaved.[71]

Murray adds insight to the relationship between African American soldiers and White officers. His outlook toward his commanding officers varied. Shortly after his enlistment John described Col. Barnes as "one of the best of men."[72] Several months later when he reported, inaccurately as it turned out, that Barnes was in prison in Washington, D.C., Murray seemed pleased by the news and hoped that "they will keep him there."[73] In one letter he called his commanding officer, Col. Henry Chipman, "the meanest man this Side of hell."[74] In telling his mother that his captain, referring to Captain Edward McKendrie, was sick and not expected to live, Murray conveyed a rather negative opinion of him when he stated that he did not consider it "much lost."[75] Elsewhere he wrote that his officers "are the Best of men they Prtect Collored men Quicken then they would white."[76] What underlying experiences led to Murray's changing opinion is unclear. Private Murray provides further awareness as to how he and his comrades perceived the attitudes that White officers expressed toward Black soldiers. Shortly after the battle of Honey Hill (November 29, 1864), Murray wrote that "the commander in this Department give the Black man the Prais of Doin the Best Fighting." Admittedly though, this praise was reluctantly given. Murray noted that "it make some of them Squirm to give us the Prais."[77]

Throughout its service, but especially when stationed in and around Beaufort, South Carolina, the 102nd USCT served alongside other African American regiments. There was also ample opportunity for White and Black soldiers to interact with one another on and off the battlefield. Murray made numerous remarks as to the relationship between Black soldiers such as himself and the White soldiers with whom they served. His commentary on racism, or lack thereof, is interesting in that

---

71. U.S. Federal Census, 1830–1880; New York State Census, 1845–1875; John Murray, CWPF.

72. J. L. Murray to Father and Mother, Detroit, December 15, 1864, CWPF. Murray misdates this letter. The correct date is January 15, 1864.

73. J. L. Murray to unnamed, Hilton Head, S.C., May 19, 1864, CWPF.

74. J. L. Murray to Mother, Beaufort, S.C., June 19, 1864, CWPF.

75. J. L. Murray to Mother, Coo Saw, S.C., October 20, 1864, CWPF.

76. J. L. Murray to Mother, Beaufort, S.C., November 4, 1864, CWPF.

77. J. L. Murray to Mother, Pocotaliga, S.C., December 7, 1864, CWPF.

he indicated that he encountered little racism and discrimination. His experience was that "the white Soldier and the Collord are on Friendly terms."[78] While in the Hilton Head area in the summer of 1864, he noted, "I have seen from one Hundred and fity thousand soldier and a Better Sett of Boys I ever saw." Murray continued, "we don't even here the word nigar I hard more in one Day at the North then I heard it in the five week South."[79] Of these same men, Murray observed that he and his comrades "eat and sleep" together and "camp alonge side of them." Being "mix up with the white Soldier," Murray often saw little distinctions made. Indeed, he once remarked that "Black man White man are also like here."[80]

Murray's commentary on such matters provides a valuable sense of what Black and White troops shared in their wartime experiences as infantry. These topics suggest that there was no sharp color line when it came to such typical soldiering experiences as receiving mail, complaining about poor food and bad weather, marching, drilling, and performing guard duty, facing the trauma of combat, and experiencing the disease-ridden army camps. They impress on readers the commonalities of army life during the Civil War. The common soldier, Black or White, marched and ate en masse, and slept and bathed in shared quarters. Disease, injury, and death were experienced by all. The fates of military life rarely respected rank or race.

Murray provided his observations of southern White attitudes toward him and his comrades. Of southern soldiers, he once commented that "the Reb hate us worst then the Devil." He admitted that race in of itself was not the sole reason for such attitudes, however. Murray said that Confederate soldiers would "fight a white man quicker then they will a Black man Johnny Say they Dont want to fight us they want fight those who maid the war they say we did not make the war."[81] Probably referring to White South Carolinians, he stated, "There kind of People I dont like I have suffered a Enough to Blow Every one Up they are not the same race as those in Floid they are like those at the north."[82] Southern white attitudes, in Murray's worldview, were best encapsu-

---

78. J. L. Murray to Mother, Crew Soil, S.C., November 18, 1864, CWPF.
79. J. L. Murray to unnamed, Port Royal, S.C., May 14, 1864, CWPF.
80. J. L. Murray to unnamed, Port Royal, S.C., May 14, 1864, CWPF.
81. J. L. Murray to unnamed, Coo Saw Island, S.C., September 2, 1864, CWPF.
82. J. L. Murray to Mother, Beaufort, S.C., November 4, 1864, CWPF.

lated in his statement that "they Say if this Country is to Be Rule By the Damn Nigars they will leave the Country."[83]

Somewhat surprising, Murray harbored extreme antipathy toward self-emancipated individuals or "contrabands" as he referred to them, whom he encountered in South Carolina and Florida.[84] His letters indicated that he was not alone in his sentiments. He revealed one source of contention between the groups: "the Contband Ridg dont like us we know to much for them our Ridge like to Drive of their Ridgement into the sea."[85] John described a physical altercation in early July 1864 between his comrades and a regiment presumably composed of southern Black refugee soldiers who, according to Murray, despised "the Black Buckey or Black Yankey." As Murray relayed the incident, men of the 102nd USCT "took Club and brick and Drove them Back" after members of the other regiment called them cowards. Murray boasted that if they had not been stopped, his comrades would have ensured that "there would not been A Cointreband Ridgement on the Island."[86] Several months later, John expressed his own harsh attitude toward southern Black laborers: "I wish Every one of them was in the army I must Stop Because it make me mad I have no good feeling for them."[87] Murray voiced an even more virulent personal animosity, admitting that "if I Could have my way I would Shoot Everyone of them I have Been into mud and water up to my waist Knight and Day Ever Sence we Been Here most of our men are in the Hospital on the Account of them."[88] It seems clear that Murray lay some, if not most, of the blame for the suffering he and his comrades endured on the enslaved refugees.

Murray offered frank criticism of the enslaved refugees whom he

---

83. J. L. Murray to Mother, Beaufort, S.C., June 19, 1864, CWPF.

84. "Contraband" was the term adopted by the U.S. military authorities and used by others to refer to wartime refugees: enslaved persons who escaped to Union lines or who followed the Union army. Murray uses "contraband" throughout his letters; however, more appropriate terminology to avoid the connotation of the term as property is "enslaved refugees" and "refugee laborers" or "soldiers." Murray uses the term "contraband" to refer both to soldiers and refugees interchangeably.

85. J. L. Murray to unnamed, Beaufort, S.C., July 17, 1864, CWPF.

86. J. L. Murray to Mother, Beaufort, S.C., July 10, 1864, CWPF. The only other reference to this incident discovered to date is a notation made by O. W. Bennett in the Report of the Guard for July 6, 1864. Regimental Letter, Endorsement, Order, and Guard Report Book, vol. 2, Book Records of Volunteer Union Organizations, 102nd USCT Infantry, 5 vols., E112–15, RG 94, NARA (hereafter Guard Report Book).

87. J. L. Murray to Mother, Crew Saw, S.C., October 11, 1864, CWPF.

88. J. L. Murray to Mother, Coo Soil, S.C., October 24, 1864, CWPF.

viewed as unwilling to do their part for their own freedom: "They Say the Government have no Buisness with them But we Can Come three thousand miles from Home and leave our Friend to Gurad and fight for them But they Cant fight for themselves."[89] Murray's comments portraying his animus against "contrabands" and soldiers recruited from fugitives from slavery convey his sense of superiority over Black southerners. Part of the duties assigned to the 102nd USCT was to scout for deserters. Murray admitted that his comrades had "some fun with them we make them Bleave we will Put the Baynett through them."[90] Clearly, his perspective as a northern Black was vastly different than, and in direct juxtaposition to, the more typical narrative of the relationship between Black northern "liberators" and the "grateful" freedmen. This intra-racial bias that Murray held against enslaved refugees challenges the idea that Black northerners in general perceived themselves as sharing a brotherhood with their fellow Black persons.

Murray's letters relate an awareness of not only the military situation of the war but also the politics of the war. He repeatedly asked his family to send him local newspapers to help keep him informed, admitting that those at home were often more up to date than the soldiers: "we Dont know Ennything abought the war in the South till it Come from the North."[91] Newspapers were often the only timely source of accurate information available regarding the course of the war and events at home. He does not often mention the receipt of any papers from home, so readers are left to wonder whether his family complied with his numerous requests. Regardless, Murray would have had access to newspapers and other reading material undoubtedly circulating through camp. Newspapers published in the area during the war that Murray and his comrades would have had access to include the *Free South*, *New South*, and *Palmetto Herald*.

Murray's letters indicate how prevalent rumors were around camp, one of which was the belief that the Union army occupied Richmond, Virginia, in May 1864, almost a year before it did. John wrote that he and his comrades voted, most of them probably for the first time, in the 1864 election. He expressed great interest in the election, telling his mother that he "should like to Here from the north to see How Elec-

---

89. J. L. Murray to Mother, Coo Soil, S.C., October 24, 1864, CWPF.
90. J. L. Murray to Mother, Coo Saw, S.C., September 18, 1864, CWPF.
91. J. L. Murray to unnamed, Hilton Head, S.C., May 19, 1864, CWPF.

tion come up."⁹² He showed an awareness of southern politics as well, stating in late November that he thought "Jeff Davis I going to Put 300,000 Slave into the Field next Spring."⁹³ His letters tell in his own words what he experienced, what he hoped for, and what he observed while he wore the blue uniform of the Union army.

In a letter dated October 11, 1864, Murray stated that he did not "feel very well But I am Araund and Stiring Abought I Hope It will Be my last time with the fever."⁹⁴ From that point on he lamented to his mother of being unwell and not fit for duty much of the time. Murray appears to have suffered from what was often described as "remittent fever," the modern diagnosis of which was likely malaria. Surgeon Vincent described malarious symptoms as "coldness, followed by flushes of fever, aching of the whole body, periodical headaches, and debility," strikingly similar to the characterization of ailments Murray continually expressed to his mother.⁹⁵ Ultimately, Private Murray was admitted to a hospital in Charleston in late February or early March 1865.⁹⁶ He never rejoined his regiment.

Private John Lovejoy Murray, Company E, 102nd United States Colored Troops, died Wednesday afternoon, April 12, 1865. Military and hospital records variously record his final cause of death as anasarca, chronic pericarditis, or dropsy from hepatic disease.⁹⁷ If a nurse, doctor, or anyone else was at his bedside when he took his last breath, no record of that, or of his final words, exist. Later that day, one of the assistant surgeons at the hospital notified Murray's commanding officer, Captain McKendrie, of his death. The 102nd USCT regiment was no longer in Charleston, so his comrades were unable to attend his burial service held the next day.⁹⁸ When or how his family and friends in New York heard of his death is unknown. They should have received official notification from a company officer or Col. Chipman, commanding the regiment, but no documentation exists to verify that. Someone, how-

---

92. J. L. Murray to Mother, Crew Soil, S.C., November 15, 1864, CWPF.
93. J. L. Murray to Mother, Crew Soil, S.C., November 22, 1864, CWPF.
94. J. L. Murray to Mother, Crew Saw, S.C., October 11, 1864, CWPF.
95. Wesley Vincent, CWPF.
96. Contradictory dates in the military records make it difficult to provide the exact date of his hospital admission. John Murray, CMSR, CWPF, Civil War Carded Medical Records, boxes 3712–13, RG 94, NARA (hereafter cited as Carded Medical Records).
97. John Murray, Carded Medical Records, CMSR, CWPF.
98. The location of Private Murray's grave is unknown.

ever, made sure that at least some of the letters Murray received and kept from his mother were returned to her along with the last few letters that she, unaware of her son's passing, wrote after John's death.

On April 5, 1865, the 102nd USCT began its last campaign of the war. It was part of an expeditionary force under the command of General Edward E. Potter. The expedition's mission was to destroy locomotives and rolling stock between Summerville and Camden, South Carolina. During this expedition, the regiment was involved in several skirmishes, including one at Bradford Springs on April 18, 1865, and one at Swift Creek the next day. Private William Smith and Sergeant Noah Hill were killed in these engagements, and at least twelve others were wounded.[99]

The 102nd USCT continued to skirmish with Confederate troops until it received news of General Joseph Johnston's surrender of his army stationed throughout North Carolina, South Carolina, and Georgia to General William T. Sherman. The men then marched back to Charleston, going into camp at Charleston Neck on April 30. From then until mustered out of service on September 30, 1865, the regiment formed part of the Union occupying force of South Carolina. The regiment remained at Charleston Neck until May 7, when it broke camp and marched for Summerville, twenty-five miles away. From there the men left by rail for Branchville on May 18 where they encamped for about a week before proceeding to Orangeburg and engaged in provost-guard and fatigue duty throughout July. At the end of July, the 102nd USCT left Orangeburg and marched about seventy miles to Winnsboro, arriving on August 3.[100]

On Saturday, September 30, 1865, the regiment mustered out of service. It remained at Charleston until October 11, when the men sailed for New York. Arriving in New York on October 14, they then crossed over to Jersey City and boarded railroad cars. From there, the journey home followed much the same route as when the regiment left De-

---

99. *OR*, vol. 47, pt. 1, 1039–40, pt. 4, 138; 102nd USCT, Record of Events, Records of the Adjutant General's Office, 1780s–1917, RG 94, M594, reel 215, NARA (hereafter cited as Record of Events); First Michigan Colored Infantry, Muster-Out Rolls, Records of the Michigan Military Establishment, RG 59-14, folders 7–11, ovs 80, Archives of Michigan, Lansing (hereafter cited as Muster-Out Rolls); 102nd USCT, CMSR; Carded Medical Records; Monthly Returns, 1865.

100. 102nd USCT, Record of Events; *OR*, vol. 47, pt. 4, 273, 274, 283–84, 358–59, 400, 466.

troit for the front in 1864. The train passed through Elmira, New York. The weary soldiers changed cars at Dunkirk on the night of October 15, stopping in Cleveland where they embarked on the Steamer *Cleveland City* for the last leg of their journey across Lake Erie. Five companies arrived in Detroit on October 17, 1865. According to the *Detroit Free Press*, the troops, who it said "fought nobly," "were received in about the same manner as the white regiments which have preceeded them." The *Detroit Advertiser and Tribune* described the men's homecoming as "a hospitable reception, consisting of a good warm meal and hearty congratulations at their safe return . . . and from a service of labor for the preservation of the Government." The remaining five companies, delayed by a storm on the lake, arrived early in the morning of October 19. A fire the previous day damaged the depot, so the men were not provided with a hot breakfast upon their arrival as was planned. But they did receive dinner at the barracks that afternoon. At Detroit, the men received their final pay and the regiment was formally disbanded.[101]

During its service four enlisted men and one officer were killed in action; sixty-five soldiers were wounded, six of whom subsequently died and twenty-two of whom were discharged because of their wounds. Various disabilities resulted in the discharge of an additional 157 men. Close to 130 soldiers died, like John Lovejoy Murray, of disease.[102] Although Murray, like so many other soldiers, Black and White, did not return home to retell his experiences to family, friends, and his community over the ensuing years, the correspondence he maintained during his months of service remain to underscore the plight of Black soldiers as they fought to purge the nation of the chains of enslavement, prove their manhood, establish their right to citizenship and equality, and save the Union. The pages that follow contain, with little editorial intervention, an unadulterated archive of one literate African American soldier's experiences, his observations of his officers, his rank-and-file comrades, White Confederates, and enslaved southerners, and insights into the health struggles that plagued Civil War soldiers.

---

101. Monthly Returns, 1865; *Detroit Free Press*, October 18, 1865, October 20, 1865; *Detroit Advertiser and Tribune*, October 20, 1865.

102. 102nd USCT, CMSR.

Editorial Note

THIS VOLUME PRESENTS, IN THEIR ENTIRETY, THE COMPLETE COLlection of known extant correspondence between Private John Lovejoy Murray, Company E, 102nd United States Colored Troops (102nd USCT) and his family and friends. The letters were written on differing sizes of paper, penned in both ink and pencil. Despite being stored in the relatively protected environment of the National Archives and Records Administration in Washington, D.C., time ravaged most of the letters: ink and pencil faded, paper tore, and ink bled on other pages. The manuscripts were transcribed using high-resolution digital images, though the physical materials in the archives were consulted as well.

Many edited works of Civil War–era letters are collections of items that originally appeared in contemporary newspapers or other publications. Such correspondence benefited from editors who made changes in the letters before publication, standardizing grammar, spelling, capitalization, and punctuation. Editors often further edited the letters to fit the needs or agenda of the editor and publication. The letters that compose this volume did not undergo such editorial revision. John's family and friends read his words at home just as he wrote them in the field. This book is about Private John Lovejoy Murray, but to know him and his experiences it is necessary to know also the 102nd USCT and the men who served alongside him. The annotations provided throughout this volume situate the 102nd USCT within the larger context of the theater of war in which it served. Most but by no means all the people, places, skirmishes, and other events mentioned in the correspondence have been identified. The intent is to add depth to Murray's story rather than detract from his voice.

In transcribing and publishing the letters, the editor wanted to remain faithful to the originals so as to allow the writers to speak for themselves in their own ways while letting modern readers share their experiences by making the letters accessible. Readability need not require extensive editorial intervention. Indeed, modernization can compromise the historical value of a document. Men and women without a formal education, like John Murray, often penned documents that might appear impenetrable to the eye but are usually understandable when read phonetically.

The letters are arranged in chapters chronologically and include brief introductory essays. When the date of a letter was in question, it was situated where it seemed to best fit based on events or other indications within the letter itself. To retain the original character of the correspondence for the reader, simple guidelines governed the transcription process. The textual body of the pages in this volume appear essentially as in the original. The nuances of Murray's language—peculiarities of grammar, syntax, capitalization, and spelling—appear without any "sic" notations so as not to disrupt the flow of the narratives to a degree that would detract from their readability. The same is true of paragraph breaks, missing or incomplete words, words run together, characters and words raised above the line, and abbreviations. The editor did, however, make some minor intrusions and adjustments for ease of understanding. In the name of saving space, the original line breaks in the letters were not maintained. Murray almost always closed his letters with instructions to the receiver as to where to direct their letters. These instructions have been removed. Any other postscripts or last-minute thoughts, however, were retained as were any words or phrases written at the tops or margins of the letters. Murray's unconventional spelling and scarce use of punctuation impart a stream-of-consciousness quality to the letters that make them difficult to understand at times. The editor employed the relatively unobtrusive device of adding silent periods at unpunctuated sentence breaks, to delineate thoughts and ideas as they occur in order to clarify these for the reader. Although most such judgments were unambiguous, there were instances in which the placement of sentence breaks required an interpretive decision. In instances where Murray repeated a word or phrase in succession, the repeated words were removed. When false starts or ordinary slips of the pen resulted in letters or words crossed out, the editor also struck them. When, however, the editor judged that the crossed-out material reflects an important alteration of meaning, the crossed-out words are signified by the use of strikethrough (~~strikethrough~~). Solidi // is used when material has been inserted above or below the line.

With these exceptions, the transcriptions are as complete and accurate as possible. The goal was to preserve the wartime experiences of John Lovejoy Murray and his family and friends so that the reader might see their experiences in much the same way that contemporary readers saw them during the Civil War over 150 years ago. The editor hopes that these near-literal transcriptions bring the texts alive to today's readers.

The primary material in this book is accompanied by a digital component, a website that allows students and scholars to interact with the volume's content. Search for this book on www.ugapress.org for links to the bonus material.

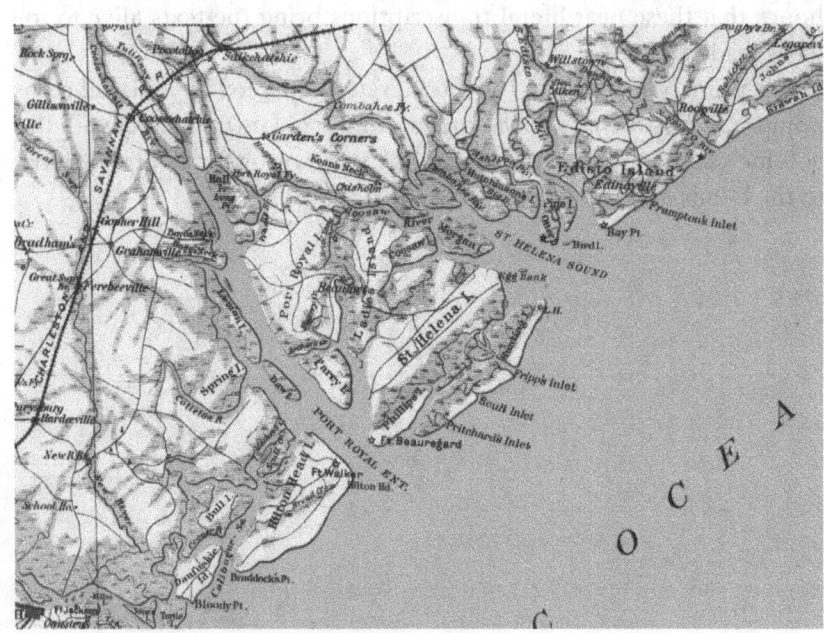

General area where the 102nd USCT was stationed.
Library of Congress; *The War of the Rebellion: A Compilation of the Official Records of the Union and Confederate Armies*, Plate 144.

CHAPTER 1

January–June 1864

*"We are maid over to the United States Ridgement
with half A Pound of Brass on our head"*

THE FIRST MICHIGAN COLORED INFANTRY OFFICIALLY MUSTERED into service on February 17, 1864, with close to nine hundred men on its roll. Colonel Henry Barnes commanded the regiment. Assigned to the Ninth Army Corps, commanded by General Ambrose Burnside, the regiment prepared to proceed to Annapolis, Maryland.[1] On Monday, March 28, the regiment marched in formation out of the training camp where the men had spent the cold winter months transforming from civilians to soldiers. The procession headed to the Michigan Southern Railroad Depot, boarded the cars, and left Detroit with little fanfare. Only family and friends came to see off their loved ones. The train traveled to Toledo, Ohio, and from there to Dunkirk, Ohio, where the regiment changed cars and continued on. At Elmira, New York, the men drew rations and changed trains yet again, this time downgrading from "good comfortable cars," to "dirty filthy hog or stock cars without fire or seats."[2] The journey continued through Pennsylvania during a heavy snowstorm that made travel even more unpleasant. An obstruction on the tracks halted the trains and left the men stranded for nearly a day without fire to keep warm or anything to eat except hardtack and salt pork. After four days and nights on the trains, almost all of it in rain or snow, the regiment reached Baltimore at sunrise on the first of April. Soon thereafter, aboard the transport steamer *Georgia*, it left Baltimore and arrived at Annapolis late in the afternoon. The weary soldiers marched three miles from town in a cold drizzling rain that turned to snow. The wagons loaded with equipment and supplies did not arrive until the next day, so the men spent the cold, snowy night without any tents and with only wet blankets draped over them for cover. About

---

1. Special Order No. 117, War Department, Adjutant General's Office (hereafter cited as AGO), Washington, D.C., March 14, 1864, NARA.
2. Jesse Madry, CWPF.

four inches of snow covered the men by morning. Thus began the regiment's service. While bivouacked at Annapolis, the First Michigan Colored continued military training at Camp Chandler.[3]

In mid-April, the regiment was transferred to the District of Hilton Head, S.C., Department of the South, under the command of Major General Quincy Gilmore.[4] The men embarked on board three transports, *North Point, Relief,* and *Nellie Pentz,* getting under way during the night of the fifteenth. After several days of rough seas that no doubt caused many of the men unfamiliar with sailing to fear that the vessels would overturn or sink to the bottom, the transports passed the Union-blockading fleet off Charleston and arrived at Hilton Head around noon on the nineteenth. There the regiment engaged in guard and picket duty on the nearby islands of St. Helena, Seabrook, Spanish Wells, and Jenkins Islands, and constructed fortifications at Hilton Head and Port Royal.

On May 18, the regiment moved inside the entrenchments at Hilton Head, and it remained there on garrison duty until June 18. The troops also received training in heavy artillery and worked in the trenches. While stationed at Hilton Head, the regiment was redesignated the 102nd United States Colored Troops.[5] In mid-June, the regiment was relieved from duty at Hilton Head and ordered to report to General Rufus Saxton at Beaufort.[6] At 10:00 p.m. the night of June 15, the men

---

3. Nelson Diary, March 28–April 1, 1864; Jesse Madry, CWPF; 102nd USCT Infantry Regimental Returns, April 1864, Record of Events, Records of the Adjutant General's Office, 1780s–1917, RG 94, M594, roll 215, NARA (hereafter cited as Regimental Returns).

4. Quincy Adams Gilmore (1825–88) graduated first in his class at West Point in 1849, was commissioned into the Corps of Engineers, and taught briefly at West Point. Tasked with various assignments during the war, he was in command of the Department of the South, consisting of North and South Carolina, Georgia, and Florida, when Charleston fell to Union forces in 1865. Warner, *Generals in Blue,* 176–77.

5. A War Department order dated May 23, 1864, officially designated Murray's regiment as the 102nd US Colored Troops. Most Black state regiments were redesignated with a USCT number but some, namely those from Massachusetts, Connecticut, and Rhode Island, retained state designations. Whether this was in part a reflection of the support, or lack of support, from the state governments is speculative at best. New England states generally encouraged the recruitment and use of African American soldiers and were among the earliest promoters of the northern-raised Black regiments. Michigan was more reluctant to promote Black soldiers. Special Order No. 85, May 23, 1864, War Department, AGO, Washington, D.C., NARA.

6. Rufus Saxton (1824–1908) graduated from West Point in 1849. He served in various posts with the Department of the South, engaged principally with the enlistment and

struck their tents and marched to the beach. From there they boarded the *Cosmopolitan* and traveled the short distance to Beaufort where they established camp about a half mile out of town.[7]

Mrs. Asher Wells   Lockport N.Y.C.O. NY   December 15, 1864
      Detroit Mich.   Jan 15th/64[8]

Dear Father[9] Mother

I have not much time to write but a few lines to you let you know that I am well and hope you are the Same. we have no Snow here But very Cold. thursday it was Spring weather but to day three Inches of Snow on the Ground But warm. I been ot of camp twice. we went with 700 men that the time to See the Coons Dress up in Uncle Sam good Clothe.[10] I have got to Stripes on my armes that what I ment when I Said I was a monkey Boy. I might have Some on my pants that when I get to get to Be Second Sargent. that will be Soon.[11] when I write again I will send you som $40 Dollars and Lue.[12] I for got her when I

---

organization of Black soldiers. After the war he served in the Freedman's Bureau, established by Congress in 1865 to assist formerly enslaved people, as assistant commissioner for South Carolina, Georgia, and Florida. Warner, *Generals in Blue*, 420–21.

    7. Dyer, *Compendium of the War*, 3:693–96; 102nd USCT Infantry Company Muster Roll, March through July 1864, Record of Events, Records of the Adjutant General's Office, 1780s–1917, RG 94, M594, roll 215, NARA (hereafter cited as Company Muster Roll); Field and Staff Muster Roll, May and June 1864, Record of Events, Records of the Adjutant General's Office, 1780s–1917, RG 94, M594, roll 215, NARA (hereafter cited as Field and Staff Muster Roll); Special Order No. 85, May 23, 1864, AGO; Special Order No. 145, April 12, 1864, AGO.

    8. The correct date of this letter must be January 1864. It could not be December 15, 1864, because the regiment was not present in Detroit in December 1864. The flag presentation described in the letter took place on January 5, 1864.

    9. Asher Wells was John Murray's stepfather.

    10. In this context, Murray's use of "Coons" (now a slur) was in reference to Black soldiers.

    11. Despite the implication here that he expected a promotion to second sergeant, Murray remained a private during the entirety of his service.

    12. Murray often mentioned Lucinda (Lucretia, Lue) Crain in his letters to his mother, and this collection includes some letters he wrote directly to Lucinda.

left. I will send its home or come home on a furlow.¹³ I got the promis. We Sent to Washington to Elected Cornel. he is a Duchman. one of the best of men. we Bought him a Sword. the Ladis of the Detroit presented the Ridgement with a Flage.¹⁴ we presented the Sword. its cost one hundred Dollars. now we a Sword for our Captain. that will be $50 Dollars. the Rigement is goin to Illnois in about two weeks.¹⁵ I Supose three others and my self will go to St. Lewis in a goin in a week If I dont get a furlow.

Tell Lue I will that mony the next time

---

13. Furloughs are formal leaves from military service, usually ranging from fifteen to thirty days. There is no evidence to suggest that Murray asked for or received a furlough while at Detroit.

14. The Detroit Colored Ladies' Soldiers' Aid Society presented a regimental flag to the First Michigan Colored Regiment in a ceremony on January 5, 1864, at Camp Ward. The regimental flag was of blue silk, decorated with a yellow silk fringe border and tassels of red, white, and blue. One side bore a representation of the Michigan State arms, while on the reverse was a representation of an eagle guarding the banner of the Union. Both sides were inscribed with several appropriate mottos. After the flag presentation ceremony, Chaplain William Waring presented a sword, sash, and belt to Lt. Col. William T. Bennett on behalf of the noncommissioned officers and privates of the regiment. The sword was said to cost about $130. These two ceremonies were witnessed by the regiment and "a large crowd of ladies and gentlemen." *Detroit Advertiser and Tribune*, January 6, 1864.

15. The regiment did not go to Illinois, nor does there ever seem to have been plans for it to do so. Rumors of all kinds traveled through army camps during the war. Murray's reports about where the regiment was going often turned out to be just inaccurate hearsay.

Detroit, Mich.   *Thursday, March 10/64*[16]

Dear Mother and Father and Grandmother.[17]   I take this oppotunity write you A few lines let you know that I am well at Presant Except A Bad Cold and hope these few lines find you the Same. we had A thunder shower here last knight. the frost is most out of the ground. Robin and Wild Duck Pigion and wilde Gees are Plenty. it is Spring weather here in Detroit. we was mustered in for our Pay last week.[18] we Are goin to Draw our Canteen and Haversack and Expect to go to St Louis[19] next week. they have benn a great meny men from Canada Enlisted

---

16. There is no definitive explanation for the lengthy interval between letters here. From January through the end of March the regiment remained bivouacked at Camp Ward where Murray presumably would have had ample time available for letter writing. No active military campaigning should have interfered with the posting of letters between Detroit and New York. Perhaps Murray wrote letters, but they were lost in transit and never received by his family, or perhaps there were letters written during this time that were not given to, or kept by, the pension office. Murray's compiled military service record provides evidence suggestive of one possibility. A "Descriptive List of Deserters Arrested," dated January 20, 1864, lists Private John L. Murray, Company E, "having absented himself from camp same day . . . without leave" as arrested by W. H. Sullivan in Detroit. The record further shows that Sullivan received a thirty-dollar reward for the arrest and return of the soldier. No other evidence that Murray deserted, or tried to desert, appears in his records. Despite the similarity of names, this record could not pertain to John Murray, Company K, as that John Murray enlisted January 26, 1864, and deserted March 6, 1864. John Lovejoy Murray appeared on the desertion list January 20, 1864. Perhaps Murray simply left Camp Ward without permission for a day in Detroit. If Murray wrote home describing or complaining about what happened, Sarah Wells might have intentionally removed those letters from the packet she submitted to the Pension Office so as not to disparage her son's name or jeopardize her claim for pension. John Murray, CMSR, CWPF.

17. Murray's maternal grandmother was Catharine Thompson, born in either New York or New Jersey. Thompson was widowed and living with Sarah and Asher Wells by 1860. She resided with them until her death in March 1878. U.S. Federal Census, 1840–1880; New York State Census, 1855, 1875; John Murray, CWPF.

18. The regiment first mustered on February 17, 1864, but the company rolls typically began as of February 29, 1864, so it is likely that February 29 is what Murray referred to here as the muster for pay. Evidence does not indicate that the men were actually paid at this time. Capt. E. J. McKendrie to Brig. Gen. L. Thomas, August 17, 1865, Letters Received, ser. 360, Colored Troops Division, RG 94, NARA.

19. The regiment never traveled to St. Louis.

and get there Bounty Deserted to Winsor.[20] and Bennett[21] will not Pay the Bounty till just Before we go Away.[22] then we will get month and Bounty Pay. I Dont Know how much I will get Down. When I get it I will Send it Care of A. G. Adams[23] Box 66. When we get to our Quarters in St. Louis I will let you know.

I Am on Duty All Knight and will Be All Day and cant write Enny more

Annapolis Maryland   ~~March~~ April 10th/64

Dear Mother and Father and Grandmother.   I take this oppotunity write to A few lines to let you know that I Am well at Presant and hope these few lines will find you in good health. we left Detroit on the 29th of march. it Commence Raining and Snowing the Day we left and it Raind for five days Steady. we got in Baltimore the first April just Sun Rise. we was four Days and four knight on the Cares.[24] we left

---

20. Windsor, Ontario, is on the southern shore of the Detroit River, directly across from Detroit. Being close, Canada was both a place from which African Americans came to enlist in the Union army and a place to which to run and hide. Upward of two hundred men in the regiment claimed to have been born in Canada or had lived in Canada before the war. At least twenty-five men deserted from Camp Ward during March 1864. Many of them, as Murray noted, fled to Canada. Reports indicate that numerous deserters were "supposed to be in Canada" as was Sherrard Bradbury whose arrest report stated that his plan was to go "over to Canada as soon as he got his bounty." Sherrard Bradbury, CMSR; Monthly Returns, 1864. For a larger discussion of Black Canadians who fought in the Union army see Reid, *African Canadians in Union Blue*.

21. William True Bennett (1836–1910) was a captain in the First USCT before he was transferred to the First Michigan Colored Infantry. He joined the regiment at Detroit and assisted in recruitment efforts and oversaw the training of the troops during the winter of 1863–64. He was promoted to lieutenant colonel on April 13, 1864. Later that year, he succeeded Col. Thomas Wentworth Higginson as commander of the Thirty-Third USCT. William T. Bennett, CMSR, CWPF.

22. It was sometimes the practice of recruiters to withhold bounties from enlistees until the men deployed to the field in an effort to prevent desertion. Murdock, "New York's Civil War Bounty Brokers"; Michael Thomas Smith, "Most Desperate Scoundrels Unhung."

23. Albert G. Adams was born in 1802 in Columbia, Herkimer County, N.Y., the son of Ruth Smith Adams and her first husband, Barney Adams (1779–1805). The 1860 census shows John Murray living in Adams's household along with his mother, Ruth, and her daughter, Lucinda. U.S. Federal Census, 1850, 1860, 1870; New York State Census, 1855, 1865.

24. Train cars.

the Depot and march Abought 2 miles and Stop and took Breakfast. it was Cold Meet and Bread and hoot Coffee. we had Been living on hard tack Cold Pork Raw at that. and then we march to the third Depot Abought 2 mils and took A Boat for our Camp Abought 44 mile just half way from washington. there is Abought forty thousand troops here in Camp. there is three Colord Ridgement here now. one N.Y. Rid one C.T. Rid.[25] we Belonge to Burnside Department the 9th Army.[26] there is Abought 30,000 Black in his Department.[27] the State of Mayrland is one Camp Ground. when we got in Camp it still Rained harder then Ever. no Cover. we went and got two Rail out on the ground and laid Dawn and Put our Blanket over us. when one Rail Ache Rod over on the other and so on till ~~Annaplis~~ Day light. it was ~~it~~ Snowing hard. Abought four Inches of Snow on the Blanket. our tents Did not Come till Abought Noon and then we haftou Pitch tent. it took till Dark and then we laid Dawn with our Clothes and our Blankes wring wet. the next Day the Sun Come out. the Next Day we was Detail on load Steemboats. If you want oysters just hitch one horse waggon up. you can get them here for ten Cent A Bushel. you Can Stand on the Wharfe and Count A hundred Boats. oysters Piled up like young mountain. Burnsid was here yesterday.[28] we have to Slick up Black Boots and Comb

---

25. The New York regiment referred to here is most likely the Twenty-Sixth USCT, mustered at Rikers Island around the same time as the First Michigan Colored Infantry. The Connecticut regiment is the Twenty-Ninth Connecticut Colored Regiment, mustered on March 19, 1864, in Fair Haven. Presumably, the third regiment of Black troops in Murray's comment was his own. 26th USCT Infantry, Record of Events, roll 215; 29th Connecticut Colored Infantry, Record of Events, roll 208.

26. The First Michigan Colored Infantry was only tangentially a part of the Ninth Army Corps. Assigned to the Ninth Corps on March 14, 1864, shortly before leaving Detroit, the regiment received orders in mid-April to report to Maj. Gen. Gilmore, Department of the South. Special Order No. 117, March 14, 1864, AGO; Special Order No. 145, April 12, 1864, AGO.

27. The Ninth Army Corps rendezvoused at Annapolis in March and April 1864. Gen. Ambrose Burnside assumed command on April 13, 1864. Organized into four divisions, the corps numbered about twenty-five thousand men. The fourth division, commanded by Gen. Edward Ferrero, was composed entirely of Black troops. Lt. Gen. U. S. Grant to Maj. Gen. G. G. Meade, Culpeper Court-House, Va., April 9, 1864, *OR*, ser. 1, vol. 33, 828; General Orders No. 7, Annapolis, Md., April 19, 1864, *OR*, ser. 1, vol. 33, 913.

28. Gen. Burnside was at Annapolis on Saturday, April 9, to complete the buildup of the Ninth Army Corps and prepare for its deployment. H. W. Halleck to Maj. Gen. Burnside, Washington, D.C., April 7, 1864; Lt. Gen. U. S. Grant to Maj. Gen. G. G. Meade, Culpeper Court-House, Va., April 9, 1864; Maj. Gen. Burnside to Lt. Gen. U. S. Grant, Annapolis, April 9, 1864, all in *OR*, ser. 1, vol. 33, 815, 828, 834.

hare. to Day was Inspection of Armes. the N.Y. Ridg was about 1,200. our Ridg 9,00.²⁹ Some of the men offer five Dollars to see A woman. they say the land is so Poor it wont groe them. talk About mud. there is no Bottom here in the Road. the Goverment waggon from four two six horses with A Contraban. tes Sunday there Captain hurry for me Dress Parrad.³⁰ Excuse Bad Spelling

Direct your letter Annapolis Maryland Camp Chandler³¹

Annapolis Mayrland   *April 11*

Direct your letter to Annapolis Mayrland
J. L. MURRAY. Co. E. 1.st. MICH. COLERD. REG³²

N. York And Conneticut Rid last Saturday Morning³³ for hilttenhead South Carlina. it is Rumor that we Are goin to Richman.³⁴ we Dont know. we Are goin to Stay here till we get our Pay. they want to give us Contreband Pay. that $10 Dollars A month. we want $16 Dollars. the N York Rid would not leave the State Before they got there Pay. they Rushed us from Detroit with out Enny knowledge if goin. it was Don Because the Coon went to Canada. About 100 men left. they would

---

29. Murray wrote "50" below this, so he might have meant 950. Regardless, his numbers were somewhat inaccurate. The monthly return for April 1864 showed the aggregate number of enlisted men present and absent as fewer than 800. Monthly Returns, April 1864.

30. Dress parade is a formal ceremonial parade in dress uniform. The schedule followed by the regiment near the end of April 1864 called for dress parade daily at 6 p.m. General Orders No. 5, Col. Henry L. Chipman, Head Qrs, 1st Mich. Col. Regt. near Hilton Head, S.C., April 23, 1864, Order Book.

31. Camp Chandler was the name of the regiment's encampment at Annapolis.

32. Looking at the original shows this to be an ink stencil rather than a stamp. This is the only letter imprinted with this personalized ink stencil. Murray could have used the stencil on the envelopes he mailed his letters in, none of which are in the pension file, or to identify his uniform or equipment. Soldiers often purchased such items from a sutler.

33. On Saturday, April 9, the Twenty-Ninth Connecticut Colored Infantry and the Twenty-Sixth USCT left Annapolis with orders to report to Hilton Head, where they arrived on the thirteenth. 29th Connecticut Colored and 26th USCT, Record of Events.

34. The First Michigan was still attached to the Ninth Army Corps at the time Murray wrote this letter; hence the belief that it would soon be heading to Richmond.

goe from one two Every Knight. Sometimes Six would go an then the Black own Detroit. it is a ~~Duck~~ Dutch and Irish City take the Nation. they Could not live together. they would Fight Ever times they went Into the City.[35] they was to Pay us our Monthely Pay our Bounty But they did not. they thought we would Be fast to tak ten Dollars A month. they give us Some the Springfield gun. you Could Not Shoot a Side of a Barn. we would not. then Cornel Benett And Barnes went to Washington. we got the Enfield Rifle Musket gun.[36] they are mark one mile and half Shoot. we had A thunder Shower last Knight to days. you Can ware over Coats when it Rain. it dont No when to Stop in this Country. there is men Enough in Mayrlan to take one half the South if they ~~y~~ use them wright. there was Seven Rid Came last Knight. I must go on Drill[37] now so good By till next

---

35. Detroit's 1860 population was around forty-five thousand, about half of whom were foreign-born, largely Irish and German. Murray was likely referring to those of German descent when he mentioned the Dutch. The Black population of Detroit in 1860 was just over fourteen hundred, less than 3 percent of the city's total population. There were a series of conflicts between the enlisted men and Detroit residents during the winter of 1863–64, when the First Michigan Colored Infantry barracked at Camp Ward. Whenever they could, Black soldiers went into the city to visit family and friends, frequent saloons and eating establishments, and shop or seek other entertainment. Often in groups, the soldiers wore their uniforms, which they expected would earn them a measure of respect, and often carried their weapons. This caused tension, especially in the east, predominantly German, side of Detroit, and fights frequently ensued. The city's newspapers reported numerous incidents, ranging from verbal arguments to saloon brawls, between Black soldiers and Detroit residents. One soldier was shot by men described as "Irish roughs" on his return to the barracks in February 1864. U.S. Federal Census, 1860; Taylor, *Old Slow Town*, 93–99; Joseph R. Smith to Henry Barnes, January 20, 1864, Letters Sent by Military Commander at Detroit, Records of the Provost Marshal General's Bureau; *Detroit Free Press*; *Detroit Advertiser and Tribune*; Elisha Robinson, CWPF.

36. The most used rifles during the Civil War were Springfields and Enfields. There were several models of Springfield rifles manufactured in Massachusetts issued to Union soldiers. The United States imported the British Enfield in large quantities from 1861 to the end of 1863. Service records indicate that many of the enlisted men of the First Michigan Colored Infantry received Austrian rifles while the regiment was at Detroit. These were likely the Lorenz Rifle, the Austrian army's standard infantry weapon at the time. Both Union and Confederate governments purchased large amounts of the Lorenz Rifle during the early years of the war. 102nd USCT, CMSR; Bilbly, *Civil War Firearms*.

37. Drill was an integral part of any soldier's daily routine while in camp. Col. Barnes ordered a battalion drill for 3:00 p.m. on April 12. Daily schedules typically called for squad drill at 9:00 a.m. and company or battalion drill at 2:00 p.m. Circular II, Headquarters, 1st Mich. Col. Regt., Camp Chandler near Annapolis, Md., April 12, 1864, Order Book; Nelson Diary, April 4, 1864, April 7, 1864, April 11, 1864, April 12, 1864.

Annapolis Maryland   April 12th/64

Loucind   this is the first ime I taking to write to you. I well at Presant and hope you Are the Same. I Am Alonge way from home. we left Detroit the 28th of March. it Rain the first day and it still Rain. we went the lake Shore Road[38] and Stope at Toledo 12 Hours. we was on the Cars four day and knight. Abought sixty in. you may think how we Sleep. we got in Baltimore just Sun Rise. we march Abought two miles. had Breakfast. it was hot Coffee Bread and Cold meet. that was Better then we had Been living on. we had Raw Pork and hard tock.[39] when we get in Camp it Rain just as hard as it Could Rain. it was Abought nine oclock at knight. we was wet as we Could Be. we had no tents. then we went and got Some Rail Put on the ground and laid down on them and Put our wet Blanket over ous. when we got up there was Abought four Inches of Snow over us. our tents did not Come till Noon. it Still Snowed and then we Pitch tents on the Snow. it took till Dark then we laid Down with our wet Clothes and Blank. you talk Abought Rain it dont now when to stop here in this Country. the mud is not quite four feet deep But very nigh it. we had A thunder shower last knight. there is Abought forty thousand troop here. tere is three Ridgement of Coler here. we Belonge to Burnside Department. he has got Abought 30,000 Black under him. Mayrland is Nothing But A Camp ground. we Are in the Smallest Part of the Camp. there is men Enough here to take one half of the South if they use them right. Burnside was here in our Camp last Saturday. tell Emona[40] to take good care of Frank E Albert.[41] our officers are all are ~~Democtat~~ Democrat Except Captain Tutle.[42] give my love to Martha.[43] It is Rool Call now. Excuse All Bad Spelling.

---

38. The Lake Shore and Michigan Southern Railway, established in 1833, was commonly known as the Lake Shore Road. It was a major part of the New York Central Railroad from Buffalo to Chicago.
39. Hardtack.
40. Emona could be Emily. If so, the reference here was likely to Emily Loveland who appears regularly in Murray's correspondence.
41. Murray seemed to be referring to two people here: Frank and Albert. Albert was Albert Adams, whom he mentioned often. It is unknown who Frank was.
42. Capt. Johnathan B. Tuttle, appointed captain of Company C on December 7, 1863, and discharged on April 24, 1864, on a surgeon's certificate of disability for disease of the lungs. Johnathan B. Tuttle, CMSR, CWPF.
43. Murray mentioned Martha numerous times throughout his letters, sometimes as Martha Wattson, but it is unknown exactly who Martha was.

April 14   Annapolis Maryland

Dear Mother   I take this oppotunity to write to you that I am well at Presant and hope you are the Same. Genral Burnside was here and Grant.⁴⁴ we showed off first but he took great Shine to us. this morning we had a Dispatch from head Quarters to Pack Up and Be Ready to Start to morow Morning at five o'clock. I spoke of Rain it Still Rain and thunder littning. we will Be on water Six or Seven Days the Captain Sayd. Our Boat went to Baltimore with Grant.⁴⁵ it just Came Back. I just got my Cloths Dry. it not any thing to wash for me But must Be Don. I Am Detail to take Care of the Sick in the Hospital.⁴⁶ I think I will Stay there Because the Rebels Ball Are Bad things to Play with. I stood guard last knight and Stop the Cornal Benett. Abought an hour he Sent for me and Releas me from guard and told me I would Do for A Solder. this morning I was Detail. I hope they will Send Us where it Dont Rain Seven Days Steady. you May have the my waggon. if you Dont want it you may sell it. Just As Soon As we get our Pay I will Send it home. I Dont want money here. tell Grand mother I lik for got her. we Are Intitle to forty Day Furlow out of A year. If I keep my heath I will Come home when we get settled. we Dont know where we Are Again to tell we Stop So good By till Nex time. I Must Pack up My Dudge and thump on harde tack And Cold Pork.

When we Stop I will Right just as Soon as we I Can. you need not answer this letter.

---

44. Gen. Ulysses S. Grant, general-in-chief of all Union troops, accompanied by Burnside, reviewed the regiment early in the afternoon on Wednesday, April 13. According to Capt. Nelson, Grant "spoke well of the regiment." Lt. Gen. U. S. Grant to Maj. Gen. A. E. Burnside, Culpeper Court-House, Va., April 11, 1864, *OR*, ser. 1, vol. 33, 838; Nelson Diary, April 13, 1864.

45. Grant traveled to Washington, D.C., from Annapolis. Perhaps Murray heard that Grant was going to Baltimore rather than Washington. Lt. Gen. U. S. Grant to Maj. Gen. Burnside, Washington, D.C., April 14, *OR*, ser. 1, vol. 33, 864.

46. A search of the Company Morning reports, Company Monthly reports, and the Regimental Order books does not reveal Murray detailed as a nurse in the hospital at this or any other time. Perhaps he requested an assignment to the hospital, but the orders never came through. Perhaps he cared for sick or wounded men for a short period but not long enough to appear on the reports. Or perhaps he embellished his service as such to those back home.

May 2/64   Hilton Head South Carolina

Dear Mother   I tak this oppotunity to Informe you that I am well at Presant and hope these few line will find you all the same health. we lift Annapolis the fifteen of April. just Before we left I Received A letter from Martha Wattson that Abert[47] was dead. I Received the letter in the Streets. we left that Knight Down the Bay. the next day I was taken sick and was sick five Day. I thought my time had come. hove up all But my Boots. we struck the Sea Abought noon. the first Knight was Rought. Sometime we thought we would go Down to the Bottom. we Pass Charleston the forth Day and landed at the head Abought 3 O'Clock in the After noon then we march in sid of the forts and Camp. I went on Post Duty the first Knight. I had foure Uncle Sam Packet Peices[48] to take care of for twenty four hours then Came to Camp the Next Day. then we had to Pack Up and take the Boat for Sea Brook.[49] that Place is on the otherr side of the Island Abought Eight miles from Camp. we are doing Picket Duty. we are in site of the Rebles. the gun Boats had A nice little time Friday. they Shell A Small Fourt and took its was in Plain Site of us. we Could See the Shell Burst in the air. we have not the Perticular of the fight. this B Picket work is very Dangerous Buisness. they have capture five of the white soldier. there was three men Shoot the twenty third of April for Deserting.[50] it is Death for a Soldier to go out Sid of the Picket without a pass. I am now in the Sunny South where Black Berry are Ripe. last Friday the Pay Muster Come to Pays Us off. Part of Ridgement took Seve Dollars amonth But I would give my time to Uncle Sam Before I would Sign the Pay Roll. they Say that Congress would Pass A Bill to Pay the Coled Soldier $12

---

47. Albert G. Adams died in 1864 in Cambria, Niagara County, N.Y. *New York, Wills and Probate Records, 1659–1999*, Ancestry.com.

48. It is unknown what "Uncle Sam Packet Peices" means. It may refer to enslaved refugees then referred to as "contrabands."

49. Companies E and F were on special duty at Seabrook. Monthly Returns, April 1864.

50. Murray is not referring to any of his comrades here. There were no soldiers in the 102nd USCT executed for desertion, or any other crime, during the regiment's service. There were, however, two soldiers from the Sixth Regiment, Connecticut Volunteers, who were executed for desertion on April 17, 1864, outside the entrenchments at Hilton Head. Private Henry Schumaker, Company C, and Private Henry Stark, Company E, were found guilty of desertion and sentenced "to be shot to death by musketry." Murray would certainly have heard of the military execution if not in attendance himself. *Palmetto Herald*, April 21, 1864; *New South*, April 23, 1864.

month.[51] they Partly Cheated me out of my Bunty By taken me away. we Dont know that we will Be Disbanded. the Ridgement was not got up wright[52] and old Barns Cant Sell us to the Government Nor can he get his Pay till we sign the Pay Roll.[53] Give my love to Grandmother.

I send two letters. Be Careful to Direct your letter to Company E. E.

May 2th/64   *Hilton Head South Carolina*

---

there was heavy firing all the after noon and last Knight from the Gun Boat. we Could See and hear the Shell Burst. they went around the Island. Good meny of the Boys ware afraid. I have ~~Nont~~ Not Seen Enny thing to Be afraid of yet. It is Rumor that the Rebels have Atacked Bufort. its is Sixteen Miles from us. the Place we are By the old kname is Port Royle. it is lazy work to Be on Picket. we have no Drill. all we have to Do is to lay around and throught the Day. about 5 o'clock is ~~in~~ Inspection of ~~arlns~~ arms.[54] our Camp is about Eight Miles from here. we have the Rates Company in the Ridgement and one of the Best Drill in the Rid. Barnes Says if he had another Rid to get up he would make them work But if he Stay here he will Slip his mind Before he wants. he Cant Rais another Rid if he try.[55] the weather is Cool this morning.

---

51. Capt. E. J. McKendrie reported that only nine of the sixty men in Company E received their pay in May 1864. Col. Henry Chipman, General Order No. 7, Head Qrs., 1st Regiment Michigan Colored Volunteers, Hilton Head, S.C., April 30, 1864, Order Book; Capt. E. J. McKendrie to Brig. Gen. L. Thomas, August 17, 1865.

52. There is no indication of any irregularities in the raising and mustering of the First Michigan Colored Infantry.

53. There was no regulation that officers would not receive pay if their men refused to sign the payroll muster.

54. General Order No. 6, dated April 27, 1864, ordered company commanders to conduct a thorough inspection of their respective companies daily at 5:00 p.m. Col. Chipman specifically instructed officers to ensure that the men kept arms, accoutrements, and clothes clean and in good order. Col. Henry Chipman, General Order No. 6, Head Quarters, 1st Regiment Michigan Colored Volunteers, Hilton Head, S.C., April 27, 1864, Order Book.

55. Whether because of the relatively small number of eligible Black men in the state by 1864 or because Michigan's government, particularly Governor Blair, lacked the initiative or motivation to do so, the First Michigan Colored Regiment was the only Black regiment raised in the state. Murray here seemed to lay the fault for this squarely on Barnes, perhaps because of a perception on Murray's part of Barnes's ineptness or dishonesty with the First Michigan Colored Infantry.

you can ware an overCoat. No firing this morning at Daybrak. we are in Gun Shoot of the Rebels. Stewed Beef and Coofee and harde tack for Breakfarst. Buter is sixty Cent a Pound. Molasse 80 Cents A Gallon. tobaco 80. whiskey 3,00 Dollars A Pints. I have not tuch a Drop of whiskey in three month and I Dont think I will. It Cant Be had Except from the Boat. you have to Be on the sly.[56] no more at Presant.

Port Royal   May 14th 1864

Black man White man are all a like here.[57]

Sunday Morning. the weather is fine. we can hear the Gun this morning. the Cornal Benett Cornal MC.Kinsty and the Genral I Dont know what his Kname is they are here.[58] they very strick in Camp. if A man look around he take them out of the Rank and tye them Up By the Fingar for two Hours. you must keep your Cloth Clean your Boots Black and Change your Shirts it twice A week. we got A kind of People Down hear you cant Under Stand. I Suppose you have Seen Frank Leslie newspaper where the Band of Music are playing An marching.[59] that

---

56. Although the U.S. Army forbade enlisted soldiers to purchase alcohol, alcohol consumption was common during the war. As Murray attested, soldiers came up with inventive ways to sneak alcohol. They smuggled whiskey in bottles with false labels, in care packages sent from loved ones at home, in loaves of baked bread, in the barrels of rifles, or even inside hollowed out watermelons. Public Acts of the Thirty-Seventh Congress, Session II, July 1862; Norris, "Forty-Rod, Blue Ruin & Oh Be Joyful."

57. Murray wrote this at the top of his letter. It was one of his first expressions about racial attitudes and experiences, or lack thereof, while a soldier in the South. At the writing of this letter, Murray and his comrades had been in the field less than two months. It is difficult to know whether Murray was referring to White and Black soldiers in the Union army or in a broader sense of the relationship between White and Black people in the general vicinity. No evidence suggests that Murray had ever visited the South before.

58. Murray was probably describing William T. Bennett, then a lieutenant colonel, and Capt. Edward McKendrie of Company E. It is unclear to whom Murray referred to as the "Genral." Henry Barnes resigned his command, and as of April 15, 1864, Col. Henry L. Chipman commanded the 102nd USCT. Murray might have thought that Chipman was a general because he commanded the regiment. Chipman, a West Point graduate, entered service in the Civil War as a captain in the Eleventh U.S. Infantry on May 14, 1861. Shortly thereafter he was transferred to the Second Michigan Infantry and promoted to lieutenant colonel. Chipman saw action at Antietam, Chancellorsville, and Gettysburg. He commanded the 102nd USCT from the time of his appointment until the regiment mustered out of service. Henry Chipman, CMSR.

59. *Frank Leslie's Illustrated Newspaper* was the country's first newspaper to include illus-

is true his Picture Dont Lie. as for Soldier they Cant Hurt them. if they Do they will Rue the Day. we are mix up with the white Soldier. we Dont Even here the word niggar. I heard more in one Day at the North then I heard in the five week South. we Eat and Sleep together. we are Camp alonge side of them. I have Seen from one Hundred and fifty thousand Souldier and A Better Sett of Boys I Ever Saw. they Dont get tanted till they get North. they are all off one mind. if you want Ennything you Can get it. we are at libberty to go Every where we might go throught the Day But when Knight Come you must Be on Hand. No more at Presant. Give my love to Grandmother and Father and all Inquiring Friend.

May 19th/64   Hilton Head South Carolina

I Received your letter the ~~19th~~ 17th. I was glad when I Red it. I got little leasure time to write to you that I am well and hope your are the Same. we left Sea Brook last Monday to our Ridgement at the Head. all the Company are ~~to gethere~~ together now. we are Drilling on heavy artilry in the fort.[60] the Gun are fourteen feet and 5 inches long. they are Sixty four Pounder. we Use Nothing But Grape and Canster.[61] we are Bilding another fourt inside Side of the other fort. we had abought seven hundred Black and one thousand white. it is three fourt of A mile. it is Nothing But Sand made from the Sea. I ~~it~~ like it on Picket Better then in the fort. they think the Reb will Call on Us. if they Do we will

---

trations. It had a circulation of over two hundred thousand during the Civil War. Murray's reference to the newspaper implied that it was available to Murray and his comrades and that his family in New York read it.

60. A need for infantry units to assist in manning the defense works in the vicinity, the result of too few artillery units available for service, necessitated instruction in heavy artillery. A company from the Third Rhode Island Heavy Artillery instructed the 102nd USCT "with a view to have them serve such works in Hilton Head District which cannot be manned by the artillery." Special Order No. 22, HdQrs, 1st Regt. Mich. Col. Vols., Hilton Head, S.C., May 25, 1864, Order Book; R. Saxton to Maj. Gen. Q. A. Gilmore, Beaufort, S.C., April 15, 1864, *OR*, ser. 1, vol. 45, 55; Col. C. R. Brayton to Capt. W. L. M. Burger, Hdqrs. Dept. of the South, Office Chief of Arty., Hilton Head, S.C., May 29, 1864, *OR*, ser. 1, vol. 35, pt. 2, 105–6.

61. Canister and Grapeshot refer to types of artillery ammunition. Canister consisted of smaller shot placed in a sheet iron cylinder that disintegrated when the gun fired. Grapeshot was smaller shot layered between iron plates and held together by a central bolt that was meant to break when the gun fired, thus allowing the shot to scatter.

meet them half way. last Sunday we took two Spy white and Six B. made them Come A Shore. they had A Pass But it was not good. then we took them to Head quarters. the Gun Boat have little fun Abought Every Day Some times twice. Evry time they See A Squad of men they will give them A few Shell. we Dont know Ennything abought the war in the South till it Come from the S North. when we heard that Richmond was takin we fired one hundred Gun.[62] it all most Split my head open. the Ship Come in one O'clock at Knight. She Had one thousand flages on her Mast. it is not Settle what they will Do with us. the old d——l Barnes they got him in Prison in Washington. I hope they will keep him there. he has mad his Brage that he has Mad forty thousand Dollars out of the Black.[63] we have thaunder shower Every Day. you Spoke abought working Lucind Place. if you Can Shape thing So you can I think it Better for you. She will give you A good Chance.[64] I must Stop. this writing on A Gun is not very good Place. give my love to Lucind Emma[65] Martha and take the Rest to your Self and Grandmother. Post Duty to Maraw

Hilton Head   June 13th   South Carolina

Dear Mother and Father   I Received your letter the 11th. I was glad to here from you. I Am well and fat as a bare. the Sunny South agree

---

62. The remarks here might be in reference to the battle of Spotsylvania Court House, part of Grant's 1864 Overland Campaign designed to take Richmond; however, the Union army did not occupy Richmond until early April 1865. Unsubstantiated reports reached the South Carolina Coast that Grant was successful in his campaign against Richmond. Capt. Nelson noted that union forces in the area "fired a national salute in honor of Grant's victory." The rumor that Grant captured Richmond in May 1864 was widespread. William Woodlin, Eighth USCT, stationed in Florida at the time, likewise wrote in his diary on May 19, 1864, that "the canoniers went up with news of the success of Grant before Richmond" and on May 21 of the "news of the capture of Richmond." Nelson Diary, May 19, 1864; Diary of William P. Woodlin, Company G, 8th USCT, The Gilder Lehrman Institute of American History, May 19–21, 1864.

63. This could be a reference to the bounty scandal that the *Detroit Free Press* alleged had occurred during the organization of the regiment. Perhaps rumors around camp were that Barnes was arrested rather than resigned his command, though there is no evidence to suggest that he was indeed detained.

64. Murray seemed to be advising his mother to take work offered by Lucinda. A later letter written by Sarah to her son mentioned her having cared for a child of Lucinda's.

65. Emily Loveland, Lucinda Crain's niece. Emily lived with Lucinda and her family from 1857 until her marriage in 1866. John Murray, CWPF; U.S. Federal Census, 1860.

with me. we are Doing Provost Guard. we guard Reb Prisnor and Deserter. they Say the Country is Destroyed By having the Damn nigar Soldier. it make them Swear when we ask them for A Pass. the Mayrland they would Drive them of there Post But they tride Us. we Shoot three of them. they Sware they will have Revenge But when they see fit to Come we will Received them kindly. our in Instruction is to shoot Every man that showe any Spunk. we went out on A Pleasure Exurtion to take A Bridge. Genral Burny[66] is the Commander of this Department. in Stead of Sending the Gun Boat Ahead he sent the transtport. the Gun Boat was four miles Behind. the Pilot was A sick. he Run her on the Sand Bar in Range of there Gun. the Reb thought they would give us A try. the first Shoot went throught the Boat. the next went in the Boiller. that Stope all work then the Command was to throw your Gun into the River. the Mayrland was Scart to Deat. they jump after there Gun. nine of them will was kill and Drown. the Conneticut Horsman lost four men. they was on Dry land. the Rest of us took A Salt water Bath then we had order to march to Camp.[67] we are Drilling on heavy artilry and Provost all together and Building forts. we have Built one and there is two more to be Built on the Island. we have marching order. we Pack up in the morning for Bufort. it is Abought 18 miles from the Head and Abought 25 miles from Charleston.

You Spoak Abought harvisting my share of my wheat. I wish you would just as soon as it get Ripe But Dont let it get to Ripe and thrash

---

66. Brig. Gen. William Birney (1819–1907). Birney entered the Union army as a captain in the First New Jersey Infantry Regiment. In June 1864 he was part of the Department of the South in charge of Black troops. Birney served in the all-Black Twenty-Fifth Corps during the Appomattox Campaign. Warner, *Generals in Blue*, 35.

67. At the end of May 1864, Gen. John P. Hatch sent out an expedition consisting of about two thousand men under the direction of Brig. Gen. W. Birney. The expedition's objective was to destroy the bridges on the Charleston and Savannah Railroad over the South Edisto and Ashepoo Rivers. The Ninth USCT, commonly called the Maryland Regiment by Murray, was part of the expedition. The *Boston*, a steamer carrying soldiers of the Ninth USCT, ran aground within range of a Confederate battery that opened fire on them, disabling the vessel and starting a fire that forced the soldiers to jump overboard. Thirteen men were killed, drowned, or missing, and seventy-five cavalry horses burned in the fire. Maj. Gen. J. G. Foster to Maj. Gen. H. W. Halleck, Headquarters, Department of the South, Hilton Head, May 26, 1864; Maj. Gen. J. G. Foster to Maj. Gen. H. W. Halleck, Headquarters, Department of the South, Hilton Head, May 28, 1864; all in *OR*, ser. 1, vol. 35, pt. 1, 7–9.

it out Right Away. there is Eleven Acre in the field. if the wheat is good it will Be Just as good as A Hundred Dollars in your Pocket.[68]

Tell Lucinda I wrote two letter to her and one to Emma and Part of one for Frank.[69] No more at Presant yours truly.

we are no more the Michigan Boys. we are maid over to the United States 102 Ridgement with half A Pound of Brass on our head.[70] you need not Answer this letter till you hear from me Again. I will write in two Days After we get Settle. it Rain hard. I work all this after noon wet to the hid. Uncle Sam got no Soul.

Beaufort South Carolina   *June 19th/64*   *Or Hilton Head 18 miles*

Dear Mother   I take this oppotunity to write to you that I Am well and harty and hope you Are the Same. we left the Head last thursday.[71] we went to Bed Abought 9 OC after B Roll Call. Abought Eleven OC Clock the order was to Strike tents in two Hours so we got up and Dress Our Self and went to work. Pack up and tore up Every thing

---

68. Murray enlisted on December 1, 1863, and was in Detroit until he traveled with the regiment at the end of March. He therefore could not have been in New York to plant any new crops for the 1864 growing season. He may, however, have sown winter wheat in the late fall of 1863 before heading to Michigan. Winter wheat is typically planted in the fall, goes into dormancy during the winter months, and is then harvested for grain the following summer. Given the timing, it seems likely that this is to what Murray was referring. United States Department of Agriculture, *Usual Planting and Harvesting Dates for U.S. Field Crops*, Agricultural Handbook Number 628, National Agricultural Statistics Service, December 1997.

69. Frank has not been identified.

70. Murray here referred to the U.S. insignia, albeit not literally equal to half a pound, placed on enlisted men's forage or kepi hats, representing the federalization of the First Michigan Colored Infantry. Murray could also have been acknowledging a statement made by Black abolitionist Frederick Douglass to encourage Black enlistment in the Union army: "Once let the black man get upon his person the brass letters U.S. . . . there is no power on earth that can deny he has earned the right to citizenship." "Should the Negro Enlist in the Union Army?", National Hall, Philadelphia (July 6, 1863) published in *Douglass' Monthly*, August 1863.

71. The 102nd USCT left Hilton Head for Beaufort on Thursday, June 16. At Beaufort, it went into a camp of instruction established by Maj. Gen. Foster to instruct Black soldiers in regimental and brigade drill and in weapons firing. Field & Staff Muster Roll, Regimental Return, Company Muster Roll, Record of Events; Maj. Gen. J. G. Foster to H. W. Halleck, Headquarters, Department of the South, Hilton Head, S.C., June 6, 1864, *OR*, ser. 1, vol. 35, pt. 1, 8–9.

that was in Camp. we did not leave till Abought 10 O.C then the Boat left for ~~Ba~~ Beaufort. it is one of the prettyes Place in the South. there is Abought Six thousand Black troops on the Island. it is held By the Colored troop. the N.Y ninty N.Y fifty Six are Station here. the Mayrland ninth the Connitcut are here. the other Ridgement I Dont know there name.[72] we are made over to the United State Reglar it is 102. we hafto ware the nomber and Bugal on our Hats.[73] we was Paid of Just Before we left.[74] I Sent $10 Dollars home. I want you to let me know wheather you Received it Because I want to Send some more. I Did not want to send much at A time. I did not get But thirty five Dollars this time. next time we Receive some Bounty. write Just as soon as you get this letter let me know. It is very sickly in our Ridgement Abought one half of the men are Sick. they Evrage Abought from three to five A Day. where we are is Very Dangerous on Picket. there was two men shoot the first Knight we Camp here of the Mayrland 9. one man is to Be Shoot in the Mass 56 Ridgement for striking an officer.[75] they are very Strick in Camp they tye men Up By the heel. Coronal Chitman is under Arest for it.[76] he is the meanest man this Side of hell. it is Sunday But it Cant Be help. we are Drill Perfict on heavy Artiry. they like to Drill us to

---

72. Although Murray wrote "NY ninty," it is unclear what unit he meant. The Ninetieth Regiment, New York Infantry, was not in the vicinity of Hilton Head during the summer of 1864. The Fifty-Sixth New York Infantry, a White regiment, was then stationed at Beaufort as was the Twenty-Ninth Connecticut Colored Infantry Regiment. The Ninth USCT mustered in at Camp Stanton in Benedict, Charles County, Maryland, in December 1863. It was at Hilton Head in March and April 1864 and then went to Beaufort for the months of May and June. The Ninth USCT is likely the Maryland Ninth mentioned. The unnamed regiment could be the Twenty-Sixth USCT, posted at Beaufort during May and June 1864. Record of Events, 29th Connecticut Colored, 9th USCT Infantry (roll 206), and 56th New York Infantry (roll 121).

73. The brass military bugle horn was the standard infantry insignia during the Civil War. Regimental numbers and company letters were also often part of the emblem worn on enlisted men's hats.

74. On Tuesday, June 14, the paymaster came and paid off the regiment through the first of May. Nelson Diary, June 11, 1864, and June 14, 1864.

75. Although it looks like Murray wrote 56th Mass., a regiment with that designation was not in or around Beaufort at the time. Murray might have meant the Fifty-Fifth Massachusetts Colored Regiment. A firing squad executed Wallace Baker, Company I, Fifty-Fifth Massachusetts Colored Infantry, on June 18, 1864, for "mutinous conduct" in refusing to obey an order and assaulting an officer. Record of Events, 56th USCT Infantry (roll 211), 55th Massachusetts Colored Infantry (roll 211), 56th Massachusetts Infantry (roll 82); Wallace Baker, CMSR; *Weekly Anglo-African*, July 30, 1864; Johnson et al., *All Were Not Heroes*, 436–38.

76. There is no evidence that Col. Chipman was ever under arrest.

Death Before we left. there is no White Ridgement Except the N.Y 9 56. we will Stay here the Rest of the Summer if nothing happen. the Provost Marshal Say we are the Best Guard Been on the Island. they want us to go to washington with Rebels Prisoner Abought Six hundred But our Commander would not let us go. the Reb hate us worst then the Devil. It is geting Dark I must Close So Good By.

tell Lue Crain I Shant write till she write to me. three ~~let~~ I sent to here And Receive ~~non~~ no Answer. give My love to Grandmother and all Inquiring Friend. we are Six Miles from the Bridge we under took to take. the Reb are Saucy But they hafto Submit to Uncle Sam ~~one~~or to the Nigar. word are to good for them. they Say if this Country is to Be Rule By the Damn Nigars they will leave the Country But they Cant leave Just yet they have Some Buiness on hand to Do. they Come in Camp Every Day not on there own good will Because they have the Black man to lead them at the Point of the Bayonett. Eighty five men got to go Down on Provost Guard in the City to Morow white Glove hafto take it. no man Cant go throught the City with out A Pass on Buiness or not. I must stop writing.

Beaufort South Carolina   June 29/64[77]

Dear Mother and Father and Grand mother   I have A little leasure to write A few lines to you that I Am well and harty as A Bear and I hope you are the Same. the weather is very hoot now. there is A Plenty of all kind Fruits here. we are ten miles from land where we do Picket. the Reb are Abought Eight Rod[78] from us. there is five Ridgement here. the N.Y 26 Mass 55 Mayrland Connetticut 26.[79] I heard from

---

77. Although the date here is difficult to read, a report in the pension file contains an excerpt from this letter confirming the date as June 29, 1864. John Murray, CWPF.

78. A rod is a unit of measurement equivalent to 16½ feet. If his estimation was an accurate one, Murray thus indicated that the Confederates were within two hundred feet of the Union pickets.

79. The regiments Murray listed here were the Twenty-Sixth USCT ("N.Y 26"), the Fifty-Fifth Massachusetts Colored Infantry Regiment ("Mass 55"), the Ninth USCT ("Mayrland 9"), and the Twenty-Ninth Connecticut Colored Infantry ("Connetticut 26"). The 102nd USCT could have been the fifth regiment, or perhaps it was the Thirty-Fourth USCT (Second South Carolina Colored Infantry Regiment). The Second South

James Hall.[80] he is well. he is at Morras Island ~~South Ca~~ in front of Charleston. they are Coming here. our Rigt is very Sickly. we Burred[81] of our Boys and one to Day. we have Marchin orders to Day. three Collord one white Ridgement that all the white troop on the Island. Beaufort is A very Pretty Place. the People in the City God made you Can under stand them. Cotton look nice. Corn Plenty. Potatoes you Can Buy them for Seventy five Cents A Peck. I Spoke of Marchin order. this is Contremanded. our Ridgement is not Agoin Because our Gun are Condem. that is the Reason we are not Agoin. the Bridge I Spoke of in my last letter. it will Be A Bloody one. they are Agointo Attack the Bridge and Charleston the Same time. I Seen A little of the Bridge Before. then we lost Seventy Horses and thirteen men kill and Drown. the Horses was Burnt up in the Boat. I Dont Care Abought Agoin this time. we will Be mustered for Pay to morrow. I want you to write just as Soon as you Receive this letter and let me know wheather you Receive ten Dollars I sent to you. I should like to Be home just Abought this time. the Boys are mad for goin Cheated out of the fun the first time But I Dont Care just now till I get near Gun Boat. now I must Stop. it is all in an uproare so good By.

I will send more money just as soon as I get answer.[82]

Carolina was posted at Beaufort in June 1864. But as indicated elsewhere, Murray held great animosity toward the Second South Carolina, so he might simply have neglected to mention it here. Record of Events, 26th USCT, 55th Massachusetts Colored, 9th USCT, 29th Connecticut Colored, and 34th USCT (roll 209).

80. The Fifty-Four Massachusetts Colored Infantry was stationed at Morris Island, South Carolina, in June 1864. Two James Halls were among the enlisted men in the Fifty-Fourth Massachusetts. According to the 1860 census, there were two African American men named James Hall, father and son, both of whom lived in the same household in Lockport, New York. The younger James is likely to whom Murray referred. Among the Hall family was a daughter, Martha. She may be the Martha that Murray sometimes wrote about. U.S. Federal Census 1850, 1860; New York State Census, 1855.

81. Buried.

82. This is written vertically along the side of the letter.

CHAPTER 2

July–August 1864

*"if they get me I have no Doubt they will
String me Between heaven and Earth"*

THE 102ND USCT REMAINED IN THE BEAUFORT AREA ENGAGED PRImarily in guard duty and drilling throughout July. From July 1 to July 14, Companies C and D occupied the camp of the Twenty-Sixth USCT inside the entrenchements at Beaufort. These companies manned the fortifications until the return of the Twenty-Sixth USCT whereupon the detachment of the 102nd USCT returned to the regiment's primary camp. At the beginning of the month, Murray's Company E removed to Battery Burnside, about a mile away. There for about three weeks, the company performed guard duty and drilled in heavy artillery.[1]

In August, the 102nd USCT deployed to Florida accompanied by other Black regiments including the Twenty-Ninth Connecticut Colored Regiment and the Thirty-Fourth USCT. Although it had a small population, Florida was an important source of cattle and other food supplies for the Confederacy. After a significant battle at Olustee in February 1864, fighting was generally limited to small raids and skirmishes.[2] It was not glamorous but it could be constant and deadly. Late in the afternoon of August 1, after a celebration marking the anniversary of the liberation of enslaved persons in the West Indies, the 102nd broke camp at Beaufort. It proceeded to Jacksonville aboard

---

1. The Twenty-Sixth USCT left Beaufort on July 1 on a reconnaissance expedition toward Charleston and engaged with the enemy on Johns and James Islands, South Carolina. The regiment returned to its camp at Beaufort on July 14 and resumed guard duty. *OR*, ser. 1, vol. 35, pt. 1, 36; 26th USCT, Record of Events.

2. The battle of Olustee, February 20, 1864, was the largest battle fought in Florida during the Civil War. A Union expedition from South Carolina intended to sever Confederate supply routes and recruit Black soldiers initially met little resistance. The Fifty-Fourth Massachusetts Colored Infantry and the Thirty-Fifth USCT were part of the Union force. When the expedition pushed deeper into the state, Confederate command sent reinforcements to bolster Florida's defenses. Confederates repulsed the Union advance at Olustee and the Union force retreated to Jacksonville. The Union suffered around eighteen hundred casualties while the Confederates lost about nine hundred men. The Confederate victory kept them in control of Florida's interior. Dobak, *Freedom by the Sword*, 65–70.

the steamer *Cannonicus*. They made a brief stop at Hilton Head where the soldiers exchanged their old arms for Springfield rifles. The expedition arrived in Jacksonville on the third. Murray and his comrades then marched inland along the Florida Railroad about twenty miles to Baldwin.[3]

While posted at Baldwin the regiment destroyed sections of the Jacksonville and Tallahasee Railroad between Baldwin and Lake City, tearing up about three miles of railroad tracks a day, burning the ties and bending the rails. It was here that Murray and his comrades experienced their first taste of hostile fire. On August 10, a Confederate cavalry unit suddenly attacked sections of the regiment on the outskirts of Baldwin. Officers deployed skirmishers and the rebels quickly retreated into nearby woods. There were no casualties on the Union side. Chaplain Waring later recalled that their time in Florida provided the men with "some experience in actual service in the field."[4]

At 3:00 in the morning on August 15, the 102nd USCT began a grueling one-hundred-mile march through eastern Florida in extremely poor weather, tasked with destroying the railroad as it went. The infantry column, composed of the Thirty-Fourth USCT, Thirty-Fifth USCT, and the 102nd USCT, advanced fifteen to twenty miles a day through low swampy country following the Florida Key West Railroad. Along the way, the regiment engaged in foraging and small raids. The stockpile the men gathered and brought in included horses, cattle, slaves, and other rebel property. One night, a herd of cattle apparently ran near the camp, alarming the men who thought it was rebel cavalry. The 102nd USCT reached Magnolia on the St. Johns River after five days of hard marching where it resumed the familiar service of picket duty and assisted in the building of fortifications. Nothing of note transpired over the next week or so. The regiment left the shady groves of Magnolia on August 29 aboard the steamer *Wyoming*.[5]

---

3. Nelson Diary, August 1, 1864; 102nd USCT, Record of Events.

4. Nelson Diary, August 10, 1864; 102nd USCT, Record of Events; William Waring to Adjutant General, Beaufort, S.C., September 19, 1864.

5. *OR*, ser. 1, vol. 35, pt. 1, 37; Nelson Diary, August 18, 1864; Monthly Returns, 1864; Company Muster Roll; Field and Staff Muster Roll.

Beaufort South Carolina July 3/64

Dear mother and Father   tis Sunday. I have all Day to my Self. I am well yet and hope I may Stay So and I hope your are the same. you Dont know what hoot ~~wet~~ weather is. Put Sweet Potatoes Into the Pure Sand it will Cook in three hours. we Cant Drill after Seven O.Clock in the marning nor Can we Drill till Abought Seven at Knight. our Camp is Split up Again. we are out on Picket. Inside it Dangers for the Eyes Shoot Every thing you see moove after Dark. A man life is nothing more than A Daze life. we would have nice time Before this if our Gun Ben good. we was in Spected and Candem. they Said they would not Send us out with Sutch Gun. ~~My is~~ mine is good Enought for me. I have Seen A little Uncle Sam Pills.[6] they make Bad nozes when they Pass. they made me leave A Boat after Setting it on fire. three Ridgement left the Island to take the Bridge Again.[7] this make the fourth time. they will have it this time. they ware three Days lading Boats with Ammunition. there will Be Abought twenty thousand troops. I saw it once I Dont want to see it Again. we got Another Bridge is troublesome. the Say if we Dont leave in five Days they will healp us to moove. genral Foster[8] went over to Mr Reb with A flage of truce. I guess he will tell them to Stay at home. there wont Be no quarters Showed to them. they have Slaughtered our folke. we Shoot Ever thing that have gray Cloth an they Do Do the Same.[9] we are at fourt Wm. one 10 Pound ~~one~~

---

6. Murray mentioned "Uncle Sam Pills" or some variation of the term several times in his letters. The context in which Murray used the phrase suggests it was a moniker for bullets, balls, shot, and shell, similar to the term "Lincoln's pills" commonly used among Civil War soldiers.

7. The Fifty-Sixth New York (White), Twenty-Sixth USCT, Ninth USCT, and Thirty-Fourth USCT were absent from Beaufort from June 30 to July 10. These regiments, commanded by Brig. Gen. Rufus Saxton, were part of a reconnaissance expedition to Johns and James Islands, South Carolina. 26th USCT, 9th USCT, 34th USCT, Record of Events; *OR*, ser. 1, vol. 35, pt. 1, 36.

8. John Gray Foster (1823–74). Foster graduated from West Point in 1846. He was wounded at Molino del Rey during the Mexican American War. Foster served as chief engineer of Ambrose Burnside's North Carolina expedition in July 1862. During the last year of the war, Foster commanded the Department of the South. After the Civil War, he served with the Corps of Engineers. Warner, *Generals in Blue*, 157–58.

9. Stories of mistreatment of Black soldiers at the hands of the enemy appeared in newspapers nationwide. Murray and his comrades were aware of such reports. The fate of the Fifty-Fourth Massachusetts Colored Infantry in its attack on Fort Wagner in July

two 20 one 32 Pounders Grape and Canster and Shell five thousand Round Each and on Beaufort River. I wish you was hear. watter mellon and tomatoes and green Corn Cotton Penuts figes lemmon and oorange are Plenty. Sweet Pattatoes and Snakes of all kindes. they Come and Sleep with you Every Knight and nothing the Scorpion to Run the whole lenght of you and for Sand flees they are thicker they Oysters Shell on the. this Bridge I Been Speaking of is Between Charleston South C and Savanah Georga.[10] no marre at Presant. I am getting Sleepy.

Dont forget to harvis the wheat in Seson and thrash it Right out and take your Away

Beaufort South Carolina July 10/64

Dear Mother I have A little leasure time to write to you A few lines that I Am well at Present But our Ridgement is very Sick. they Die from two to five A Day.[11] they Cant Stand this hoot weather Down

---

1863 was widely known. They undoubtedly heard the stories of the battle of Olustee less than six months before Murray's letter. Evidence suggests that Confederate soldiers killed wounded Black soldiers left on the battlefield there. The men in Murray's regiment were also aware of Fort Pillow, Tennessee, where, in April 1864, Confederates under the command of Nathan Bedford Forrest executed scores of Black Union soldiers after they surrendered. Murray was not alone in his sentiment that he and his comrades would give no quarter to rebel soldiers. Shortly after John penned this letter, a private in the Fifty-Fifth Massachusetts wrote: "As far as this regiment is concerned, we will ask no quarter, and rest satisfied that we will give none." Another soldier in the same regiment expressed a similar statement, writing "there will be but little quarter shown to rebels." *Detroit Free Press*, August 4, 1863, July 31, 1864; Jenkins, *Climbing Up to Glory*, 37; To Mr. Editor, Headquarters, 55th Reg. Mass. Infantry, Paltka, Fla., April 10, 1864, *Weekly Anglo-African*, May 14, 1864; To Mr. Editor, Camp 55th Mass. Vols., Folly Island, S.C., Jan. 12, 1864, *Weekly Anglo-African*, January 30, 1864.

10. There were a number of bridges and trestle works along the Charleston and Savannah Railroad in the path of the Johns Island expedition. Which specific one Murray referred to here is unclear.

11. July 1864 was indeed an unhealthy time for the soldiers in the vicinity of Beaufort, but if Murray was referring only to his regiment, the records do not validate his comment that two to five men died each day. Nine enlisted men of the 102nd USCT died between July 1 and July 9, the day before Murray wrote this letter. Murray might have meant the number of deaths more generally. Monthly Returns, 1864.

South. the themometer stand from one 100 to 110 Degree Days After Days.[12] our Ridement had Alittle fun one Day last week with the Contreband Ridgement. they dispise the Black Buckey or Black Yankey. we was Showed A little favor Abought goin on the last Expdition. they Call us Coward. we told them that we Could fight with out Being Drove Into Battle. that mad them mad. they Come at us like tigers But they left just as soon. they went to there quarters and got there Gun. we took Club and Brick and Drove them Back. if they let us Alone we would Drove them Into to Sea. there was two men kill of the Contreband.[13] our men Knock Down the Conoral the Majer Lieutenant. if our Ridgement been Altogeather there would not Been A Contreband Ridgement on the Island. the New York Boys[14] will Stick By us till the last. the Mayrland 9[15] Shoot Into the Second South[16] to make them fight. that what made them mad. our Ridgement is Split up Again. our Company is Split up. one half is on one Part of Island and the other is in Another B Part Doing Picket. the Reb have not Don what they Said they would Do. they give us five Days to leave the Island. if I we Did not they would help us off. But they lie. the Boys left last week took the Bridge. Did not loose A man this time. then they went to Charleston. they fought three Days and half got within Eight miles of the City on main land.[17] we got the Best kname of Enny Ridgement Been here

---

12. Capt. Nelson noted that the temperature was over a hundred degrees for several days in June and July 1864. Nelson Diary, June 20, 1864–July 3, 1864.

13. The "Contreband Ridgement" Murray referred to was the Second South Carolina Colored Infantry, under the command of Col. James Montgomery. The First and Second South Carolina regiments were redesignated as the Thirty-Third USCT and Thirty-Fourth USCT a few months prior, but Murray continued to refer to them either by their initial designations or simply as the "contraband" regiments. Despite Murray's assertion that two men were killed in this incident with the 102nd, Officer of the Day 1st Lt. Bennett reported that the disturbance was "quieted without any serious results." Tensions between northern and southern African Americans is not often mentioned in Civil War accounts, but this incident suggests that perhaps regional prejudices held by some Americans could be almost as powerful a force as racial prejudice. General Orders No. 44, Head Quarters, Department of the South, Hilton Head, S.C., March 26, 1864, *OR*, ser. 1, vol. 35, pt. 2, 29; Report of the Guard, July 6, 1864, Guard Report Book.

14. Twenty-Sixth USCT.

15. Ninth USCT.

16. Murray's statement that the Ninth USCT fired into the Second South Carolina to force them to continue fighting in a recent engagement with the enemy insinuated that the men had not conducted themselves in a soldierly manner. No records to substantiate Murray's allegation have been found.

17. Perhaps not surprising, Murray's descriptions of this expedition against Charleston

and the most Independent and Ratest Because they are not Afraid to Stop Nice Cloth.[18] the Contreband Dost not look A man in the face. we get Paid of next friday at Sixteen Dollars Amonth and Some Bounty.[19] Keep track of the Post office. your letter Come quicker to me then mine dose to you. no more at Presant. it Very hoot and Sultry. we have two Days of thunder and lightning But no Rain. we are station at fourt taylor the other at fourt Burnside.[20]

Northen Black   Southern Black   Cant live together[21]

---

and the railroad leading to Savannah and its results were somewhat different than the official reports. Gen. Foster left Hilton Head on the evening of Friday, July 1, with a force of about five thousand infantry, one hundred cavalry, and two sections of artillery. The detachment entered the mouth of the North Edisto River on the morning of the second and landed a force on Seabrook Island under orders to push forward to the upper part of Johns Island, seize the ferry, cross over, and destroy the railroad. The federal troops did not fulfill the main objective of the expedition; namely, the destruction of the railroad and bridges. The total loss for the expedition was 33 killed, 133 wounded, 143 missing, 3 sunstruck, and 18 drowned by the accidental upsetting of a boat on the Stono River. Asst. Adj. Gen. W. L. M. Burger to Brig. Gen. Saxton, Headquarters, Department of the South, Hilton Head, S.C., June 28, 1864; Maj. Gen. J. G. Foster to Maj. Gen. Halleck, Headquarters, Department of the South, Hilton Head, S.C., June 30, 1864; Maj. Gen. J. G. Foster to Maj. Gen. H. W. Halleck, Headquarters, Department of the South, Hilton Head, S.C., July 7, 1864; Maj. Gen. J. G. Foster to Maj. Gen. H. W. Halleck, Headquarters, Department of the South, Hilton Head, S.C., July 12, 1864, all in *OR*, ser. 1, vol. 35, pt. 2, 14–15, 16–17, 155, 157–58.

18. "Nice cloth" denoted officers. Murray indicated that members of his regiment on picket or guard duty were not reluctant to challenge officers. Note the contrasting image John then made in regard presumably to the South Carolina regiments of which he often disparaged; namely, that they do not look "a man in the face."

19. Murray wrote this letter on Sunday, July 10, 1864. The "next Friday" would have been Friday, July 15. His statement suggested an awareness of recent congressional legislation that increased the pay of soldiers to sixteen dollars per month. Evidence does not suggest that the men were actually paid at this time, however. Regimental Order Books.

20. Fort Taylor and Fort Burnside, also referred to as Battery Taylor and Battery Burnside, were gun batteries situated to protect Union troops occupying Beaufort. Fort Burnside contained two 8-inch guns: one 30-pdr Parrott and one 24-pdr gun. Fort Taylor housed two 30-pdr Parrotts and one 24-pdr howitzer. Report of Charles Suter, Chief Engineer's office, Hilton Head, S.C., June 8, 1864, *OR*, ser. 1, vol. 35, pt. 2, 117–19.

21. Murray's somewhat cryptic postscript here inferred an increasing perception, or perhaps reality, at least in his eyes, of ill will between Black Union soldiers and the southern Black population, be they enslaved refugees, conscript soldiers, or other segments of the southern Black population. Murray certainly demonstrates considerable hostility toward Black southerners.

Beaufort South Carolina   *July 17th/64*

we will change our Name soon[22]

I have got time once more to write A few lines to you that I Am well at Presant and hope you and the Rest are Doing well. our Ridgement is geting Some Better But there is Agreat menny Sick Boys. our Ridgement has Been Broak up Again and my Company was Devided one half at Battery Taylor the other at Battery Burnside on the Bank of the River. we was Abought two week there. flees and gnat are worst then Reb. it was A Pleasant Place in A Pine Grove. we had two Places to Guard. one at Fourt Duane. that Place was mounted with Eight Gun and A high loge fence. there is forty thousand Reb twenty miles from here. we hafte Sleep with one Eye open with Sixty Round of Catrage. we are all together now But we have marching orders. it wont Be Straing that we will Be Sent home. they are Agointo Pay us this week Seven Dollars Amonth But we wont take it. the New York Boys are gointo Do the same. they say they Cant fight for that. all the Northen Ridgement gointo Stack Arms. the State of Michigan has Call us home. we are goin to the Head Again. if they Cant get us to take Seven Dollars we will Be in New York next week on our way home to Guard Reb Prisnor in the State. the State of Michigan is Paying for our Baurd and Clothes. they wont give us no new Gun.[23] the Contreband Ridg Dont like us. we ~~no~~ know to much for them. our Ridge like to Drive of there Ridgement

---

22. The regiment had been redesignated the 102nd USCT almost two months prior, and Murray had been instructing his family to direct their correspondence to the 102nd, so why he made note of a possible name change here is unclear. If he had any understanding that his regiment's affiliation was going to change again, he made no clear communication of this. Perhaps there is a connection between this comment and his discussions elsewhere of what he perceived as strife between Michigan, the U.S. government, and his regiment.

23. Murray was not the only one uneasy about the condition of the regiment's weaponry. Just two days prior, Col. Chipman ordered his company commanders to make a thorough inspection of the men's guns "to find out what parts of guns if any are missing or lost and attend at once to furnishing such parts as far as possible." Other comments made elsewhere by Chipman and Capt. Nelson express similar concerns. An editorial in the *Detroit Advertiser and Tribune*, written by "Van," mentions an inspection of the men's guns on July 20, 1864, "with the view to have them condemned and give us new ones. Men and officers are delighted with the project of getting a good arm upon which they can depend." Circular, Headquarters, 102nd USCT, Beaufort, S.C., July 15, 1864, Order Book; *Detroit Advertiser and Tribune*, August 3, 1864.

into the Sea. they are twelve hundred stronge. we are not got five hundred Able Body men.[24] they want us to go in front of Charleston But we cant see it. give us our Sixteen Dollars then we will fight like A man But not for less. Congress has Pass the Bill for All Colord troop to have the same Pay and Ration. our officers are leaving the Ridgement.[25] the Prvost Marshal Say we are the worst Ridgement Been on the Island But the Best he Ever Saw to Do Duty. he Says they ~~went~~ wont let A man Pass when they have A Right to Pass. he told us that the Reson they Dont like us Because we wont Knuckle to some Potickler Person. we are to over Baring. now I must stop my time is up So Good By.

We will Change Kname Soon. if Sixteen Dollars Dont Come this week will tell the story.
Dont foget to Put Company E[26]

Beaufort South Carolina   *July 22th/64*

Blacks shot at the Lieutenent. He Would not give the Counter sign.

Dear Mother   I take this oppotunity to write A few lines that I Am well as A Buck. I never felt Better In the world then I do now at the Presant time and hope you are the Same. we had A very heavy thunder Shower last Knight. the Rain Poured Down in torrance. I was on Guard. the Grand Round[27] Came Around just as the Rain Commence. the Countersign was Lake Shamplain. we are on Provost. they cant Do

---

24. The regiment reported 487 enlisted men present for duty in July 1864. Monthly Returns, 1864.

25. Beyond the change in command from Col. Barnes to Col. Chipman, few changes actually took place in the regiment during this time. 2nd Lt. George Stoneburner, Company K, resigned from the regiment in June, and 1st Lt. H. D. Benham, Company B, died July 3, 1864. Several officers were either sick or on detached service when Murray wrote this letter, so perhaps he mistakenly thought they had left the regiment. Monthly Returns, 1864.

26. This indicates that Murray knew of the second John Murray in his regiment and wanted to ensure that the letters were delivered to the right person.

27. The Officer of the Day, usually a captain, conducted grand rounds typically between midnight and 2 o'clock a.m. to inspect the guards at all the various posts, ensure that they remained awake and alert at their duty stations, and properly challenged anyone approaching their post for the correct countersign of the day, a measure designed to ensure no enemy entered camp.

with out us if we are so Bad for Shooting. one of the Boys Shoot at one of the Lieutant Twice. he would not Stop But they Brought him up to A Stand. he had the Countersign But he was to Drunk to Answer then we took him to the Guards Hous.[28] the Provost want to know what kind of Boys we ware to Shoot Aman when he had A Pass. the Countersign was Lake Shamplain. they Began to Be Scart of the mich Boys now we are on Duty. the Paymaster is around But the Cornal told him that he need not come to Pay off this Ridgement with out Paying it of at Sixteen Dollars A Month. we Swore that we would give our time to Uncle Same Before we would take it. our officers get Afraid of us. they would Read on Dress Perrade Every Day Abought mutany to Scare the Boys But it would not take. they Paid the Mass Rid off at Sixteen Dollars.[29] the N.Y. Boys will have it and the Conn and the mayrland 9 will not take Seven Dollars. the Northen Boys Stick together titer then ticks. Cornal Chitman time is out in this Department.[30] Cornal ~~Bent~~ Bennett time is out at ~~the~~ Hilton Head.[31] the State of Mich has called us home. it Seems that they cant Do Enny thing with us yet But they will make out in time. the State I Gues will hold us the three years. if we Do go home I Dont think She will Disband us. we will do Provost Duty in the State. in the last Battle the New York Boys lost 70 men kill and mising. the ordley Sargent was A nice man. the Second South Run.[32] we can here heavy firing at Charleston Every Day. A new Expidition is to Be got up next week for the Bridge and Before Charleston. it will Be four time to take the Bridge But fail. it will take 15,000 men to take

---

28. No official report of this incident appears in the records. The Report of the Guard for July 21, 1864, shows Murray detailed on guard duty and the countersign as Lake Champlain. A. S. Merrill, the Officer of the Day did not record anything of note in his report, and the only addition to the men in arrest from the twenty-first to the twenty-second was Private John Willis, confined for "crossing a sentinel." Willis was released a day later. Report of the Guard, July 21–23, 1864, Guard Report Book.

29. Either the Fifty-Fourth or Fifty-Fifth Massachusetts Colored Regiment.

30. Col. Chipman continued to command the regiment until its muster out in September 1865.

31. Lt. Col. W. T. Bennett was detached from the 102nd USCT at the end of May 1864 to serve as chief police officer on the staff of the Brigadier General Commanding, Department of the South, Hilton Head. Bennett served on various detached assignments until promoted to colonel of the Thirty-Third USCT in December 1864. It is unlikely that he returned to duty with the 102nd USCT. William T. Bennett, CMSR.

32. Although Murray again implied that the Second South Carolina (Thirty-Fourth USCT) acted cowardly in a recent engagement, likely the St. Johns expedition of which it was a part, evidence does not support this accusation.

it. I Dont care Abought goin Again. it was to Rough this jumping one
Board is not safe two menny men in the watter wont Do. So Good By
till next time.

the next letter Send the number of your Box. Dont forget to Put Company E and the number of Box.

I want you to send me some Postage Stamp.[33] they are Scarce in this
City. you cant Get them for Love nor money. Send abought 50 Cents
worth. I will Pay you Back next Pay Day. that will Be next week if Sixteen Dollars come.

Beaufort South Carolina   *July 29/64*

I have not much time to write. I thought I would answer the letter I Receive the twenty Seventh Inst. I am well at Presant and hope you are
the same. there is Some troble abought this Rid at ~~Wshishing~~ Washingtoon. ~~we~~ they Dont Know Ennything abought the Mich first nor the
United State Vollenteer. we are not on Record. they cant Do Ennything
with us But they wont let us go. the state has called us home Mishigan Delr.[34] the state has call us home. the transport has Been here. our
leading men Sent them Back.[35] we will Be home Before long. I Dont

---

33. Murray frequently commented on the scarcity of postage stamps and asked his family to send him some. Postage, ink, and paper were sometimes difficult to come by. One of the letters sent by his mother, now a part of this collection, included a three-cent stamp (see chapter 5). Presumably, she sent others when she was able.

34. Probably Detroit. The last phrase is written along the side of the page with a line designating where it goes in the letter.

35. Although Murray made similar comments elsewhere, there is no indication that this was anything more than rumor. Evidence shows that such speculation as this surfaced in other Black regiments, showing the power of rumors as a real force. In a letter to the *Weekly Anglo-African*, a soldier in the Fifty-Fifth Massachusetts Colored Infantry stated that "there is considerable speculation among the men now, arising from rumors of the two regiments (54th and 55th) being recalled to Massachusetts and disbanded . . . if we stay our nine months without pay . . . the majority of our men seem to be placing great confidence in it." Additionally, Murray seems to be saying that transports arrived to take the regiment back to Michigan but that the officers refused them. There is no corroborating evidence of this incident either. Whether such fears were the result of some insecurities common to all African American troops or those raised initially as state regiments is unknown. To Mr. Editor, Camp 55th Mass. Vols., Folly Island, S.C., January 12, 1864, *Weekly Anglo-African*, January 30, 1864.

think they can Keep us. time will tell. I know Dought we will winter in Detroit are some Part of Mich. we Expict Pay Soon. to Day we had A genral Inspection By the Inspector. I went on Guard yesterday at Eight O'Cl and Came off abought two O'C to Day and allmost Dead for the want of Sleep. Day befour yesterday I went over the River on lady Island. that is A Pretty Place. there is some talk of goin to New Orleans to Do Provost Dity.[36] there is abought five thousand Johnnes or Reb you ar better A quainted By that Knames. you would like to Be here to here and See the Yankey Shell Burst in the air and the Small Ball Sing around your head. our officers are afraid of us. they think we will Shoot them. they think wright. they thought they would Scare us just like they Do the Contreband Rid. there is one human white man left in our Rid one in the State that is the Govener.[37] I should like to go to New Orleans Before we Come Back. I Shant Put to much confendence in Enny white man. this war never will Be stop as longe as there is money to Be made at it. the City of Charleston is Burnt.[38] when we leave here we are goin to Washington City then home. they are trying hard to Keep us. I want you to answer this just as soon you Recieve this. now I must Stop. it is geting Dark So Good By till next time. Every mail I send three or four letters. we have two mail once A week. Send me the number of your Box. Excuse Bad writing not much time.

July 31		*Beaufort South Carolina*

Marching Orders. if i get killed good By   J.L. Murray

not much time to write. we got marching orders to Pack Up. we are goin to fight Johnny. this time we are goin to Charles to Be Slatghtered.[39] our Gun wont go. if we Do go to Charleston we will Stack

---

36. This appears to be just another camp rumor.

37. The governor of Michigan was Austin Blair, whose term began on January 1, 1861, and extended throughout the war. A lawyer turned politician, Blair helped establish the Republican Party in Michigan and served in both the Michigan House of Representatives and Senate before the war. While a Michigan senator, he introduced legislation to allow Black men the right to vote. After the war, Blair served in the U.S. House of Representatives (1867–73). Taylor, *Old Slow Town*, 40.

38. Charleston did not burn this early in the war and was not yet occupied by the Union.

39. Murray's tone in this letter is more morose than elsewhere. It certainly sounds as

our arms. this will Be the first Battle we have had. the Cornal Sent to the Head for new Gun. he said he Did not want his men and himself to Be Slaterd.[40] we got three Day Ration. the Bugal is A Blowing So Good By. if I Dont get Shoot I will write just as Soon we get Back. Give my love to Lue and Emma.

Uncle Same wont let us go till we have A fight then they will Pay us off. five O'Clock in the marning orders light marching orders.[41] the New York Boys will Guard our Camp while we are gon. yonge Degrawe the Boys usto work for Mr. Brumley Charles Lockety Chancy Leverton. they are in the Conn Rid.[42] they went just Before I did. they are well and harty. Breakfast call. cold mule and Bread and Coffee maid out of Bean and other trash. no more but at Presant.

Mule Muat to Eat[43]

---

if he was preparing for a battle and possible death. Why exactly John thought he and his comrades were going "to Be Slatghtered" is unknown, but the poor quality of their guns seems to have played a role in his fears. Perhaps word was that the regiment was going on an expedition toward Charleston as other Black troops had earlier in the month. Those units had sustained casualties and Murray wrote previously about their losses.

40. Capt. Nelson also commented about the state of the rifles, writing in his diary that the regiment's "guns are good for nothing." On July 25, he noted that his men "made rather wild shots," at target practice, presumably because of the condition of their weapons. Nelson Diary, July 25, 1864.

41. The 102nd USCT, along with the Twenty-Ninth Connecticut Colored, as well as the Ninth, Twenty-Sixth, and Thirty-Fourth USCT regiments, had orders to be ready to embark aboard transports to Hilton Head. Instructions to the men were to carry three days' rations, one pair of socks, a rubber or woolen blanket, and twenty extra rounds of ammunition. Asst. Adj. Gen. W. L. M. Burger to Brig. Gen. E. E. Potter, HeadQuarters, Department of the South, Hilton Head, S.C., July 30, 1864; Brig. Gen. Wm. Birney to Maj. Gen. Foster, Headquarters, Department of the South, Hilton Head, July 30, 1864, all in *OR*, ser. 1, vol. 35, pt. 2, 200–201.

42. According to the 1860 federal census, William Bromley was a forty-five-year-old barber in Lockport, N.Y. Elias Degraff (Degroff, Degraugh) and Charles Dockhrity (Dockrity, Daugherty, Dougherty) were privates in Company H, Twenty-Ninth Connecticut Colored Infantry. Chancy Leverton has not been located in either the census records or the rolls of the Twenty-Ninth Connecticut. Elias Degraff, CMSR; Charles Dockhrity, CMSR; U.S. Federal Census, 1850, 1860.

43. Murray's lamentations about the soldiers' diet in this letter indicate a shortage of supplies, possibly the result of preparations for the impending expedition. His comments have not been corroborated elsewhere, though a comrade attested, albeit years after the war, that the men were on half rations in June 1864 and "in consequence the men's hunger led them to eat almost anything that they could get hold of." Andrew Vineyard, CWPF.

August 14th/64   Balding Station Florida

Dear Mother   I have not got But A short time to write to let you Know that I Am well. After A heard march my limb have not got over cramping yet otherwise I feel well. and you and Grandmother are well. I went out on Picket the next knight. Johnny was Around trying our Post. he found out Some Body Elce was in the Beside him Self. we Squrmishing most all knight with them. they thought they could Drive us in the Same they Did the first South.[44] they found out it could not Be Don. they Did not Drive us nor twice the number. what Johnny got to Do he Dost in hurray and off. I had A Ball Split the wood on my Gun and Cut Into I had tied on my Back.[45] my Dog tent fell to the ground. the Bullet whistle Around my head like hail Stone. we gave them one Volley. they left to Parts Unknown. we took five Prisoner we would Riddle with Ball if our Cornal would let us. he want us to set Example for them not Disgrace our Self By killing them. I want Revenge what they have Don at fourt Pillow.[46] I came Down here to fight. if they get me I no Doubt they will String me Between heaven and Earth But they Shant take A live with out I loose my Arm or leg. my mess mate we have Pledge our Self to Stick By one other till the last. we are Duty Bound never to Be taken A live. I have not Been A fraid in All the Play Spell we had yet. I Dont know what I may Do when I got to face those

---

44. It is unknown exactly to what Murray was referring here in regard to the First South Carolina Colored Regiment (Thirty-Third USCT). But he again insinuated that soldiers of the South Carolina Colored Regiments acted unsoldierly, and it shows that John's hostile attitude shown elsewhere was not just directed against the Second South Carolina.

45. Although Murray does not fully complete his thought here, the bullet likely cut the pack on his back. The Company Muster Roll for September and October 1864 notes that Murray owed the government $2.14 for "the loss of knapsack." From his description it does not appear that this was the incident between Confederate cavalry and the 102nd USCT on August 10, 1864. There was likely additional skirmishing between the lines during the Union column's march in Florida. John Murray, CMSR.

46. Fort Pillow, Tennessee, was a two-mile line of entrenchments that faced inland on the bluffs above the Mississippi River. Approximately six hundred Union soldiers, Black and White, manned the fort, occupied by the Union since June 1862. On April 12, 1864, two brigades of Nathan Bedford Forrest's Confederate cavalry, about fifteen hundred men strong, captured the fort. The Confederates killed between 246 and 264 Union soldiers. Another 31 died of wounds. Two-thirds of the dead were Black soldiers. Afterward, an army-investigating committee interviewed several dozen witnesses who alleged that Forrest's men shot unarmed Black soldiers who were trying to surrender. Dobak, *Freedom by the Sword*, 206–8; Cimprich, *Fort Pillow*; Jenkins, *Climbing Up to Glory*, 38.

Big Siege Pieces with grape and canester. it might make my hare curl once more Around. it Rain Every Day Sence we Been in Florida. So Good By.

Jacksonvill Florida   19 August/64[47]

Dear mother   I take this oppotunity write A few line to you that I am well at presant and hope these few lines will find you well. we left Beaufort August 1. the Boys had a good time Before they went away. we went to the Head and stop all Knight and got our new Gun and left there the next Day abought four O'Clock in the afternoon.[48] the next day we arived at the mouth of St John River. About 1 O'C arived at Jacksonvill. we stop there all knight. left at Day light for Balding Station. we march 25 miles that Day. the Sun was Scalding hott. I give out abought 10 O'C and left the Ranks and went under a tree. tride to Set Down But Could not and Down By a tree. my feet Becam numb to my Knees and Comencing Cramping. Some of the Boys Rub my leg. my load was to much for me. I had Seventy Round of Catridge my Knapsack and Blanket and Seven Days Ration on my Back.[49] I

---

47. Since the regiment was only at Jacksonville for one night, arriving on August 3 and leaving the next day, this letter was not composed entirely at Jacksonville. The date on this letter is also extremely difficult to read so the 19th may not be an accurate transcription. Perhaps Murray wrote this letter over a number of days. Alternatively, John mistakenly wrote Jacksonville when he meant Magnolia. On August 19, the regiment was at Magnolia.

48. An order by command of Maj. Gen. Foster, dated August 1, 1864, stated that "the exigencies of the service requiring the arms of the 102nd USCT to be exchanged the comdg officers of said regiment will turn in to the Ord Department at once the old arms of his regt they having been condemned by the A.A. Insp. Genl. D.S. and will receive new arms in their place." The timing suggests that Foster's order was the outcome of the general inspection that Murray wrote about in his letter dated July 29. As much as Murray discusses the poor quality of their guns, it is interesting that he did not write more about the new weapons the men received at Hilton Head. Order Book; Nelson Diary, August 1, 1864.

49. Capt. Wilbur Nelson confirms that "it was a very hot day and the march was a hard one." Even in light marching order, carrying three days rations, a blanket, a gun, and ammunition, the heat would have made for a difficult march. Murray's service record notes that he was "absent from camp without leave" sometime in July or August, but neither this nor the Company Morning Reports and Remarks provide specific information as to this incident. Murray's recorded absence could be related to the debilitating march. Pension records reveal that several men of the 102nd USCT suffered sunstroke on this

throwed away Everything Except my Gun and Equipment. the Ridgement got in Camp aboght 2 hour Before I Did. we Stop at Balding till the fifteenth. we tore up abought ten miles of Rail Road there where we Saw the Souther Elephant.[50] after we tore up the Bridge and Burnt it Johnney Came Up on the Rear of us commence firing on us But we Soon Stop there fun. the next Day they Commence at the Second South. Johnney Drove them But Ralleed Again and Drive them. one man was Slightly hurt.[51] the next Day Mayrland 9th Rid[52] and abought 50 mounted Infantry went up to work. through the Knight Johnny had Plant two Pieces of artilry on Cars. just as Soon they come in Sight they Commence throwing Shell. one Shell Burst and Kill one of the Infantry. they Striped him of his Cloth Bured three Inches Under groun. we went up to Reinforce them But Johnny had gon. we Burnt Everything we Could See. we Did not leave Even A hog pen. we left Balding Station march A Raid through Florida. it was warm. we march two Days through Swamp and water four Inches to four feet Deep. Did not See But two Houses. we Stop at Vermilion Station. we Kill forty Head of Cattle for our super and Breakfast then we started for the next Day journey. we Burnt the Place and Captured four Reb. the third Day we took fifteen Counterband mostley woman and Children.[53] then

---

march, the effects of which they felt for years. Nelson Diary, August 4, 1864; John Murray, CMSR, CWPF.

50. The term "seeing the elephant" refers to experiencing enemy fire.

51. On August 12, 1864, about six miles west of Baldwin, a Confederate force of infantry, cavalry, and artillery attacked several companies of the Thirty-Fourth USCT as they worked to destroy railroad track. Two men belonging to Company I were wounded in the legs by canister shot. 34th USCT, Record of Events.

52. This was not the Ninth USCT that Murray usually called the Maryland regiment. The Ninth USCT was with the Army of the James, X Corps, serving in Virginia, as was the Eighth USCT. There was an Eighth Maryland Infantry (White), but it, too, was stationed in Virginia at this time. *OR*, ser. 1, vol. 35, pt. 2, 200–202; 8th USCT, 9th USCT, Record of Events.

53. Col. William Noble, Seventeenth Connecticut, was in command of the infantry column composed of the Thirty-Fourth, Thirty-Fifth, and 102nd USCT, with a detachment of Third Rhode Island Heavy Artillery that left Baldwin on August 15. In a subsequent report, Col. Noble detailed the cache brought in by various scouting parties sent out during the march, including horses, stock, enslaved persons, and other rebel property. Brig. Gen. Hatch noted the arrival of Noble's command at Magnolia with the comment that they brought with them "about 75 contrabands and some few horses and mules." Capt. Nelson also recorded that the "fruits of the raid are some 60 negrows, 2 old guns, and 10 mules." Several times in this letter Murray mentioned capturing or bringing in "contraband." More than a year and a half after the Emancipation Proclamation, any enslaved persons captured or otherwise coming into Union lines would have been freed.

abought five hundred Cavelry left us and one Rid went another Road. they come across Gorrilla Dickson[54] with Eight hundred men. Dickson got in A Small town Call Gainvill abought 2 hours Before our men Did. they found out we was A coming. he moved out in the woods and corn field. our men on saddle ther horses went in Search of the fodder for the horses. Dickson had to Pieces of artilry our Boys had But one. the main force had four Pieces. Johnny open on them. they Maid A Charge on them three time and Diven Back. our Boys Drew there Battry of the ground and Spiked Befour it was captured. one shoot from our Battry Dismount one of there. gaud menny kill on Both side.[55] the Countreband they Dickerson Butcher in the waggon. our genral would

---

Perhaps because of his bitterness, made clear in other letters, toward refugee slaves, Murray did not embellish his correspondence with any discussion of how he and his comrades released their brethren from the bonds of enslavement. Nonetheless, Col. Noble praised the men for "liberating slaves." Thomas Miller, Company K, and London Floyd, Company D, who enlisted in the 102nd USCT at Magnolia may have been among those enslaved persons thus freed. Murray does not acknowledge the enlistment of them or any men in Florida.

Report of Col. William H. Noble, 17th Connecticut Infantry, Magnolia, Fla., September 4, 1864; Report No. 3, Itinerary of Military Operations, January 1–November 13, 1864, Department of the South; Report of Brig. Gen. Jno. P. Hatch, Commanding District of Florida, Jacksonville, August 19, 1864, all in *OR*, ser. 1, vol. 35, pt. 1, 36–37, 427–31; Nelson Diary, August 19, 1864; Thomas Miller, London Floyd, CMSR.

54. John Jackson Dickinson was a captain in the Second Florida Cavalry. Dickinson commanded about two hundred mounted men and employed guerilla tactics. He was responsible for defending an area in Florida along the St. Johns River. Gen. Hatch reported that the Union cavalry force scouting in the vicinity of Magnolia engaged in frequent skirmishes with Dickinson's cavalry. Report of Brig. Gen. John P. Hatch, Headquarters, District of Florida, Jacksonville, August 15, 1864, *OR*, ser. 1, vol. 35, pt. 1, 426.

55. On August 15, the mounted portion of Gen. Hatch's force, under the command of Col. Harris, Seventy-Fifth Ohio, started on an expedition. The force consisted of the Seventy-Fifth Ohio, Fourth Massachusetts Cavalry, and one section of Light Battery A, Third Rhode Island Heavy Artillery. Moving south, the column arrived at Gainesville on August 17, where a severe engagement took place. The Union cavalry force, too far in advance of the infantry to receive any support, sustained heavy losses when attacked by Capt. Dickinson's troops. A small detachment of the Third Rhode Island Heavy Artillery consisting of fifteen enlisted men, one howitzer, and thirteen horses were part of the engagement. After suffering the loss of nearly all their horses, the artillery unit fell back. During the retreat, the enemy charged them and captured the howitzer and remaining horses. Only three of the fifteen men escaped. After this engagement, the remaining Union forces in the north-central Florida area withdrew to the garrisons at Jacksonville and St. Augustine. Gainesville remained in Confederate control for the duration of the war.

Maj. Gen. J. G. Foster to Maj. Gen. H. W. Halleck, HeadQuarters, Department of the South, Hilton Head, S.C., August 26, 1864; Report of A. L. Harris, Col. 75th Ohio Vol-

not Reinforce them. we was Abought four miles from them. the next Day we Captured 30 Countreband and a number mules and Seven Barrel of Sugar. we had all the figs and mellons and Peaches we could Eat and Sweet Potatoes. Down north you talk abought Starving the Johnny out. you Dont know Ennything abought it. there is Plenty of corn and Pottaoes and Rice. Every thing in Propotion that the land Ever Raise. Sugar Corn and Cotton look Better then it Dos now. the old Setter Says Crop never was Better Rice cant be Enny Better.[56]

August 20th/64   Magnolia Florida   just in camp. very tired. we Been on a March Seven Days. Brought with us in Camp 150 Countreband nine Johnny 17 mules and Six Horses five Big wagons two top Bugges three white women and one girl. Rested two Days and then we Built a heavy fourt of Six Seige Gun. we left Magnolia 29th. arived at Beaufort 31st.[57]

---

unteers, all in *OR*, ser. 1, vol. 35, pt. 1, 22–23, 434–35; 3rd Rhode Island Heavy Artillery, Record of Events (roll 186); Denison, *Shot and Shell*, 268–69.

56. Murray's observations here, and elsewhere in regard to bountiful harvests and availability of food, seem a striking contradiction to the general perception that the southern people were starving and that Union forces just had to wait them out.

57. On Tuesday, August 29, the 102nd USCT left Magnolia for Beaufort, arriving on the thirtieth, not the thirty-first as Murray wrote. 102nd USCT, Record of Events.

CHAPTER 3

September–October 1864

"we get Everything the white man get So we cant Complain"

ON AUGUST 30, 1864, MURRAY AND HIS REGIMENT ARRIVED BACK at Beaufort, assigned to guard the nearby islands of Port Royal, Lady, and Coosa. The routine of camp life for the next several months revolved around picket, guard and fatigue duty, drills, and inspections. The regiment, in separate detachments, served along a line some thirty miles in extent. Several companies quartered on various plantations along the Broad River. Murray's Company E performed picket duty and guarded public property on Coosa Island.

Perhaps due to the monotony and boredom that comes with guard duty and incessant drilling, the early fall was fraught with more disciplinary problems than usual. The most common infraction was sleeping on post. At his court-martial Private James Henson, Company A, explained that he fell asleep while on duty the night of September 2 because he was sick. He further attributed missing an inspection about a week later to the fact that, not able to eat anything, he went to get some milk. On the night of September 14, the sergeant of the guard discovered Private Oliver Winslow, on duty as a sentinel near the enemy lines on Port Royal Island, asleep at his post. Sleeping on post was a serious offense, particularly during war, and Winslow, like Henson, was court-martialed. Both Privates Henson and Winslow were sentenced to hard labor in confinement for the rest of their enlistments and forfeited ten dollars of their pay per month.[1]

Soldierly misconduct often involved alcohol. Around midnight on September 27, William H. Washington and Creed Calloway, both members of Company D, illicitly acquired some whiskey and, somewhat intoxicated, "caused considerable disturbance" in the soldiers' barracks located on the upper floor of the Barnwell Plantation house, Port Royal Island. An altercation broke out when the drunken soldiers resisted the

---

1. James Henson and Oliver Winslow, Courts-Martial, Case #LL-2768, Court-Martial Case Files, Records of the Office of the Judge Advocate General (Army), RG 153, NARA.

efforts of Sergeants Madry and Dickson to subdue them. In addition to repeatedly shouting expletives at the officers, Washington struck Sergeant Dickson in the face and Calloway struggled with Sergeant Madry. In the end, Privates Washington and Calloway were placed under arrest and court-martialed. They were sentenced to hard labor for the rest of their enlistment and fined twelve dollars per month during their confinement, but a technicality later negated the findings of the courts-martial and the men were restored to duty without loss of pay.[2]

An incident involving civilians occurred about three weeks later. Privates Augustus Bullard, Nelson Hardee, and Thomas Johnson, all members of Company A, left camp with their guns and went to a nearby plantation house where they allegedly threatened to kill its residents, Lucretia Simmons and Emma Cohen. The soldiers carried off a number of chickens, leaving their heads on the ground, with blood and feathers strewn around. A court-martial found the soldiers guilty only of being absent without leave and sentenced them to a fine of ten dollars each.[3]

Moments of excitement sometimes interrupted the boredom of camp life, such as on September 19 when the men thought they heard firing on the picket line. Having "got up a scare," members of the guard investigated, only to discover that it was a false alarm.[4] The long, monotonous hours on picket duty were again disturbed on September 28 when the men of Company A, on picket duty at Ladies Island, more fully grasped the value of diligence. That night, a detachment of Confederates from the mainland attempted to storm the island in three boats. The rebels tried to land several times, but Union soldiers repulsed them at each advance. There were no casualties among the 102nd USCT during this in-

---

2. Washington and Calloway were tried and sentenced for assaulting an officer, but upon higher review it was decided that they should have been charged with a lesser offense. The Judge Advocate General ruled that because Sgts. Madry and Dickson were noncommissioned, they were considered soldiers not officers. At the original courts-martial, both men were found not guilty of the additional charge of theft, so the entire sentence was "left to rest upon an irregularity and is therefore inoperative." On May 18, 1865, an order was given to release Privates Calloway and Washington from confinement at Fort Marion, St. Augustine, Florida, where they had been since sentenced at the end of October 1864. William H. Washington and Creed Calloway, Courts-Martial, Case #MM-1876; CMSR.

3. Privates Bullard, Hardee, and Johnson were court-martialed on charges of being absent without leave, threatening to kill, and robbery. They were found guilty only of the first charge and fined ten dollars apiece. Augustus Bullard, James Hardee, and Thomas Johnson, Courts-Martial, Case #LL-2768.

4. Nelson Diary, September 19, 1864.

cident though one man, Corporal William Blake, had three holes shot through the cape of his great coat.[5] On the afternoon of October 16 four Confederates ventured too near the Union held shore in a boat and pickets from the 102nd USCT fired at them, causing the rebels to come ashore. Three were taken prisoner. The fourth tried to run but was "shot through the head and killed."[6] Other than these minor incidents, much of the fall months passed relatively quietly.

Sept 2th/64   Coo Saw Island S. Carolina

---

we left Beaufort yesterday morning. this Place is abought 25 miles Up the River 35 miles from Charleston. we are Doing Picket Duty. we are one miles from main land. Johnny are very troublesom. Uncle Sam Pills and the Black man they Dont like. the will fight a white man quicker then they will a Black man. Johnny Say they Dont want to fight us. they want fight those who maid the war. they Say we Did not make the war. I Did not Receive no mail till I got Back. I found three letters for me. the letter you sent the fifty cents worth of Stamp I Did not get. I got the one had three Stamp in and was glad to Receive them. we was Paid of in Florida in the Swamp.[7] there was no mail Sent from there. I tied it abought fifty dollar in my Packet to mail at Beaufort. Comming across the Sea my Packet was cut out the money takin. one man lost Eighty Dollars in the Same way. one Captain $200 Dollars.[8] we was Paid Sixteen Dollars month.[9] we was mustered in for our next Pay yesterday. for

---

5. Company Muster Roll, Company A, September and October 1864.

6. Nelson Diary, October 16, 1864; Henry L. Chipman to Adjutant General, State of Michigan, from Beaufort, S.C., November 1, 1864.

7. The regiment received their pay at Magnolia on August 20, 1864. Nelson Diary, August 20, 1864; Wm. Waring to Adjutant General, Beaufort, S.C., November 10, 1864.

8. No other direct mention or evidence of this thievery has yet been found elsewhere in the records of the regiment. An incident in camp at Beaufort was likely related. On August 31, 1864, Capt. Edward Jewett discovered that Private Wesley Blackman had stolen over a hundred dollars from his comrades. A search of his person revealed the money in the collar and wristbands of Blackman's shirt. There is no specific reference to the theft having occurred during the transport from Florida, but the timing of the incident suggests that it did. Edward E. Jewett to J. H. Baker, Commissioner of Pensions, Niles, Michigan, February 15, 1872, Wesley Blackman, CMSR, CWPF.

9. Given the extent of dissatisfaction with the unequitable pay he expressed through-

our Back Pay and Bounty it will Bee $157 Dollars. I will Send most of it home to you. I want you to Put it ~~to~~ So it will Do you Som good. we Paid of the fifteen of November. we are goin to stope here Sixty Day then hard telling what Uncle Sam will do with. he give us a free Ride all the By Pond and around his Planttion. I Been a marching of thousand miles sence I left home. the State Sent for us Again while we was in Florida. there is no Danger of fighting or Being in Battle Except we Run across Johnny in Some of our Raid. I must Stop. I am getting. I was on Picket last knight. now I tell you abought Florida Rattle Snake. we kill one that weight forty Eight Pound. he had thirty nine Rattle. he was Kill in the Dismal Swamp. A number of such old Settlr we Saw and other of Differance Kind from Eight to thirteen feet longe. St John River is full of Allegator and torped one of our Boat was Blown up.

Coo Saw Island   Sept 4/64

Dear Mother   I am at Presant well. I Dont Know how long it will Be so. it is very Sickley Place.[10] ~~there~~ they are taking with the fever. in three or four Day they are Put in the Ground. it last one month. to Day I went Up to Morgan Island where Part of our Boys are Doing Pick Duty.[11] our Squad Do Picket on lady Island and Coo Saw. I like the Place very much. our Duty is nothing But Knight work to watch Johnney. he sleep Daytime and travel Knight. his Jack Ass is no good to him now he cant Swim. we are making Slab Shanty for winter quarters.[12] there is talk of Sending us to Florida after Dickson. our Captain is A fraid Uncl

---

out his communications, it is rather surprising that Murray did not make more of the fact that he and his comrades finally received sixteen dollars per month.

10. The area around Beaufort and Hilton Head was an unhealthy one at that time of the year as evidenced by the number of men reported sick and absent. The regiment's monthly returns for September 1864 show one hundred and thirty-three enlisted men present sick and another fifty-six absent sick. Within days of Murray's letter, Maj. Gen. Foster reported that the health of the Department of the South was "growing rapidly worse. The number of sick in hospital[s] is increasing." Monthly Returns, 1864; Maj. Gen. J. G. Foster to Maj. Gen. H. W. Halleck, Headquarters, Department of the South, Hilton Head, S.C., September 6, 1864, *OR*, ser. 1, vol. 35, pt. 2, 273–74.

11. Morgan Island is in St. Helena Sound, just across the Coosa River from Coosa Island where Murray's company was stationed.

12. Winter huts, or shanties, were semipermanent shelters built out of the surrounding materials: trees, mud, leaves, and soldiers' canvas tents. Many had small fireplaces with chimneys. Soldiers often dug out a few feet of earth so that the floor of the shanty was

Sam will give us Another Ride on his fish Pond. we are Making Up our Eating line. I cant get Enough to Satisfy me. we Did not have half Ration on our Seven Days March. we was one month in Florid Swamp. we ownley lost one man while on our Raid.[13] you must Excuse my Pen and Ink. we halfto send to Beaufort for Everything we get. we have not got settle yet. we are living in Dog tents at Presant.   No More. at the mail come to us Regular. the Boat Dont Come But twice A week with our Ration. So good By.

the next time I will have Some Ink

Sept 7th/64   Co Soil Island South Carolina

Dear Mother   I take this Presant oppotunity to write to you that I Am well and hope you are the Same. I went Down to lady Island Day before yesterday where Company A Doing Picket. the wind Drove us over the other Side of the River. Johnney Saluted us But Don no Damage. we had no Gun But A Revolver. our Company are gointo Be Station all on one Island. now we are on four Island Doing Picket Duty. we Cant tell where we will winter. the Same old talk of goin to Mich. all Kind of Report Sence we got Back. the Cornal is goin Home next week.[14] we are to Stay here till he Come Back. we have not Draw no Clothes yet. Dirty and Ragged. we got no Shooes to ware But one Shirt. we go Around without Shirt throught the Day and Drink quinine and Whiskey once Day.[15] Sence we got Back they mak us Drink the

---

below the surface, making for a bit more room and providing additional protection from cold winds.

13. William Porter, Company F, reported missing and presumed taken prisoner on August 17. Monthly Returns, 1864; William Porter, CMSR.

14. Col. Chipman began a thirty day leave of absence on September 13, 1864, to attend to business matters in Detroit. He was a partner in a produce and commission business and his partner, who managed the business during the war, had recently died. During Chipman's absence, Maj. Nelson Clark commanded the regiment. Monthly Returns, 1864; Special Order no. 328, Department of the South, September 13, 1864, Henry Chipman, CMSR; Nelson Diary, October 12, 1864.

15. Quinine is an alkaloid synthesized from the bark of cinchona, a tree native to South America. Its primary use during the war was to counteract some of the symptoms of malaria and other fevers. While not a cure, soldiers were often given routine doses of quinine, sometimes mixed with whiskey, prophylactically. Hicks, "Popular Dose with Doctors"; Churchman, "Use of Quinine."

Stuff. if you have A Cold or Cut finger or A Sour toe quinine. the Captain Say this Pay Day is the last Pay we Receive ~~in~~ Down here. Probley the next will Be in Mich. if So I will Be home on A furlow this winter But it is to good to Bleave. I Am getting tired of Riding on Uncle Sam mill Pond. I have Been menny thousand miles on it. we Been within four hundred miles of Hati and twelve ~~mil~~ hour Rid of Cuba. Hati is owlney fifty miles from Cuba. I Rather fight Johnney then go Back to Florida. two third of that State is not fit for Cattle to live in let A long Human Being. we was in the State one Month. it Rain Every Day we was there Except one. that was the Day went to Balding Station. A hotter ~~Caruntry~~ Country Cant hardley Be found. one week week to Day Sence we got Back. no more at Presant So good By.

the mail Come. Every time it Come in ther is no Post office here. our letters we have to Carry to Beaufort. we cant get Ink yet.

S.C. Coo Soil   Sept 11th/64

Dear Mother   it is Sunday. I have a little time to write to you a few line to you that I Am well and hope all of you are the same. there is nothing new at Presant But Very warm and Sultry. we are Recruting Up fast Sence we Came Back.[16] Plenty to Eat and Drink. we have for two Days Very heuvy firing all around us.[17] Sherman is Driving Johnney out of Georjey.[18] they are Comming into South Carolina. we had and order to capture Every Small Boat is Between Maryan Coo Soil. I Expict we will hove to Sleep on our arms. we have got ownley forty five men to Guard fore Iland. we are Abought ~~four~~ one miles from main land. we have to Guard the Contreband Beside the Draft Scare them almost to Death. A litle more of Camp talk. the State of Michigan Dont

---

16. The 102nd USCT received almost ninety new recruits in September 1864, most of whom came from various recruiting rendezvous depots in Michigan. Monthly Returns, 1864.

17. Murray was likely referring to the frequent shelling of Charleston from Morris Island and elsewhere in the vicinity.

18. Georgia. Toward the end of August 1864, Gen. Sherman began his last campaign to take Atlanta, a flanking movement to the southwest of the city and Confederate forces. Confederate general John B. Hood evacuated Atlanta on the night of September 1. Federal troops marched in the next day. News of Sherman's capture of Atlanta reached the 102nd USCT about a week later. Nelson Diary, September 8, 1864.

want Exknowledge us as Citzen and Uncle Sam wont give them Cridet for us. he Say he will take us and make us citzen to the United State or the State must take us home.[19] we get Everything the white man get So we cant Complain.[20] we will get our Back Bounty State and Goverment and our Back Pay. we was mustered in for ~~our Bount~~ it. my State Bounty is four hundred and fifty Dollars. my other if I should Stay will Be three hundred more. in all will be $750 Dollars Be Side Sixteen Dollars a month.[21] we was Paid of at that once in Florida in the Swamp. we had no use for it. there was no mail nor we Did not Receive no mail till we got Back. I had fifty Dollars sole out of my Pocket. the Pocket was cut out and others had great Deal more. I Save it to Send home to you. I dont know when we will get Paid of again. I will Send it all home. I will Send you ten Dollars now I Save for my Self. So Good By till next time. The next letter I will Send you my likness for all.[22] one for Grandmother in Parteculur.

Be Shure to write if you Dont get Enny letter from me Because I might not Be in the State longe.

---

19. The basis for this statement, and similar ones found throughout the collection, is somewhat speculative. The enlisted men of the 102nd USCT may have felt a lack of support from Michigan. African Americans could not vote in Michigan and there was no statewide effort there to grant equality of any sort. Gov. Austin Blair, albeit a Republican, had not initially been supportive of Henry Barnes's request to establish a Black regiment. There was greater state support for the New England Black regiments than those in the northwestern states, Michigan included. Murray's attitude was likely in part a reflection of the support, or lack of support, from the state governments and reflective of less prejudice and more abolitionist sentiment in the New England states generally.

20. Murray's comment here suggests that, at least at the time of its writing, he saw little difference in the treatment of Black soldiers from White soldiers insofar as the supplies and equipment provided to them. His attitude is somewhat surprising giving his frequent prior complaints concerning the inequity in pay. Perhaps, since Congress rectified the inequality by then, Murray saw fewer inequalities.

21. Murray's estimate as to how much bounty he was due to receive is rather high. But if Murray believed himself owed upward of $700, this explains why he remonstrated in his correspondence so often about bounties.

22. In several letters, Murray promised to send his "likeness" or picture home. If he ever did, the photograph did not become part of his pension file. There are no known extant images of John Murray. During the war, photographers set up shop when soldiers were in camp. Carte-de-visite photographs, so called because they were the size of visiting cards, were quite popular. Soldiers likewise requested their loved ones to send them images. Murray repeatedly asked for Lucinda to send him her likeness. There is no indication that she ever did.

Coo Saw   Sept 18th/64

Dear Mother   I though I would write another letter to let you Know how I was getting along. I am well and harty as can bee and hope your are the Same. I left Home last Friday Knight abought Eight in the Evening for St. Helena ten miles from this Place on A Raid for Small Boat. we got twenty five Boat on Saturday. ~~So~~ we come Back to Coon Island and Stayed all Knight. we left with the tide abought three in the marning for Comp. we have now Seventy five Boat Under Guard. we have an order to go and cetch Contreba[23]. those who are Drafted they Run away Into the Swamp to hide from Us But they cant cant get away from Us. the Caverly and the New York Rid Collord[24] an our own are on the Scout for them. I Spect we will have Some fun with them. we make them Bleave we will Put the Baynett through them.[25] If we Dont go to Atlanta Georgey in two ~~week~~ or three week most likley we will Say here. our Captain is trying hard to get this Place. I hope will Because it is a very Pretty Place. we Expect a fight at Charleson and Savanna Georga in fiunt and Rear of Both Places. we wont have ~~muet~~ mutch to do ownley Stand Pick Duty and Scower the Island. there is abouth Eighteen Islan on the Sea Cost. I Dont want to go North this winter to Stand Guard Because it will Kill all the men off. I am Sleepy. I Did not Sleep last Knight. I was on watter Rowing Boats and watching Reb. no more at Presant so good By till next time. I want you to Send me Some more Stamps. I Did not get them you sent.

Monday the 19th   I am goin to Beaufort to Day if nothin happen. I have got to Be quite a Boatman. Steam is Plaid out in this ~~Pl~~ Part of the Country. I am tring to get on a Gun Boat. so Good By.

our Ridgment is Collard men But white offcers.

---

23. Murray reached the end of the page here, and he likely tried to squeeze in the rest of the word "Contreband," but the ink is now smudged beyond recognition.

24. The New York regiment Murray referenced was the Twenty-Sixth USCT. The Twenty-Sixth remained stationed at Beaufort while the 102nd USCT went on the Florida expedition and were there when Murray and his comrades returned to the Beaufort area. Most of the Twenty-Sixth USCT was stationed at Fort Duane near Beaufort. Companies D and F were at Battery Burnside and Battery Taylor. 26th USCT, Record of Events.

25. Apprehending deserters was a regular part of picket duties. Despite Murray's previously expressed ill will toward refugee soldiers in particular, his comment here that he and his comrades would put them, whether they be soldiers or laborers, to the bayonet to scare them seems patently harsh.

Coo Saw   Friday   Sept 30th/64

Dear Mother   I receive your letter this morning abought Daylight. I was very glad to Hear from Home that you was well. I was out on Guard last Knight. It Rain most all Knight. My Health never was Better. we are now on the advance Picket toward Charleston. Knight Before last Johnny Came over in Small Boat to See Us But the Picket keep them at Sea.[26] the Gun Boat was here But the tide went out left here on ground. we Dont have much to Do. we have Inspection Every Day. the weather is Very warm now. I not Been to Beaufort yet to get my likness taken. just as Soon I Can get time I will have them taken. there is great many Camp Rumor abought our Ridgement But nothing Importent abought our Staying here. we Dont Know Enny thing abought leaving Untill the Cournal Come Home. you want to kow what the Govener name of Michigan Blair. our Cornal name is Chitman. Captain MacKinsy Belonge to our Company.[27] we are in Genral Foster Department.[28] If we leave here I will write to you and let you know when we go away. But I want you to write to me If I Dont write to you. Some times we get into Some Place we cant Send mail out. If I get kill our Captain will write to you. he is Bound to write if Enny one get Captured or Kill. he has all the Kname and Resident of all the man So you need not Be afraid of not hearing from me in Some way or other. there has Been Some talk of Sending us to Florida Again. Dickerson is very troublesome Down there.[29] if we Do go Dawn there I wont take nothing But my clothes. if we Stay Dawn here   I Should like to Come Home this winter. if we Stay Down here it will Be Imposible of think-

---

26. This is in reference to the incident of September 28 when the picket at Ladies Island repulsed a detachment of Confederates who attempted to storm the island by boat.

27. The officers of Company E at this time were Capt. Edward J. McKendrie, 1st Lt. A. Andrews, and 2nd Lt. O. A. Davis. McKendrie, to whom Murray likely referred, joined the regiment in February 1864 from the Sixteenth Michigan Volunteer Infantry regiment, where he held the rank of first sergeant. Monthly Returns, 1864; Edward McKendrie, CMSR, CWPF.

28. The 102nd USCT was part of the Department of the South then commanded by Maj. Gen. John G. Foster.

29. Rebel raids, many of them conducted by Capt. Dickinson's men, continued to be a threat to Union forces in Florida. The Union conducted at least two expeditions in Florida during the fall of 1864, but the 102nd USCT was not involved in either. Maj. Gen. J. G. Foster to Brig. Gen. J. P. Hatch, Headquarters, Department of the South, Hilton Head, S.C., October 31, 1864, *OR*, ser. 1, vol. 35, pt. 2, 319–20; Report No. 3, Itinerary of Military Operations, January 1–November 13, 1864, Department of the South, *OR*, ser. 1, vol. 35, pt. 1, 37.

ing of Sutch a thing. So good By till next time. if you see Lue tell her to write to me.

Govener name is of Mishigan is Mr Blair. our Cornal name is Chitman. Captain Mac Kinsy Belongs to our Company. whe are in Genral Foster Department.

~~Cruu~~ Crew Saw   Oct 6th 11/64[30]

Dear Mother   I Reced your letter the twenty fifthe. I was glad to Heare from you and that your wer well But for my Part I Dont feel very well But I am Araund and Stiring Abought. I Hope It will Be my last time with the fever. I Have not Don Enny Duty for three weeks. Enfact I Have not Don Enny Duty for the last Six weeks worth Speeking abought. we are not afraid of Johnny now Because we Have Plenty of men at the Presant time. we Have abought Seventy four men In Camp and Eighteen In the Hospital[31] But they are waiting for A Discharge from that Place. our Comp Is free from Sickness at Presant. cooller the weather get more Healthy It Is. we Had Some Frost last Knight the first of the Seson. ~~It Put make me feel~~ It Put me In mind of old times when I usto Shuck Corn with gloves on. But now we are getting So lazy we Cant Cook our onwn vituals nor Hardly wash our Hands and face. we ownly Do Duty at Knight. Come off at Day Break and then we Shoot of our Gun and Clean them and Rest the other Part of the Day. Probly we Dont go on But once A week. there Is Some firing Can Be Heard Day and Knight But So far of we Dont notice It. we Cant Hear Ennything what goin on. you Hear Before we Do. If you get A pape you will Have to Pay twenty five Cents for It. we Dont Run after these Kind of Folks Enny more. they Have taken most all and Prest Into the Servis of the United State. I wish Every one of them was In the army. I must Stop Because It make me mad. I Have no good feeling for them.[32] Excuse all Bad Spelling.

---

30. The date of this letter is likely October 6, 1864.

31. In October, Company E reported sixty-nine enlisted men present, fifty-one of whom were present for duty. Fourteen were absent sick. The rest were detailed on various duty assignments. Monthly Returns, 1864.

32. Given previously stated sentiments, Murray was likely referring to Black refugees, either soldiers or laborers.

Beaufort S.C.   Oct 17/64

Dear Mother   I Recd your letter with Pleasur and was glad to Hear that you were well. for my Part I am getting Better of the fever But very week. my limb I Cant Hardly Stand on them. I Am Under the Doctor Care at Presant But I am in hope of getting Better Soon. it is a new thing for me. there is not mutch new at Presant. Comp H Captured three Reb to Day and Shoot one.[33] there is Very Heavy firing all Day of in the Direction of Charleston. the Johnny are getting Bold. we got to Put a Stop to them. our Cornal has got Home. we have But Eleven Days to Do Duty.[34] our time is most Up then it is Hard to tell what will Be Don. Camp talk is we will go to John Island in lake Erie to Guard Reb Prisoners.[35] it is very Sickly. they Die of like Sheep. my Head Ache Some So I Must Stop. So good By till next time. I hope I will Be Better next time your here from me.

Coo Saw   Wensday   Oct 20/64

Dear Mother   I am turned over to Duty Again. I am quite Smart again But my Head Is not Strait. I was Very sick with the fever for abought two weeks. I was Burnt up with with the fever. If I took all the Medican the Doctor give me I would not Be Here. my nerves are all Un Strung with medican. I think In a few Days I will get over It. I went to the Head yesterday on the Gun Boat *Thomas Walker*.[36] got Into Camp this morning at Daylight. our Ridgement is In Bad Condition. Most all our Sick with the fever. there is great menny has Died of

---

33. The day before Murray wrote this letter, a small group of Confederates ventured too near the Union side and pickets from the 102nd fired at them. Three were taken prisoner and a fourth was shot. Henry L. Chipman to Adjutant General, State of Michigan, Detroit, from Beaufort, S.C., November 1, 1864.

34. The regiment was not scheduled to be mustered out. Men who volunteered before the regiment left Detroit enlisted for three years. Most of those who joined after the regiment left Detroit enlisted for one year, but their enlistments would not have been nearing an end yet. Perhaps Murray thought the regiment was slated to move to another theater of the war. If so, this was yet another camp rumor.

35. Johnson's Island, located on Lake Erie near Sandusky, Ohio, housed a prisoner of war camp primarily for Confederate officers. Between 1862 and 1865, there were more than ten thousand Confederates confined at the camp.

36. There was not a Union gunboat named *Thomas Walker*. Murray likely traveled to Hilton Head aboard a vessel that he misidentified as a gunboat.

In a few Days.[37] our times is most out in the Island. we had two month to Stand Picket But we cant leave Because the Hosptal Is full of our men. we have Cool Knight But Warm Days. there is another Expidition In this Department.[38] the New York Boys are goin. there is a number of Lockport Boys Down here. one young man work for Wm Brumly[39] ~~is~~ Driving teem for the Goverment. Johnny are getting troublesom. the Gun Boat Shell them Every Day. they are fighting all around us. we can here Heavy firing Day and Knight. we whip them In Every Place. Johnny Say he Is getting tired of fighting. they have Compromise with our Picket not to fire on one other.[40] we trade of tobaco ~~for~~ and Hard tack for Sweet Pottatoes alltho they tresspass on our ground so we take them to Head Quarters. we have had abought 160 men Sent to our Ridgement with In two weeks so It make It light the Rest of the Boys. we Expect to Be Paid of within a few Days. our Captain is Very Sick not

---

37. Murray's comments on the health of his regiment during October suggest a rapidly changing health status. In his October 11 letter, Murray made a point of telling his family that the camp was "free from sickness." Less than a week later he reported that it was "very sickly" and the men were dying "like sheep." His letters of October 20 and 27 make it clear that the general health of the men remained poor and that most all were "sick with the fever." It was only at the very end of the month that Murray reported that though he was still sick, the men were "getting better." Other sources substantiate Murray's statements concerning the health of the soldiers. Chaplain Waring's report for the month of October 1864 stated that "during the greater part of the month they had more than the ordinary amount of sickness and deaths." Capt. Edward McKendrie wrote that "full one half of my 105 men were sick with a malignant fever." Wm. Waring to Adjutant General, Beaufort, S.C., November 10, 1864; Edward McKendrie to James Turner, Commissioner of Pensions, Detroit, August 19, 1889, CWPF.

38. The expedition Murray alluded to here was likely that leading up to the engagement at Honey Hill at the end of November. There was no other major expedition involving troops from the Beaufort area at this time.

39. In 1860, sixteen-year-old Elias Degraff (Degroff, Degraugh) was an apprentice in William Bromley's barbershop. Elias was born in Vienna, New York, but he and his family had lived in Lockport since the mid-1850s. He enlisted in the Twenty-Ninth Connecticut Colored Infantry at Hartford on December 19, 1863. From April 1864 through August 1865, he was detailed as a teamster. U.S. Federal Census, 1850, 1860; New York State Census, 1855; Elias Degraff, CMSR; 29th Connecticut Colored Infantry, Record of Events.

40. Confederate and Union soldiers, generally those on picket duty, sometimes engaged in unofficial truces during which they exchanged goods between picket lines. Coffee, tobacco, and newspapers were common items of trade. Capt. Nelson recorded such contact between Union and Confederate soldiers while encamped in the Beaufort area during September and October. Nelson Diary, September 12, 14, 17, 25, 1864, October 2, 15, 31, 1864.

Coosaw Oct 24th /64

Dear Mother I thought I would write to you let you know how I was getting along I am quite well at present So I am to my Company again I hope these few lines will find all of you well we have been Cavil Krigt at Present almost evry the Reb are very troubled Every Knight there Is Some doing on the Island we have to make a Raid Every Day But we Dont See them we found out where they Sleep In the woods we are called up two or three times a Knight fall In line of Battle they come upes In Small Boat the Gun Boat John Adams Run up and Down the River must Evry Knight we have our Sunday Dawn here yesterday we went out after deserters and Collecting the Contrebond they are not Draffed But fell Into Army If they Dont have a Pass we fetch In 15 yesterday they say the Government have no Business with them But we can come three thousand miles from Home and leave our Friend to Guard and fight for them But they Cant fight for their Self If you Buy Enything from them they will Charge you Double Price they Know Enoug for that they think they cant work Enny more on Plantation they have Been free to Long If I Could have my way I would Shoot Evry one of them I have Been Into mud and water up to my waist Knight and Day

Ever Since we Been here Most of our Men are In the Hospital on the Account of them they are Afraid of the Reb will Slaughter them and So they Will If they over Power us we have twenty new Recrutes from Michigan we have got Seven Day more to Stay Here then our time will Be up will you Pleas Send me Some Stamps Stamps they are very Hard thing to get halt of So good By my nerves are not Steady yet

S. L. Murray

Direct your letter to Beaufort S. C. 112th United States Col Comp. E. E.

Expected to live. not much lost he think Black man cant get Sick.[41] Every Day has his own Day. So Good By till next time. Excuse Bad writting my Hand is not steady yet.

I hope I will Be all Right next letter.

Coo Soil   Oct 24th/64

Dear Mother   I thought I would write to you let you know How I was getting alonge. I am Quite well at Presant So I am to my Company again. I hope these few lines will find all of you well. we have very Cool Knight at Presant allmost frost. the Reb are very troublesom. Every Knight there Is Some Johnny on the Island. we have to make A Raid Every Day But we Dont See them. we found out where they Sleep In the Woods. we are Called Up two or three times A Knight fall In line of Battle. they Come over In Small Boat. the Gun Boat John Adams Run up and Down the River most Every Knight.[42] we have no Sunday Down here. yesterday we went out after Deserters and Contreband. the Contreband they are not Drafted But Press Into the army If they

---

41. Murray's comment suggested that Capt. McKendrie had a reputation for not believing, or for scrutinizing, enlisted men's reports of illness. Not surprising, Murray saw it as rather ironic when the captain himself fell sick. It was not necessarily the case that McKendrie believed Black soldiers to be less subject to sickness and disease than White soldiers as Murray here insinuated. It was somewhat common for officers to be suspicious of privates feigning sickness to be excused from duty. Nonetheless, when Black soldiers suffered from disease or fatigue, some White officers readily ascribed to the prevailing rhetoric at the time that Black people were inherently weaker and less able to resist disease. During his court-martial, Oliver Winslow defended falling asleep on post due to the fact that he was sick but added that his captain thought he was "fooling him" and refused to excuse him from duty. Likewise, James Henson testified at his court-martial that he told his lieutenant that he was sick but that the officer did not believe him. Undoubtedly, there were other such instances. Monthly Returns, 1864; Edward McKendrie, CMSR, CWPF; James Henson and Oliver Winslow, Courts-Martial, Case #LL-2768.

42. In October 1864, the Union gunboat *John Adams* operated in the South Atlantic Blockading Squadron. The gunboat was stationed off Morris Island inside the Charleston Bar where it served as the flagship of the inner blockade. The 700-ton vessel had 8 guns and a crew of 118. As a part of the blockading squadron, the *John Adams* would have moved along the waterways in the area, alert for Confederate blockade runners attempting to get in or out of the Port Royal–Charleston area. Murray mentioned this particular gunship numerous times in his correspondence. *Official Records of the Union and Confederate Navies in the War of the Rebellion* (Washington, D.C.: Government Printing Office, 1903), ser. 1, vol. 16, xviii (hereafter cited as *ORN*); see also Browning, *Success Is All*.

Dont have A Pass. we fetch In 17 yesterday. they Say the Goverment have no Buisness with them But we Can Come three thousand miles from Home and leave our Friend to Guard and fight for them But they Cant fight for them Self. If you Buy Ennything from them they will charge you Double Price. they Know Enoght for that. they think they Cant Work Enny more on Plantation. they Have Been free to longe. If I Could have my way I would Shoot Every one of them. I have Been Into mud and water up to my waist Knight and Day Ever Sence we Been Here. most of our men are In the Hospital on the Account of them.[43] they are afraid of the Reb will Slaughter them and So they will If they over Power us. we have twenty new Recruits from Michigan. we Have got Seven Days more to Stay Here then our time will Be Up.[44] will you Pleas Send me Some ~~Stap~~ Stamps. they are very Hard thing to get Holt of. So good By my nerves are not Steady yet.

| Coo Sioil | Thursday | Oct 27th/64 |

Dear Mother   I thought I would write A few lines to you that I Am not very well at Presant. My Sickey Has all Un Strung my Sistom. My Head and My Bones trouble me very much.[45] It will take Some time Before I will get Strait. I Dont Know wheather I Ever will Be Sound. the Quine I have taken Has gon all through my Sistom. I Dont Do Much Duty now. we have twenty one men in the Hospital now. we Have twenty new men In our Comp from Michigan. they Enlisted for one year.[46] our time is Meast out. we Have till next tuesday then I Dont know what will Be Don with Us But there Is one thing Sirting. we wont

---

43. The root of Murray's attitude toward Black refugees becomes a bit more apparent here. He projected blame for the hardships he and his comrades experienced as soldiers on to the refugees. His personal perception that formerly enslaved persons were not doing their part to secure their own freedom grounded his frustration, annoyance, and infuriation.

44. Illustrating the persistence of camp rumors once again, Murray thought, incorrectly, that the regiment would soon be rotated out of its current duty station and moved elsewhere.

45. Common side effects of quinine include headache, ringing in the ears, trouble seeing, and sweating. Murray complained of many of these symptoms during his recurring illnesses. William Woodlin, a private in the Eighth USCT, noted that quinine, "if taken in large doses . . . is apt to effect the head unpleasantly and produces vistigo deafness and stiffness of the joints." William P. Woodlin, Diary, July 2, 1864.

46. Company E received twenty-one recruits during October 1864. Most of them en-

Be In the Army three years. the Reb are very troublesom. Every Knight the Gun Boat John Adams Run Up and Down the River. Uncle Sam Is getting up an Expidition to go into Florida. I Dont know wheather we will go or not. I Hope not I seen Enoght the first time. If we are goin north I Rather Stay Down Here then go north. It will kill of all the men with Cold. It Is Rumor ~~the~~ Here that Charleston Is Burnt Down.[47] we Can Here Heavy firing Day and Knight. my time Is very Short So I must Stop writting. So Good By.

Dont forget to Send me some Stamp. I want to write Every mail so you Can know How I get Along. Excuse all Bad writing.

Coo Soil   Oct 31/64

The gun Boat John Adams runs up and down the river for the Johnneys.

Dear Mother   I Have a little leasure time to write to you that I am not very well at Presant. I Have Been very Sick with the fever again. I had one Chill It lasted one Hour. It like to Shook all the teeth out of my Head. I could not walk But the worst thing to Come was the fever. It lasted me two Hours. It all most made me Crazy. I am So week that I Cant Hardly ~~wall~~ walk. you would not know me now I am so Poor. the weather Is very fine Here. we Have very little Rain But Cool Knight. I think we will Stay Down at this Place all winter. our offices are trying to keep this Department. we Dont Have much to Do ownly to Keep of Johnny at Bay. they try us Every Dark Knight. the Gun Boat John Adams Plays up and Down the River Every Hour. our men are getting Better and our Compny Is getting most fill up. we Have lot of new men from Michgan. we Have Abought Eighty fit for Duty. that make It Easy for the old men. But Some of them Better Stayed at Home. they not

---

listed for three-year terms, but five or so enlisted for one year. Monthly Returns, 1864; 102nd USCT, CMSR.

47. If Murray here meant that the city had burned to the ground, that was indeed just a rumor. Nonetheless, by the fall of 1864, Union troops had been bombing Charleston for over a year, so it was already in many senses, a city of ruin. A large fire, probably caused by Union shells, broke out in Charleston on September 17, 1864, burning for several hours. Brig. Gen. R. Saxton to Capt. W. L. M. Burger, Headquarters, Northern District, Department of the South, Morris Island, S.C., September 27, 1864, *OR*, ser. 1, vol. 35, pt. 1, 81.

Hardly wean from ther Mother. they are not large Enough to Cary ther Gun.⁴⁸ I Bleave I told you Before that we had no Sundy. the Pay Master Came Here yesterday and Paid of the Company. I ~~Dig~~ Did not Receive no Pay. the Captain Did not mak out my Back Pay Right. we was mustered In for pay to day. we Dont get It till next January then I will Have abought one Hundred Dollars.⁴⁹ But I will Baraw Some and Send It to you Because I think you kneede It. you Say it was very Bad seon. I know you Cant Rais ~~Mitch~~ mutch.⁵⁰ I Have not mutch use for It. very little will Do me. If I Had not lost that fifty Dollars on the Boat It would help you very much. If I Ever go on a Raid Again and get Paid up I will Put my money in the Soles of my Boot and mail It there Before I will let Enny Black man cut my Pocket out again. we get Some of our Bounty the ~~me~~ next Pay Day. that will make my quite large. I have not mutch more to Say. there Is not Enny ~~me Darms~~ newes Down Here But there is lot of of fun all around us. we Can Here Heavy firing all abought us and See the flash of Uncle Sam Iron Rod and His fever Pills.⁵¹ He think Can Stop Johnny from Shaking So much. I Have not mutch more to Say So good By.

Plas Send me Some Stamp.

---

48. According to their enlistment papers, more than half the new recruits assigned to Company E in October were eighteen or nineteen years of age. Given the frequent inaccuracies of the enlistment papers (and Murray's observations of their youth), some of the new recruits may have been even younger than that. 102nd USCT, CMSR.

49. Troops mustered for pay by companies. Company commanders were supposed to pick up the pay for those men on detached duty, sick, or on leave. A formal review and inspection was often conducted as part of the muster for pay. This pay muster roll was then sent to the adjutant general. The soldiers actually received their pay at a separate muster. It appears that in this case, Murray's company commander might have made a mistake on the payroll muster and hence Murray did not receive the appropriate amount due him. Capt. Nelson noted that he signed the payrolls for his company for July and August on October 28, 1864, and the next day the men received their pay. Nelson Diary, October 28, 29, 1864.

50. Statements such as this provide a glimpse into the financial situation of Murray's family back home. Murray's comment spoke to the financial need of Black families and what soldiers did to help relieve their struggles. The pension file only contains a few letters from Sarah to her son, but these letters made it clear that the family was indeed experiencing difficult times (see chapter 5).

51. "Uncle Sam Iron Rod" was a moniker of sorts for artillery that Union forces shelled Confederate fortifications with. At the time of the writing of this letter, the Union was keeping up an almost continuous artillery barrage against Charleston.

CHAPTER 4

November–December 1864

"give me the Black man Against the World"

THROUGHOUT MOST OF NOVEMBER, THE COMPANIES OF THE 102ND USCT continued performing picket duty, guarding public property, and practicing infantry drill on the islands of Coosa, Port Royal, and Ladies. At the end of the month, Colonel Chipman received orders from Brigadier Saxton to form a detachment of men for an upcoming expedition under the overall command of General Foster. Foster's orders were to break the Savannah and Charleston road around Pocotaligo in support of General William T. Sherman's advancing army. Foster assembled a striking force of five White and six Black infantry regiments. The three-hundred-man detachment from the 102nd USCT, under the command of Colonel Chipman and Captain C. S. Montague, conducted a night march on November 29, arriving at Beaufort at 4:00 a.m. There the men embarked on a transport and proceeded up the Broad River to Boyd's Landing, reaching their destination at around 11:00 a.m. Once disembarked the force marched about five miles to Honey Hill, a fifteen- to twenty-foot rise on which the Confederates under the command of Major General Gustavus Smith had hastily constructed earthworks from which to defend against the Union's advance.[1]

Lieutenants George Southworth and Volney Powers commanded a detail from Companies G and H responsible for stopping and returning stragglers. Lieutenant Colonel William Ames (Third Rhode Island Heavy Artillery) deployed another detail from Company D and led by Captain A. E. Lindsay, to retrieve three cannons abandoned by Battery B, Third New York Artillery, after two of the battery's officers and most of its horses and cannoneers were either killed or wounded. The field pieces remained exposed within 150 yards of the rebels' earth-

---

1. November 30, 1864, Engagement at Honey Hill, near Grahamville, S.C., Reports, *OR*, ser. 1, vol. 44, 419–38; Maj. N. Clark, June 25, 1865, Orangeburg, S.C., Letters Received by the Commission Branch of the AGO, 1863–1870, RG 94, NARA.

works. Before reaching their target, Lindsay was killed and First Lieutenant Alvord seriously wounded. Command of the detail fell to First Sergeant Jesse Madry who, unaware of the company's objective, filed the men into the woods without accomplishing their goal. Company A, under the command of First Lieutenant Orson Bennett, made a second attempt to retrieve the artillery pieces, successfully hauling the pieces off by hand and ropes while under heavy fire. The men were later praised for saving the artillery pieces from capture by the enemy "in the coolest and most gallant manner."[2]

The 102nd detachment remained at the front that evening along with the 127th New York, covering the Union retreat. The detachment was then tasked with removing wounded men to the nearest landing, about three miles away. They finished their duties and bivouacked for the night around 2:00 a.m. Two men from the 102nd were killed in action and eighteen others wounded. The participating Black regiments, including the 102nd USCT, gained respect from White troops for their courage shown at Honey Hill.[3]

Following the engagement at Honey Hill, the detachment remained with Foster's expeditionary force and participated in further demonstrations along the Charleston and Savannah Railroad meant to keep Confederate reinforcements from harassing Sherman's left flank during his March to the Sea. On December 9, the Union force battled with Confederates about ten miles north of Honey Hill at Deveaux Neck. The 102nd, alongside the 56th and 154th New York Infantry regiments, fighting on the front line, took the brunt of the rebels' assault. In the battle at Deveaux Neck, the 102nd USCT suffered one killed and forty-three

---

2. November 30, 1864, Engagement at Honey Hill, near Grahamville, S.C., Reports, *OR*, ser. 1, vol. 44, 419–38; Maj. N. Clark, June 25, 1865, Orangeburg, S.C., Letters Received by the Commission Branch, AGO; Report of Capt. C. S. Montague, Commanding Detachment of 102nd USCT in the action of Honey Hill, S.C., November 30, 1864; H. L. Chipman, Col. 102nd Regt. U.S.C.T. to 1st Lt. L. B. Perry, 55th Reg. Mass. Vols., January 27, 1865, Hd. Qrs. 102nd Regt. U.S.C.T., Deveaux Neck, Letters Received by the Commission Branch, AGO.

3. Order Book, November 29, 1864; 102nd USCT, Record of Events; Report of Capt. C. S. Montague, Commanding Detachment of 102nd USCT in the action of Honey Hill, S.C., November 30, 1864, RG 94, NARA. After the expedition, Col. Chipman submitted the names of several officers for having distinguished themselves in battle. No specific mention of any individual privates and their heroism or bravery was made. 1st Lt. O. W. Bennett was awarded the congressional Medal of Honor for leading the detail that recovered the artillery pieces.

wounded.⁴ The regiment remained divided, with various companies on picket duty around the Port Royal area and the detachment remaining out in the field with General Foster's expedition, until the new year.

<hr>

Nov 4ᵗʰ/64   Beaufort South Carolina

<hr>

Dear Mother   I take Plauser In answer your letter. I Rec'd those Paper with an welcom Heart.⁵ My Health Is Consiable Better. I am Improving very fast. I Hope this letter will find you the Same. It Is very Cool to Day. We Had two Days Rain. I keep very Close. I Do not Do Enny Duty now But I Expect to soon. I told you that we would stay all winter But we are goin to Stay two month longer. that will Be the first of Jan. I Hope By that time we will Be trying to get Home. there Is more sign of ~~we~~ going. ~~think of try~~ they are trying to get the Collord Ridgement out of the Field. there Is no new at Presant. Everything is at A stand like A Cat watch one other But we have to watch the Reb those Dark Knight.

Wright Sound Georgy⁶   Nov 9ᵗʰ/64⁷
we had A Plesant Ride. we laid their fine Day. Saw nothing nor Don nothing But then we came Home. the Sound Is Abought Eighty miles from Beaufort. there was But Seventeen men out of our Comp. I was one of them. I have travel menny thousand miles Sence I left Home. If my Health keep good I just as leaf to travle around In the army as to

<hr>

4. The regimental casualty list shows forty-three men wounded at Deveaux Neck. Other records show between thirty-seven and forty-three wounded. 102nd USCT, Regimental Casualty Lists.

5. Murray frequently asked his family to send him the *Lockport Journal*, published from 1859 to 1871 as the *Lockport Daily Journal & Courier*, and the *Buffalo Express*, printed as the *Buffalo Morning Express* between 1859 and 1866. Local newspapers from home were a source of information regarding the course of the war and helped maintain a connection with family, friends, and community.

6. Wright River is located between Turtle Island and Jones Island, branching off the Savannah River, not far from the Hilton Head area. It is unclear how or why Murray went to Wright Sound.

7. This is not the beginning of a new letter but a continuation of the November 4 letter.

Be on A Farm. It is A good School to Enny one to see the world and Folks But these kind of People I Dont like. I Have Suffered a Enough to Blow Every one Up. they are not the same Race as those in Florid.[8] they are like those at the north. they are Human. I Sent you twenty Dollars. write and let me Know wheather you Red[9] It. I have not Recd Enny letter for the last three mail. we Receive mail one A week. I allways Send one or two write soon. no more at Presant So good By.

I must Put in little more abought Some of these officer In this Department. they are the Best of men. they Prtect Collored men Qucken then they would white[10] But the North may fight them Reb till they get gray and then they Cant whip them. Even If they Do It will take fifty Thousand men to Keep them Into Subjection. there will Be Gorrilla Band for ten years to Com In this Department. It is held By Collord troops. we Have Plenty of Prvition and So Has the Reb. you Cant Starve them out no use trying.

Crew Saw   Nov 9th/64

Dear Mother   a few word more to let you know that I am well at Presant and I Hope you are the Same. since we Had the Frost the weather Is very warm and Pleasant. It make the oranges Ripen faster then they Did Before. they charge ten cents a Piece for them. fifty cents a Pound for Butter for Egg. Seventy five cents a Pound for Butter. two Dollars a Bushel for Pottatoes and twelve Shilling for a Peck of Peanut. that the Unreasonable Price they charge Soldier. The Provost Marshal Has Put a Stop to Selling at Such Prices. Last Knight was the first Duty I Have Don In three week. next week I am Agoin Into George to Burn a Bridge. I Expect Some fight with Johnny. I Dont know How menny of our Ridgement will go But there will Be But few. the new York Boys

---

8. Murray might be referring to southern White people here.
9. Received.
10. Murray's attitude here contradicts sentiments he previously expressed regarding the White officers of his company and regiment. In earlier letters, Murray was sharply critical of his White officers. He made negative statements about Capt. McKendrie, spoke ill of Henry Barnes, and criticized Henry Chipman for harsh discipline. What accounted for Murray's change of heart by the writing of this letter is unknown.

are goin. I Should like to Have Some fun. In Florida that ownly mad us mad. we will Be gon two week. we are goin to take two week Ration. If we Dont Have Enny more then we Had Before we will see Hungrey times. there Is abought fifteen Hundred Johnny at the Bridge. we are goin to take them By Suprise. there Is a longe Swamp on one Side. the Rail Road Is on the other Side. the Swamp Is abought four miles through mostly water. It Is Abought 100 miles By water and Eight By land.[11] I Hope we will all of us will get Back to our Company again. the Cornal Say Every man take care of Him Self let others alone you may come out Safe But I want you to look to your Self and fire low the Day Is ours. I must stop In Spection at four So good By.

Dont Stop writing Because I am goin away. It wont Be long.

Hell Gate[12]

Crew Soil   Nov 15th/64

Dear Mother   I gues you will get Sick of answering all my letters. I thought I will let you know How I was getting longe. Yeasterday I Had a chill and Fever through the Knight. I was most Burnt Up with the Fevor. to Day I feel Some Better But It leaves a Person Very week. I Dont know what It will Do to me. I never Been Sick Before I came Down Here. It work on me Harder then it Dost on Enny the Rest of the Boys. It me Sick. I cant Eat nor Drink fer three or fore Days at a times But when I Do Eat Ennything I make It Suffer I cant get Enough to Satify Hungar. I Have got Back that Place they Call Hell Gate. It Is a Pretty Place But to close to Johnny. you can See Eight or ten Gun Pointing at you. If you got courage Enough to Run into the claws of a lion this Is the Place for you But for my Part I dont want the Job. I did not Stay But three Day. the last Day the Bay Became Rough at lasted till we got

---

11. There were likely rumors circulating as to pending military operations. Murray may have believed that he and his comrades would soon be leaving to lend support to Gen. Sherman's army.

12. Given Murray's description, it seems likely that "Hell Gate" was some place on water and close to Confederate fortifications, perhaps either the Charleston Harbor area or the Savannah area around Wright Sound. He gives no indication as to the meaning behind the name "hell gate."

out of the Bay I was. the weather Is very fine But cold at Knight with Heavy Frost. trees look as Green as as Ever. Flowers never look Better. oranges just getting Ripe. Sweet Potatoes are not Dug yet. you can get them fresh from the Ground. water Mellon are In Blossom and the third ~~grath~~ crop are on Hand. There I no newes Down Here at Presant. I Should like to Here from the north to See How Election come up.[13] Pleas Send Buffalo Express and the Lockport Journal and I will Be much oblige. you need not send Enny more writting Paper Because I can get Plenty of Paper But Stamp Cant Be got In this Department. there Is to menny Soldies. they get from 1,00 Dollar to Dollars at a time. It would take a Boat load of Stamps to Suply all. I must sop my Heard getting out of tune So Good By.

S.C Crew Soil   Nov 17th/64

Dear Mother   I Shant write that I am well Because I am not. I Been Sick with the old Complaint with Chill and Fever. I Been for four Days sick. this South Carolina Fever Is the worst kind of Sickness. you cant Eat nor Drink nor take Medican. I Have A chill once In two week. I Dont get over It for one week then not In time to Do Duty Befour It come on again. It Use me Rather Rough. I Shant go to the Hospital If I can Help my Self. when you go there you Cant get away till you are Discharge with Piece of Paper. you can get out of the Rid Just as Quick as you can out of the Hospital. they are very Strick. If you go Down Into the City without a Pass they find It out they will Put you to Bed for one week. they wont let you get Up. If you lay Down with your clothes on In your own Bearth they will take of all your Cloth and Send you to Bed for one week Sick or well. the weather Is Fine. It cant Be Enny Bether. I Find out By Being on wathes[14] I am more Subject of taking the Fever I am on Land. I am goin to Keep of the wather If I can. I Should like to Have you Send me Buffalo Express Lockport Journal and write and let me know How Lection went at the North. the Native careed to Day Here. no more at Presant So good By. my Head Is getting light my Hand Unsteady.

---

13. Tuesday, November 8, 1864, was election day.
14. Water.

A little more to tell you. I Had my letter Closed But the ~~mail~~ news Come In that Sherman Is within 15 miles of Charleston In the Rear and the Fleet In the Frount.[15]

We are goin to Have Genral Inspection to Morrow. I was goin to Send One Dollars to get Paper with But I cant now. we Have to Have Black Boots and Paper Collar and white Gloves. I want you to Send the Paper. I will Send Some Money next time.

~~I Send you one Dollars to Buy two Papers the Rest I suppose you know what to do with It~~

Crew Soil   Nov 18th/64

Dear Mother   I thought I would write a few lines to let you Know ~~tat~~ that I am well and Harty. I hope these few lines will find you the Same. we Had very good time at Beaufort at Election.[16] the Contreband took the Poles. if A White man talk abought voting for M.C[17] they would Drive Him from the Poles. Every Black man voted in this Department. But our officers are all Democrat of the worst Kind. they could Put in our votes if they would. the Contre[18] came very neigh getting

---

15. Gen. Sherman's army left Atlanta on November 15, 1864, on its infamous March to the Sea. Two days later when Murray wrote this letter, Sherman was not within fifteen miles of Charleston. Rather, he was nearing Georgia's capital of Milledgeville. Confederates evacuated Milledgeville on November 21 and parts of Sherman's army began marching in the next day. The "fleet" referenced by Murray was the South Atlantic Blockading Squadron stationed around Charleston's harbor. Maj. Gen. W. T. Sherman to Maj. Gen. H. W. Halleck, In the Field, Savannah, Ga., January 1, 1865; Report No. 3, Itinerary of the Union Forces, November 1–December 21, 1864, all in *OR*, ser. 1, vol. 44, 7–14, 25–55.

16. The 1864 election was the first in U.S. history in which soldiers in the field participated. Most Black soldiers voted for the first time in their lives. Murray and many of his comrades would not have otherwise voted in the election as most northern states restricted the franchise to White males. It was, as African American soldiers like Murray observed, a significant distinction. Alonzo Reed also asked his mother to tell him "if the colord men vote at home all the colord men voted down here." Alonzo Reed to Mother, November 15, 1864, Alonzo Reed Letters, 1864–1866, Rubenstein Library, Duke University.

17. George B. McClellan was the Democratic Party candidate in the 1864 Presidential election.

18. "Contre" is written at the edge of the sheet, and it looks like Murray tried to squeeze

up a Riot. they would not let a white man say little M.C. they are free in good Earnest. they are geting very Saucy But they are very fraid of Rid. the white Soldier and the Collord are on Friendly terms. I Receive your letter 12th. I was very glad to Here from you and Grandmother and Father. I wish I could Be Home this winter. Uncle Sam Is getting Up very Heavy Expidion. they are goin to take Every man they Can Spare In this Department But I gues we wont go Because we are on the out Sid Post and we are to Stay there till the first of January. Uncle Samiel wont take Enny men from the front. we are on the Advance Post to Charleston. if we get Releas from Picket I will let you Know But there Is not much Danger of that. our Ridgement gain very fast. we Have now Eighty men. yesterday there was Abought 39 men came from Michigan. they are all Drafted.[19] we will have Soon one thousand men if they come in as fast as they Do now. I want ~~you~~ to tell you some of my Exploit this last week. I have Been Running on the Gun Boat John Adams. we Had good times. She Shell one of Johnny Villages But Don not much Damage.[20] But now I am to my comp again. the weather Is warm and Pleasant through the Day But cool through the Knight. we Had one Frost But Daun ~~In this~~ no Domage. I dont Know But I will Be one the Gun Boat next week. no more at Presant So good By. you must Excuse this letter Be cause my Hand Is not Steady nor It wont Be for Some time. I want you to let me know wheather you Receive that mone.

Crew Soil S.C   Nov 20th/64

Dear Mother   I Have Plenty of time write A few lines to you. I feel Better. I Hope you are Doin well. It ~~Complaint~~ commence Rain last knight and It Rain now But we Have Very good weather long. Backtroops are coming Into the Head very fast. we Expect to get Up A large

---

the end of "contraband" on the line.

19. Between thirty and forty new recruits joined the regiment at Beaufort in November, about half of whom arrived right around the day Murray wrote this letter. At least ten, and perhaps more, of the new arrivals appear to have been draftees. Most of the others were substitutes. Perhaps Murray included substitutes in his definition of "drafted." 102nd USCT, CMSR; Monthly Returns, 1864; Descriptive Book.

20. Company and regimental records do not list Murray tasked to daily or special duty with this, or any, gunboat during his service.

Raid Soon Into George take one of the Island the Reb heare. It Is Reported that Abought 30,000 men In this Departement. If we are too Belave I supose we will Have to go But I Dont think we will. If the Ridgement Dos go I aint got Strenght Enough to go. But we got all we can Do. the Reb are geting trouble Some. we Have to Sleep with my Clothes on. knight Before last we was Call out In Battle ~~of~~ and fell In line. went throught the woods. there Is abought one Full Brigade on the other Side of the River. But we Dont Have much to Do ownley to Eat and Sleep. our Gun Boat Is out of Repare So we are In Danger. we Put on more Guard But we cant keep of all the Reb that Can Come ~~of~~ over In Small Boat. I Saw one of our ~~lo~~ Lockport Boys. He Is In the Conneticut Rid as Driver.[21] of all the Collord Rid Been In this Department the Mch Is the Best Becaus they are So Strick on Duty But they wont let us Do Provost Duty Enny more Because they are afraid we will Shoot them. the Genral like us Becaus we are so Strick. the Folks Entered complaint. they are afraid of their lives. I like Picket Duty Better then Ennything Else. If I was well they would Send me to Some Place I Dont want to go. It fall on me for all Short Boat Ride Becaus It not very Plesant Place to go. to Menny large Gun. I must Stop writting this time. I cant write long at A time So good By.

S.C. Crew Soil Nov 22th/64

Dear Mother   It is with Pleasure I sent Down to write A few lines that I Am well. I Hope these few line will find you Enjoying good Hearth. there Is not much news at Presant. we Heave Had two Days and Knight Rain with Some Snow this morning. It Is quite Cool so you want your over coat on. this weather Pick Up A Person Quite close. I suppose you Have Heard that Mayrland Has Freed Her Slaves.[22] It wont Be long Before South Carolina will Be Free By the Point of the

---

21. Elias Degraff (Degroff, Degraugh), Twenty-Ninth Connecticut Colored Infantry. Elias was detailed as a teamster. Elias Degraff, CMSR.

22. Although slavery had been in decline in Maryland since 1810, proslavery forces retained the institution and the 1860 federal census recorded approximately eighty-seven thousand enslaved persons. As a loyal Union state, Maryland was exempt from President Lincoln's Emancipation Proclamation. In November 1864, a new state constitution prohibiting enslavement passed, effectively freeing enslaved persons in Maryland. U.S.

Bauyanet. Sherman Is Pushing them Hard. Farugut Doin the Same on water.[23] I Hope It will Be soon. the next Place will Be Savannah George that will winde up this Department then I Dont know where we will go to. we are not In So much fear now Sence the Gun Boat got Repared.[24] when She was lying Still Johnny were troublesom But we Use some Poweder on them. If we can keep them from landing that all we want. It wont Be longe Before we will go and See them. My health Is getting Better. I Expect to go to Wright Sound Again. there Is some Fun Some Place But that not for Private to know. Jeff. Davis I goin to Put 300,000 Slave Into the Field next Spring. He tell them He will give them fifty Acre of land A Piece.[25] we Have got Abought Eight Hundred men in our Ridgement now.[26] Michigan Is Drafting all the Collord men She can get Hold of. you need not call It Draft But Prest Into the Army. there Is no Honesty Abought It. It will Be so all over the Country Before longe. the men they must Have Before this ware Is Stop. we are Expecting to get Paid of Again. the Captain He say the Paymaster Is

---

Federal Census, 1810–1860; State Constitution of Maryland, ratified November 1, 1864; see Fields, *Slavery and Freedom*.

23. Murray may have meant Rear Adm. J. A. Dahlgren, commander of the South Atlantic Blockading Squadron, providing naval assistance to Gen. Foster's expedition and to Gen. Sherman's movements. David Farragut was in command of the West Gulf Squadron. *ORN*, ser. 1, vol. 16, 57–70; Browning, *Success Is All*, 215–16.

24. The gunboat Murray usually spoke of in his letters was the USS *John Adams*; however, there is no indication that the *John Adams* was out of service at this time. Sources do show another vessel mentioned in a later letter, the USS *Pawnee*, as disabled and under repairs from mid-October until the beginning of November 1864. Report of Commander T. H. Patterson, USS *James Adger*, Off Charleston Bar, October 7, 1864; Distribution of vessels of the South Atlantic Blockading Squadron, October 15, 1864; Report of Rear Adm. Dahlgren, regarding general matters pertaining to his command, No. 543, Flag-Steamer *Philadelphia*, Port Royal Harbor, S.C., October 29, 1864, all in *ORN*, ser. 1, vol. 16, 9, 16–17, 34–36.

25. The Confederate States of America debated arming African Americans, free or enslaved, for much of the war. While most southern leaders opposed freeing enslaved persons and arming them, the idea drew converts as hope for a Confederate victory waned. With Gen. Robert E. Lee's endorsement, a bill allowing for the enlistment of enslaved persons passed the Confederate Congress and President Jefferson Davis signed it on March 13, 1865. The bill did not, however, offer land to enslaved persons who fought for the Confederacy as Murray here suggested. See Levine, *Confederate Emancipation*; Gallagher, *Confederate War*.

26. According to the November returns, the entire regiment numbered 795 enlisted men present, about 650 of whom were present for duty. Monthly Returns, 1864.

at the Head. He will Be to Pay our company In abought one week. no more at Presant. write let me know all the news. So good By.

S.C. Crew Soil   Nov 25th/64

Dear Mother   I Receive ~~your letter~~ yours and Aunt letter yeasterday Thankgiving Day. I was very glad to Hear From Home. I Hope you are all well But for my Part I am not well. I went to Beaufort yesterday. My Head Comence Acheing So I Could not Hardly See. ~~tow~~ to Day Is not much Better. the Head Ache Is A new thing for me Sence I Had the Fever. I have It Very often. I caught cold the other night. the Reb Bother us So Bad that we Had to get up See what we Could Do. I was In So Big Hurray I did not Put on my clothes. I was out all Knight. It was cool and Heavey Due. I caught Cold. It Is most time to Have Another chill. now the war news. Sherman was Bumbading Charleston. It keep us Awaik most All knight. we could Hear Heavy Firing all Around us. the Reb are Plenty cross the River. we Have Abought thirty thousand at Head. they talk of getting up an Expedition go Into Georga to take Savannah.[27] If Sherman tak Charleston there wont Be no Fighting Don there. U must Excuse this Short letter and all Bad Spelling. no more at Presant My Head Ache to Bad.

SC Crew Saw   Nov 29th/64

Dear Mother   I Have not much to tell But I am Sick. Been in my Birth for Six Days But I feel Better to Day. the Captain want me to go to the Hospital But I cant See the Point. last knight abought 30 men was Detail ~~of~~ out of our Comp on Another Rade But ~~Im~~ I am not well Enough to go.[28] I Had Rather Be well and go Fight Johnney then Be

---

27. Murray was not alone in his suspicion that planning for an expedition was afoot. Around this same time, Capt. Nelson noted in his diary that he believed an expedition was being raised but was unsure whether the 102nd USCT would take part in it. These instincts proved correct. On November 11, Sherman instructed Gen. Foster to break the Savannah and Charleston road around Pocotaligo so as to prevent Confederate reinforcements from striking his left flank. Nelson Diary, November 26, 1864; Dobak, *Freedom by the Sword*, 76.

28. Thirty enlisted men and one officer from each company were detailed for this

in Camp Sick. I Dont Know wheather I Ever will get Better Untill we moove from this Place. I Have not Don Eny Duty So long It will Be A new thing for me to commence Again if I.[29] It will Be All the Better for If. they Have taken aboght 30 men out the Companey But I am A fraid Part of the men wont come Back again. these Raid close at Home are not very Healthy for Enny Body to Be on. they are goin Into Georga. I Expect they will go to Savannah.[30] the mail Is goin out So I must Stop. give my love to Evey Body.

S.C. Crew Soil   Dec 1th/64

Dear Mother   I thought I would let you know what goin on In camp. I spake of Some of the Boys Being Detail to go on another Raid. they left yesterday with good Cheers. I Have Been very Sick So I Could not go But If I been well I would went. But It all for the Best. I Dont think one Half will Come Back Again. It Is Pretty Surring times Abought Here. they are Fighting all around us. we Have Plenty of Mucick[31] knight and Day. we can See the Smook In Every Direction. abought four O'Clock yesterday we Saw A large twon on Fire. the Blaze was Distinkley Seen from our Comp. we Have not Heard Ennything abought It yet. we cant tell wheather It was Burnt By the Reb or

---

expedition. On November 29, Brig. Gen. Saxton instructed the detachment to march to the ferry for transport to Beaufort. The detachment from the 102nd USCT, under the command of Col. Chipman and Capt. C. S. Montague, left Beaufort the next day to join Gen. Foster. Foster's orders were to cut the Charleston & Savannah Railroad near Pocotaligo. Called the Coastal Division, the expeditionary force consisted of three brigades commanded in the field by Brig. Gen. John Hatch. The First Brigade, led by Gen. Edward Potter, consisted of the Fifty-Sixth, 127th, 144th, and 157th New York Infantry regiments and the Thirty-Second, Thirty-Fourth, and Thirty-Fifth USCT. Col. Alfred Hartwell commanded the Second Brigade, composed of the Fifty-Fourth and Fifty-Fifth Massachusetts Colored Infantry Regiments, the Twenty-Sixth USCT, and the detachment from the 102nd USCT. Col. William Ames led an artillery unit made up of Batteries B and F, Third New York Artillery and Battery A, Third Rhode Island Heavy Artillery. Regimental Order Book, November 29, 1864; Report of Brig. Gen. John P. Hatch, U.S. Army, Commanding Coast Division, *OR*, ser. 1, vol. 44, 421–25.

29. Company morning reports show Private Murray on the sick list from October 5, 1864, through the rest of the year.

30. Despite Murray's prediction reflecting camp rumor, Foster's expedition did not go to Georgia to meet up with Sherman's troops. The 102nd USCT, however, did go to Savannah in March 1865.

31. The noise of battle, particularly from the artillery.

By the Union Boys. I am left with one mate as an old Granney. He Says that man Have the Same Sickness as A Horse. He Has Been Sick. He want A little white oak Bark A littles Quinine opium and little wormwood tea.[32] If you Have A Pin you cant keep It. He want to tast Everything you Have to Eat. If It Is good He will get Some. He will Say aint that good But after all. I Have got the Best mess mate In comp. two of my Best mate are gon. I am afraid they wont come Back again. we Have no Hard words Sence we Been together But my temper get A Stray few word I am Don. I Expect to Do Duty to Knight If call on. Sence I Have Had the Fever I have turn fool. last Knight I could not Sleep. I ownley thought of the Boys and got the Head Ache. I Rather Be well and Be Fighting then Be Sick lying In Camp. after all we Have But very few Sick men In our Rid. I wish I Could Be Home this winter to See you all. we cant get A Furlow In this Department. to far from Home. If we Should get one It would Be 20 or 30 Days Furlow. It take four Days and Knight to go to New York then It would take twelve Hours to come Home. But the worst would Be getting A Boat to go Back. Some time we would Have to wait A week or two. I must Stope my Head and Hand getting Unruly So Good By.

write Soon.

Crew Soil   Dec 2th/64   S.C.

Dear Mother   I Set Down to write A few lines that I feel very well at and Hope these few lines will find you and the Rest of the Famley well. Sence our Boys went Away they Have Had very Hard Fight with the Johnny. the very next Day they was Push In to Hard Fighting. they Fought 3 Hours with out Stoping. Abought 300 men were Brought to

---

32. Soldiers often complained that the treatment was worse than the disease itself. Common treatments during the Civil War included quinine, opium, calomel, blue mass, castor oil, turpentine, silver nitrate, and ipecac. Most of these came with serious side effects. Calomel and blue mass, for example, were mercury based and caused mercury poisoning, inflamed gums, and loose teeth. An unknown number of soldiers returned home addicted to opium. When possible, soldiers self-treated with a variety of herbal remedies. White oak bark was used as a tea for diarrhea, fever, or cough or applied to the skin in a compress to relieve inflammation. Wormwood tea was used for various digestive ailments. See Bollet, *Civil War Medicine*; Devine, *Learning from the Wounded*.

Bufs Beaufort that were wounded. our Cournal was wounded.³³ one Captain In one of the other Compney was kill. Allso non of our Boy was Hirt we Have Heard of to Day. at Daylight the Ball Commence. we Have taken the Bridge and Fourt. this Is the fourth time It Has Been th tride. It was the main Bridge Run from Charleston to Savannah George. It was Iron Built Tressel work. I wish I was well Enought to went But I was not. Dec 3th/64 the 54th Mass and the 55 Mass were cut all to Pieces. the Reb Built A Big fire Before the Fourt to Prtect It. they Made A Charge through It. great Menny were Burnt.³⁴ It Is Said that Abought four Hundred was Brought to the Hospital.³⁵ we are Doing A Big thin Down Here. the Reb think there Chance are not good. the Second Day we got the worst of It. they Done Us Some But the Boys of the Gun Boat turned In Help. If they Had not we would Been whip. the Reb had 14,000 we Had 8,000 all told yesterday fight.³⁶ we Have not Heard from. we Have the Best of Summer weather. Everything look As green as Ever. the Robin and malking³⁷ Birds Sing

---

33. Col. Chipman was not injured in the fighting at Honey Hill. This likely was just a rumor that got back to the men before a more accurate account of casualties was available. 1st Lt. H. H. Alvord was the only officer of the 102nd USCT wounded at Honey Hill. Alvord was wounded in several places: once by a minié ball to his right ear, then by grapeshot in his left hip, and finally by a minié ball that struck him in the back of the head. Henry H. Alvord, CMSR.

34. Confederate colonel Charles Colcock ordered his South Carolina troops to set fire to the tall grass and weeds in front of their position. The fire quickly covered the field, and a strong wind carried the blaze to the Union troops, making the Union advance difficult. Official reports of the battle as well as later recollections of soldiers describing the fight at Honey Hill speak of the harrowing experience fighting the brushfire. Report of Brig. Gen. E. Potter, commanding First Brigade, Headquarters First Brigade, Deveaux's Neck, December 11, 1864; Report of Col. William Gurney, 127th New York Infantry, both in *OR*, ser. 1, vol. 44, 425–29; David Spears, Company A, 55th Mass. to Dr. B. G. Wilder, April 26, 1918, in Trudeau, *Voices of the 55th*, 173; Hudson, "Confederate Victory at Grahamville."

35. Records show 137 casualties for the Fifty-Fifth Massachusetts and 43 for the Fifty-Fourth Massachusetts. Report of Col. Henry L. Chipman, 102nd USCT, commanding the Second Brigade, Headquarters 102nd USCT, December 4, 1864, *OR*, ser. 1, vol. 44, 432–34; Trudeau, *Voices of the 55th*, 27.

36. Maj. Gen. John G. Foster's expeditionary force consisted of five thousand infantry, cavalry, and artillery, and five hundred sailors and marines. Foster estimated the enemy's force at nearly equal to that of the Union's, but in reality the Confederate force consisted of approximately fourteen hundred Georgia and South Carolina regulars and militia under Gen. Gustavus Smith and Col. Charles Colcock. Report of Maj. Gen. John G. Foster, Department of the South, including operations November 28–December 7, 1864, *OR*, ser. 1, vol. 44, 420–25.

37. Mockingbirds.

Sweetly. 5 pm the Fight comence again. Gnat and Mosketo are So Bad I must stop for the Knight.

Dec 7th I am not very well at Presant. I went to Beaufort Sunday come Back Monday and Had A chill. the Fight still goin on. one of my mess mate got Shoot in the Arm.[38] we Have not heard Ennything from the Rest of the Boys. they went Into the 54 Rid. they made A Charge and got cut all to Pieces. I Supose our Boys the same. the Union lost 1000 Men and Abought 70 officers.[39] we Dont know How menny the Reb lost. we Have not Heard from Head Quarters In four Days But I Expect our Rid Is Cut all to Pieces.[40] we Have not got But 20 men In camp. last Knight we was Keep Awake all Knight longe. the conteband keep up Such nois we went over on lady Island to See what the matter was. our Force and Sherman are close to gether. you can Here His Guns In Georga and South Carolina. all the Fighting Will Be Don this winter. we are Right In the Worst of it. we Dont know How Soon the Sick will be In It. I am sick one Day and well the next. I must Bring my letter to A close So Good By. I will let you Know Eney Day Fight If I can.

---

38. Based on Murray's description, Joseph Morgan is most likely the wounded soldier mentioned here. Private Joseph Morgan, Company E, sustained a musket ball wound to his right forearm at Honey Hill. Morgan was among the wounded transported to Beaufort after the battle. There he received treatment for his wound and returned to duty by the end of January 1865. 102nd USCT, Regimental Casualty Lists; Monthly Returns, 1864; Joseph Morgan, CMSR, CWPF.

39. According to Foster's report of the battle, there were 754 killed, wounded, and missing. Hatch's casualty report shows 746 casualties: 89 killed, 629 wounded, and 28 missing. The Confederates suffered one hundred or fewer casualties. *OR*, ser. 1, vol. 44, 420, 425; Hudson, "Confederate Victory at Grahamville."

40. The 102nd sustained two killed and seventeen wounded at Honey Hill. Capt. A. E. Lindsay and Private John Wade were both killed on the field. The most serious among the wounded was Joseph Marshall, shot in the back of his neck. Marshall was taken from the field to the hospital steamer *Cosmopolitan* and then sent to the General Hospital at Beaufort where he died on December 22, 1864. David Strother, wounded in both his neck and abdomen, also had his left thumb shot off. Isaac Johnson was shot in both of his arms and his right hand. A surgeon later amputated the middle finger of his right hand, but at least three shot, deemed too dangerous to remove, remained lodged in his arm for the remainder of his life. Corporal Philip White received a gunshot wound through his left shoulder, and a shell fragment injured a nerve in Ezekiel Thompson's right arm. A shell struck John Gray in his right thigh. Surgeons initially suggested amputation. Although ultimately spared the loss of his leg, he suffered great disability for the rest of his life. The remainder of the casualties suffered less serious wounds. 102nd USCT, Regimental Casualty Lists; Muster-Out Rolls; 102nd USCT, CMSR; Joseph Marshall, David Strother, Isaac Johnson, Philip White, Ezekiel Thompson, John Gray, Carded Medical Files and CWPF.

Pocotaliga S.C.   Dec 7th/64

Dear Mother   We Was Broak of our Rest last Knight By the contreband. we was call up and fell Into line of Battle. It was Reported that our Picket was Captured. they was on Lady Island on the other Sid of the Crick at an old Fourt. we went over and found them all Sound. they Had not Heard nothing nor Seen nothing. Some Body went to one of these Native House and want to get In. they Said they Had A Sick Soldier and want to come In. they would not let them In So they gave the Alarme that the Reb was comming. one of my mess mate Has got Back with A wounded Arm. the other one I Supose is Dead. we Have not Heard Ennything from them Sence they went Away. we are ownley 20 miles from where they are fighting. we can see the Smoak Plainly. our Folk Keep up Firing all Knight. this after noon we will Hear from them If nothing hapen. It so Reported that our Rid Is Cut all to Pieces. the 54 Mass Chusseth want our Rid to goin with them. we Have very nice weather Down Hear. Everthing look green as Ever. I went to Beaufort Sunday and came Back Monday. I Saw Some of our Union Boys that was wounded. Some Had there Under Jaw Shoot off. Some Ear and leg an Arm nose. Some Shoot through the neck. It was A Horable Sight to See. my Sickness ownly Save me. 5 Pm It Reported that our Folks Has taken Savanah But It Is not Sirtain yet.[41]

Dec 8th Nothing In Particular from our Boys. Heavy Firing all knight. we Have August weather Down Hear. there Is no Mail goes out of this Department till the Fighting Is over. last Knight we Had A thunder Shower. I Am not Able to Do Duty yet. It Been Almost three month Sence I Been fit for Ennything. It will Be Some time Before I will Be fit for Much Duty.

28th no news from the Front. our men Hold the Bridge. I Hope our folks will kill Every Johnney In the South. you cant whip them till Every man Is Dead. If you Drive them out of one Hole they will go In Another and fortify them self. they are Devlish Coward. they wont come

---

41. When Murray wrote this letter, Gen. Sherman had not yet reached Savannah. Sherman's army moved from Atlanta at a rate of about nine miles a day. On December 12, one of Sherman's scouts reached Beaufort, re-establishing communications with the rest of the Union army, cut off since leaving Atlanta. Nine days later, Sherman's troops arrived at the outskirts of Savannah. The Confederates abandoned the city and Sherman occupied it on December 22. Maj. Gen. W. T. Sherman to Lt. Gen. U. S. Grant, December 22, 1864, in *OR*, ser. 1, vol. 44, 6–7.

out In open Field and Fight. there would not Be A Johnny left to tell the Story. It Is warm times Down Here. Fighting all Around Us. Plenty of Music to Sleep By. you would Allmost think they was In Camp. the Smook In Day time look like Dark Cloud Arising. at Knight you would think A Thunder Storm was A comming Past. Johnny and the Black man. this Department Is Black. we are under Genral Butler.[42] He Is A fighting man and So Is His men. the commander In this Department give the Black man the Prais of Doin the Best Fighting. It make Some ~~Squrm~~ of them Squrm to give us the Prais. give me the Black man Against the World. we Have Abought 150,000 In the Field. nothing more at Presant. give my love to Every Body.

I Receive A letter from Martha Watson to Knight.

S.C. Crew Soil   Dec 11th/64

Dear Mother   It Is with Pleasure to write to you when I feel well. I am Quite Smart By Spell. I Hope you and the Rest of the Famly are Enjoying the Best of Health. we cant Hear Much from the Fight Although we are In +30 mils of them. our Ridgement Is not cut up as Bad as was Reported. we Had five Boys wounded But non kill.[43] we Have the Best of weather for the Business. Johnny are A set of Coward. they wont come out of there Hole to Fight. If they are out they will Run Back to there Hole then they will Slaughter our Men By the Hundred. the ownley way Is to make A Charge on them. they cant stand that. If It was not for that they would whip our men. they think It Is there last chance. our Army Is Burning Up Everything come In there way. they will Fight till the last man. our Ridgement get great Prais. the white Rid Depend Upon the 54 Mass. If they give Back there Aint men Enough In the North to Drive them Into Battle. our Boys are with them. If Black men cant whip them there Is no use of Enny other tring. the officers give up that the Collord troop are the Best men to Fight. they Dont want to Say

---

42. Presumably, Murray meant Maj. Gen. Benjamin Butler, but the 102nd USCT was not under Butler's command structure at the time.

43. Murray was referring to the battle at Deveaux Neck that occurred on December 9, not Honey Hill. Five men from Murray's company sustained injuries at Deveaux Neck: James Baza (right breast), Andrew Batts (left breast), Nathan Davis (arm), George Appleton (hand), and John Theuston (face). 102nd USCT, Regimental Casualty Lists; CMSR.

So. this Is the fourth time they Have tride to take this Bridge. now they Have got It But who took It. It was taken By the Black through A large Fire where they could not get there own men to go. It Is Reported there Is Abought 13,000 men at Beaufort In the Hospital. I Saw last Sunday 6,00 when I was there. If I Been Well Probly It would Be my fate or worst. But I Should like to Be there with my mess mate. we Had A thunder Shower last knight. It some cool to Day But Clear. I Been wating for the mail. It goin to very Cold to knight. the wind Blow from the north. the last of this month is Pay day. It Is Very Hard to tell wheather we will Be Paid of this month or not Because the Boys are at the Frount. there Is no Rid at Beaufort nor at the Head. If they Do Pay of I will Send Some Money In my next letter. I cant tell How much But It will Be Some. Pleas Send me the Buffalo Express and the Lockport Journal. Good By till next time. give my love to Every Body.

our time Is out on Picket this month But we may Stay all winter. If we leave Here we will go to see Johnny where the Rid Is But they may come Back.

S.C. Crew Soil   Dec 14th/64

Dear Mother   I Receive your letter to Day. I was glad to Hear that you was well as Expected. I am Quite Smart to Day Except A Slite Head Ache. there Is Some Hard Fighting In this Department. Sherman Has got Savannah By Burning It. we Have taken the Bridge Between that Place and Charleston. our Ridgement Is Fighting yet. we Have Abought 6 men wounded. two of my mess mate were wounded. there Is non kill out of our Comp. we Have Heard of our Folks Has lost 800 kill and Abought 600 at Beaufort. we cant Hear Ennything of Enny Important Although we they Have Been Fighting within 20 miles of us. there Is no mail goes out till after the Fight. we can whip Johnneys If they are In there Hole But we loos two men to there one. Charleston Is the last Place In this Department. our Cornal give our Boys great Prais. He Says they Dont Know what Retreat Is. they wont take no Prisoner. we Have the Best of weather for the Buisness. for the last two Days It Has Been Cool and Frosty But It Is Summer weather. Every thing look Green. I Dont Know But we will all Have A Hand with Johnny yet. If my Health Is good I will go with the Rest. I was not well Enough to go when the Rid went. you want to know wheather I Receive Enny Stamp. I get Every one. I have not lost But two sence I Been Down Hear. one I lost when I was In Florid with A lot of Stamp. you need not send Enny Paper Because I can get Plenty But Stamp are Hard thing to get Holt of at the Postoffice. Soldiers will go and get from two to three Dollars worth and It Run them Short. I Receive one letter from Lue one letter from Aunt and one letter from Martha W. I Have Answered them. I Sent two to Lue In Box 655. If they are Put in your Box Send them to Her and tell Her to write to me and Emma. You can Hear the Cannon Roar Knight and Day. It Been So for two weeks. Some times It will jar the Earth so you will Have Quear Feeling. the Pawnee Hold the Bridge.[44] She Is 64 Gun Boat. I wish I was well So I Could See the Elephant. I Have Seen the tail, when I was In Florid But It was sharp work for the Eyes. Johnneys are Dangerous with Fire Armes. So no more at Presant. I will Send you the Particular Just as soon our Rid Come Back. Give my love to Every Body.

Heavy Firing can Be Heard.

S.C. Crew Soil   Dec 16th/64

Dear Mother   I am well as can Be Expected. las knight I was Sick with the Headach and I hope these few line will find you well and the Famley. I Receive two letters to day and was glad to Hear from Hom. I get all the letters you Send and the Stamp. I Receive 13 Stamp By this mail. you think I Dont Send you Enny letters. there Is not A mail go out But what I Send Some two or three letter. the mail Has not Been out for two weeks Because we Have very Hard Fighting In this Department. Part of our Boys Has Been kill and wounded. In A Month Probley the Fighting will Be to End. we cant Hear Enneything from our Rid. you will get the new sooner then we can. they Have Been Fighting within 30 miles of us. two of my mess mates Have Been wounded. one Shoot In the Arm. the other was Shoot through the Hand.[45] His

---

44. The USS *Pawnee* was a sloop-of-war built in the Philadelphia Navy Yard shortly before the Civil War broke out. Beginning in February 1863, the *Pawnee* operated with the South Atlantic Squadron. The vessel was part of the expedition on the Broad River in late November 1864. *ORN*, ser. 1, vol. 16, 68–74; Browning, *Success Is All*.

45. George Appleton was the only member of Company E who received a wound at

S.C.

Coosaw Dec 25th /64

Dear Mother I wish you a Merry Chrismas and a Happy one It will Be a Dull one for me But I am well and harty and I Hope these few lines will find you and the Rest of the Family well We Have Quite Sturring times now In this Department our Rigt Has Been out for three weeks fighting mos't Every Day the first Day our falls lost Eight Hundred men there Is About Six Hug at Beaufort In the Hospital gave Meny of our Boys out of our Rigt were kill and maunded I was Down to Beaufort Yesterday to See two of my Ships mates who was wounded We Can't Hear Enny thing from the Rigt But land more and Plenty of Smack We Have taken the Bridge at Pocotaliga and fort By Hard fighting the Johneys are like ground Hogs you get them out of one Hole they will go Into Another It Cost great meny life to Rout them out Sherman Has got Savannah with out fighting for It He Is now In S.C. fighting the Best to know How the Reb See Hard times It wont Be long Before the war will Be D.Stop Down Here surely one more Place of Enny Account In this Department that Is Charleston Is taken Savannah Sherman lost ninty men He Say If He was Another man He wont leave a Stunt In

George for the Reb to Get to Day It Is Very Bad Cheving for great meny of our Soldiers It will Be the last they See It Is like Heavy thunder Every minute we are About 20 miles from them they keep moving Slowly to the East I wish I had Been well Enough to went with the Rigt But I might been kill Before this time no more at Present So good By

D. S. M.

We wont get Paid of not till our Rigt Come In we may not Be Paid till the last of Feb Direct your letter As the Same Comp E

Gun was Shoot all to Pieces. one Shoot Struck Him In the Shoulder and one In the Hip. our comp Drew of two Pieces of Reb Battery. I was Sick so I Could not go. I Should like to went. last kinght two of our Picket was taken of there Post By the Reb. we Sleep with Both Eyes open. Johnny Have got Abought ten men to our one But we can whip them. they are Reinforce from Charleston But cant get Enny Short of Sending to Fortust[46] Monroe. Sherman Is Shelling Savannah. By this time He Has got the Place. we Hold the Bridge So Johnny cant cross.

You Want to know who our Lockport Boy was. His Name Is Elias Degraugh. He Is In the Connetticut Ridgement. He Drive team.

you must not think I Dont Send Enny letter. I Send from three two five letter Every mail. our mail Has Been Stop for A time. no More at Presant so good By.

When the mail dos Come In you will Have Plenty of them

S.C. Crew Soil   Dec 25th/64

Dear mother   I wish you A Merry Chrismas and A Happy one. It will Be A Dull one for me But I am well and Harty and I Hope these few lines will find you and the Rest of the Famley well. we Have Quite Sturring times now In this Department. our Rid Has Been out for three week Fighting most Every Day. the first Day our Folks lost Eight Hundred men. there Is abought Six Hun at Beaufort In the Hospital. gaud menny of our Boys out of our Rid were kill and wounded. I was Down to Beaufort yesterday to See two of my mess mates who was wounded. we cant Hear Ennything from the Rid But laud nois and Plenty of ~~Smuck~~ Smook. we Have taken the Bridge at Pocotaliga and Fourt By Hard Fighting. the Johnny are like ground Hogs. you get them out of one Hole they will go Into another. It Cost great menny life to Rout them out. Sherman Has got Savannah with out Fighting for It. He Is

---

Deveaux Neck such as that described here by Murray. Appleton was admitted to the General Hospital at Beaufort on December 11 with a perforating gunshot wound of his right hand. He was returned to duty on February 2, 1865. The medical records do not mention any injuries to the shoulder or hip as Murray describes. 102nd USCT, CMSR; 102nd USCT, Regimental Casualty Lists; George Appleton, Carded Medical Files.

46. Fortress.

now In S.C. Fighting the Best He know How. the Reb See Hard times. It wont Be long Before the war will Be ~~D~~ Stop Down Here. ownley one more Place of Enny account In this Department that Is Charleston. In taken Savannah Sherman lost ninty men. He Say If He loos another man He wont leave A Stump In Georga for the Reb to ~~lay~~ set on. to Day It is very Bad Chrismas for great menny of our Soldier It will Be the last they Every see. It Is like Heavy thunder Every minute. we are Abought 30 miles from them. they keep mooving Slowly to the East. I wish I Had Been well Enough to went with the Rid But I Might Been kill Before this time. no more at Presant So good By.

We wont get Paid of not till our Rid come In. we may not Be Paid till the last of Feb.[47]

Crew Soil SC   Dec 27th/64

Dear Mother   I set Down By Candle light to write a few line that I am well at Presant. I Hope these few line will find you well and Famley. we Have the Best of weather In this Country for winter. you can go Barefoot most of the time. our Ridgement Has not come In yet. we Have Abought 70 men In the Hospital. there was two men kill we know of. Sherman Has got Into Sooth Carolina. He Is Burning up Every thing come In His way. we can see the fire from our camp. In less then a month He will Have Charleston.[48] you cant Sleep Knight Because there Is So much nois. our Picket Duty is Most Don on the Island. the next Place will Be Main land. our Head Quarters will Be at Savannah Georga. I Dont Know wheather we will Stay Hear Enny longer then our time or not. If we leave I will write to you and let you know where we will go. It might Be at Richman But Genral Foster Belonge In this Department. we are under Him. when our Rid come In we will Be Paid of. no more at Presant.

My love to all.

---

47. The 102nd USCT was paid on February 28, 1865. Company Muster Rolls; 102nd USCT, Record of Events.

48. Charleston did not surrender to Union forces until February 18, 1865, and Gen. Sherman did not occupy the city.

CHAPTER 5

January–March 1865

"Dear son if I never see you Enny do strive to meet me in heaven"

THE COMPANIES ON PICKET DUTY ON PORT ROYAL, LADIES, AND Coosa Islands returned to camp at Beaufort on January 19, 1865. After several days of heavy rain that prevented them from moving, the men embarked on a steamer Sunday, January 22, and sailed up to Boyd's Neck, making camp at Deveaux Neck. The detachment with General Foster's expedition rejoined the regiment at Deveaux Neck two days later. During February 1865, the Coastal Division, including the 102nd USCT, slowly moved toward Charleston, destroying railroads, farms, and other installations that might aid Confederate forces. On February 7, the regiment crossed the Salkehatchie River and marched five miles along the Charleston and Savannah Railroad toward Charleston and then bivouacked. Major Clark, with Companies B, E, and I, conducted a reconnaissance mission near Cuckhold Creek on February 9. There the detachment engaged Confederate cavalry in a brief skirmish. The rebels opened up with artillery, causing Major Clark's forces to fall back about three miles. Records do not show any Union casualties in this skirmish. Three additional companies from the 102nd USCT arrived the next day, bringing along three pieces of artillery. With this support, the 102nd advanced some distance before camping for the night. The regiment continued moving slowly, destroying track and bridges as it passed. At one point about twenty enslaved refugees fled the rebels and came into Union lines.[1]

The regiment reached the Ashepoo River on February 14 and burned several houses in the vicinity before building a bridge across the river. The soldiers then marched to the Edisto River on the twentieth, and from there continued their slow advance toward Charleston. After another three days marching, the 102nd reached the Ashley River oppo-

---

1. Nelson Diary, February 9, 1865; Monthly Returns, 1865. Capt. Nelson wrote that he hired one of these men, Jim, as a servant.

site Charleston and set up camp at Charleston Neck. There, the men helped build Union defenses. On February 15, 1865, Confederate general P. G. T. Beauregard ordered Confederate forces to evacuate the city of Charleston. Three days later, after being under a continuous siege by Union forces since July 10, 1863, and threatened by Union forces, including those of General William T. Sherman, the mayor of Charleston surrendered the city. After the Confederate evacuation, Union troops moved into the city where war had started four years earlier. Black troops from the Twenty-First and Thirty-Third USCT Infantry regiments and the Fifty-Fifth Massachusetts were among the first to enter Charleston. Additional African American regiments, including the 102nd USCT performed occupation duties in and around this important southern city as the war drew to a close.

Picket and fatigue duties at Charleston Neck continued for the regiment until early March when it received orders to move to Savannah. The right wing of the regiment, under Colonel Chipman's command, embarked first, arriving at Savannah on the eleventh. Meanwhile, the left wing, under the command of Major Clark, remained in Charleston several days awaiting transportation. It arrived at Savannah on the fifteenth, joining the right wing on the outskirts of the city. Once there the men resumed the familiar routine of picket and fatigue duty. On March 28, the 102nd USCT received orders to proceed to Georgetown, South Carolina. This time the left wing departed first, boarding the *Planter* and arriving at Georgetown on April 1, while the right wing remained in Savannah awaiting transportation.[2] From this point on, the 102nd USCT engaged primarily in occupation duties as the war came to an end.[3]

---

2. The *Planter* was a Confederate cargo steamer that transported cotton before the war. Its enslaved crew, led by Robert Smalls, commandeered the *Planter* in May 1862 and delivered it into Union hands outside the defenses of Charleston harbor. The vessel subsequently became part of the South Atlantic Blockading Squadron. The *Planter* helped support Sherman's army in Savannah and returned, with Smalls at its helm, to Charleston harbor in April 1865. See Miller, *Gullah Statesman*.

3. Monthly Returns, 1865; Muster-Out Rolls; Record of Events.

Crew Saw SC Jan 1ᵗʰ/64[4]

Dear Mother   I wish you A happy New Years. I Hope you are all well and Harty. as for my Self I am allmost well as I Can Be. last Thursday we had A Thunder Shower. It lasted all Day. yester Day we Had Some Rain. last Knight It was very Cold. to Day the weather Is fine But cool. we Keep In our Shanty. we cant See the Difference Between New Years then Enny other Day. our Boys must Suffer very mush at the Frount. they Have not Come In yet.[5] Sherman Has not got By yet.[6] Just as soon He get By they will come in. we Have lost two men out of the Hospital that were wounded.[7] we Have not Heard How Menny Has Been Killed out of the Ridgement. there Is Abought 600 men In the Hospital at Beaufort the last time I was there. we Can Hear Heavy Firing In Every Direction. for the last three Days there Has Been Plenty of nois. we cant Hear Ennything from our Boys Unless we get a new York Paper. they Have Been Fighting within 20 miles of us. we could Hear the musketry very Plain. there Is Some talk of takig Abought Six Ridg out of this Department. I Hope ours will not go Because It Is So Cold. we would Suffer like Dogs Because our Blood So thin. In South Carolina Snow Dont very often fall. It will Be Something new for ~~See Snow~~ me to See Snow fly Again. It Rather A Dull New Year for me. I wish I could get A Squar meal again. we are Fasting to Day. our Ration Run out two Day ago. we Have Been living on old Flour that Has got worm In as large as your fingar. you must not Say A word ~~go~~ Against It.

---

4. The correct year was 1865.

5. The detachment out in the field with Gen. Foster's expedition did not rejoin the regiment until January 24, 1865, at Deveaux Neck. Monthly Returns, 1864, 1865.

6. On January 15, 1865, Sherman sent Gen. Oliver O. Howard and his Army of the Tennessee to Beaufort to take position on the railroad from Charleston to Savannah. Capt. Nelson's diary indicates that the Seventeenth Corps was in the vicinity of the 102nd's camp in mid-January. Sherman' March to the Sea Chronology, Civil War Library; Nelson Diary, January 10–13, 1865.

7. Three men wounded during the regiment's recent engagements died by the time Private Murray wrote this letter. Joseph Marshall, wounded in his right shoulder at Honey Hill, died December 22 from typhoid pneumonia. At Deveaux Neck, Alexander Johnson sustained a gunshot wound to the right orbit, penetrating his brain. He died on December 22 at a General Hospital in Beaufort. A minié ball perforated Andrew Batts's left lung at Deveaux Neck. He succumbed to his injury on December 27. Joseph Marshall, Alexander Johnson, and Andrew Batts, CMSR and Carded Medical Files; 102nd USCT, Regimental Casualty Lists.

If you Do you will get tied up By your fingar.⁸ I want you to Have for me when I come Home lot of Pottatoes and Plenty of Pork. Sweet Pottatoes I Dont like. no more at Presant. give my love to Every Body. I want you to let me Know If Lucinda Has gon West Again. I Have written four letter to Her two In your Box and two I Directed to Her.

Crew Saw SC   Jan 4th/65

Dear Mother   I Have Som time to write A few lines to you that I Am well at Presant and Hope these few lines will find you well and the Rest of the Famley. there Is not much news at Presant In camp ownley they are goin to Send Home the wounded Soldier. the main Part to new york.⁹ Some of our Boys out of our Rid Dont want to go. at Beaufort the Hospital Is full now. we think they are goin to Evacuate the Island. our Rid Have not come In yet. Sherman Is Burning Everything In He Come Across In this State. we can Hear Him at A Distant Every Knight. we Have the Best of weather. we Have one or two cold Knight and Plesant Day. to Day the weather Is like Sumer weather. you can go Barefoot most of the time But I Dont think you can Do It at the North. we Dont Have no Snow In this country. I Dont Know But I will go to Savannah In A few Day. I cant tell How long It will Be. I See you northern Folks Dont think we Have Savannah. we Have not much force In the State at Presant. the State of South Carolina Have to get Her just Due. I Hope they wont leave A House Standing In the whole

---

8. Although no record asserting that any of the men in Murray's company or regiment suffered such punishment has been discovered, Black soldiers, as did White soldiers, complained of receiving punishments, including being bucked and gagged or made to stand in the hot sun for hours at a time, for the slightest infractions. B. W., Morris Island, S.C., July 8, 1864, *Christian Recorder*, July 30, 1864.

9. Soldiers expected to need a lengthy recovery period and those likely to be discharged rather than returned to service were often transferred to general hospitals in northern cities. Many of the men wounded at Honey Hill and Deveaux Neck were moved to DeCamp General Hospital, on David's Island in New York Harbor. By late 1862, DeCamp was the Union army's largest general hospital, housing more than twenty-one hundred patients. It included a main hospital, quarters and barracks, storehouses, stables, shops, bakeries, and cookhouses. The hospital steamer *General J. K. Barnes* left the Beaufort area on January 1, 1865, carrying many of Murray's wounded comrades. The *Barnes* arrived in New York harbor on the fifth. 102nd USCT, CMSR; Carded Medical Files; *New York Times*, May 8, 1862; August 31, 1862; September 11, 1862; January 6, 1865; *Brooklyn Daily Eagle*, September 25, 1862.

State. when we get Don we are coming north to clean up the Dirty work that left undon. then we will See If we cant keep Piece. the old Saying Is to whip our children at Home then we can keep Piece Abroad. I Should like to Have few of them northern men Down Hear In Frount of Some Battle. I think It would Stop Some of there talk. most of the Folks Dont know what It Is to Be In Battle and they Dont care as long as there are out.[10] we Have lost kill and wounded Abought 1500 men In one Day and Half. most of them was lost the first Day. when you find Johnny In His Hole you must Fight Hard to get Him out. It cost great menny life But we can whip them In Enny Shape. we will Have the Johnny whip out of this Department this winter. I Suppose we will go to Richmond In the Spring. then It will Be Sharp work for the Eyes. I Dont care Ennything About the Small Gun But the Grape and canester are Bad thing front and charge on. no more at Presant so good By. give my love to Every Body. If you see Lucinda and Emma tell them to write to me. my love to them Allso and Jane.[11]

Crew Saw SC   Jan 11th/65

Dear Mother   I Recd your letter Dated on the 19th Inst on the 10th of this month. I was very glad to Hear from Home. It Been Abought three weeks Sence I Recd Enny letter from Home. I maid up mind I would not write Enny more untill I got an Answer from Some of them. yesterday we Had A very Heavy thunder Shower all Day. to Day It Is very cold But Plesant weather. your letter you Sent the Stamp In I Have not got them. I will get them After Awhile. Every Sence our Rid Been out the mail Has not Been not Regular. our Rid Is at the Froant

---

10. Murray's attitude here was one shared by many of his comrades. Soldiers, Black and White, resented those men and women who criticized the war or espoused peace while remaining safe in their homes far from the battlefields and the hardships soldiers experienced. Peace Democrats, or Copperheads as they were derisively known, especially were the targets of soldiers' ire.

11. According to the 1855 New York Census, Jane Broadhead (Brodhead) lived with Lanson (Alanson) Hollenbauch (Hollenbeck, Hollenback), his wife Susan, and their children Richard and Sarah. The Wells-Murray family had a friendship with the Hollenbacks, so Jane Broadhead seems a likely candidate for the Jane whom John Murray spoke of here. Sarah Wells later wrote of a Jane Ann Van Buren, but no one by that name has been located. It is possible that the two Janes were the same woman whose marital status resulted in a name change. U.S. Federal Census, 1850, 1860; New York Census, 1855, 1865.

yet. there Is great menny of our Boys wounded But few Kill. they are Sending them to New York all Sick and wound. Part of Sherman men are at Beaufort getting there Pay.[12] we wont get Enny Pay Untill our Ridgement come In. It Quite Still Abought Hear at Presant. we Cant Hear Enny Firing. It would Quite Strange to See Snow In this Country. I Receive A letter from Mrs. Hawley[13] at the Same time I Recd those Papers you Sent and Mrs. Allen Sent.[14] tell Mrs Allen I am much oblige to Her for that Paper She Sent to me and give my love to them all. I want you to tell me what kind of weather you Have In your country. you Say that Aunt[15] take out my letters out of the Postoffice. I Dont want Enny one take my letters out ownley those Have A Right to take them out Because I Sometimes Send money In them. I want you to get It. when you Receive Enny I want you to tell the amount of money you Recd. I Expect to Send Home considrable when we get Paid of. I Have got Six month Pay and Back Pay coming to me this time.[16] no more at Presant. give my love to all Incuiring friend.

---

12. A notation made by Capt. Nelson in his diary on January 6 stated that part of Gen. Sherman's army was landing on the island. The next week Nelson wrote that the Seventeenth Corps was in the vicinity, laying pontoons across the Coosa River at the Ferry. Nelson Diary, January 6, 10, 12–14, 1865.

13. Rheuma Hawley. Rheuma (Rheumah) Hannah (Hotchkiss) Crain was Lucinda Crain's older sister. Born in 1807 or 1808, Rheuma married twice. Festus Isham, her first husband whom she married in February 1827, died before 1850. Rheuma then married Lyman Hawley. Rheuma had one child with each of her husbands: Clarissa Isham, who died in 1857, and Lucinda Hawley, born in 1841 or 1843. After the death of her second husband in 1867, Rheuma lived with her sister Lucinda. U.S. Federal Census, 1800–1880; New York State Census, 1845, 1855, 1865.

14. A family of color named Allen lived in Lockport in 1860. The Allen household consisted of George Allen, a forty-two-year-old barber, his wife Mahetable, and their children Charles, Rosana, and Frederick. Also a member of the household was sixty-four-year-old Rosana Hollenbeck, George Allen's mother-in-law. Letters written by Sarah Wells to her son establish Richard Hollenbeck as a friend of John's. The Mrs. Allen referred to in this letter is likely Mahetable Allen. U.S. Federal Census, 1850, 1860; New York State Census, 1855, 1865.

15. Asher Wells had two brothers: Calvin and Bartlett (Bailey). Calvin's wife was Sarah, and Bartlett was married to Elizabeth. No siblings for Sarah or John Murray's birth father, Alonzo, have been identified, so the "aunt" may have been a fictive aunt rather than a blood aunt. A letter from Sarah Wells to her son referred to "Aunt Jane," so it seems probable that the aunt mentioned here was Jane.

16. When the regiment mustered for pay on Tuesday, February 28, the men had six months' pay due them. Private Murray was not present for this pay. He was admitted to the hospital two days earlier. Murray's service record indicates that, at the time of his death, he had been paid only through June 1864. Nelson Diary, February 28, 1865; John Murray, CWPF.

CHAPTER FIVE

Crewsaw SC   Jan 17th/65

Dear Mother   I Have A little time to write you A few lines to let you know that I Am well and Harty Except A Bad Cold. I Hope these few line will find you and Father and Grandmother all well. Sherman men Has left Beaufort last knight.[17] there was abought 30,000 men. last Knight Some 45,000 men came Into Beaufort. they are goin through to Main land. they were A Rough Seet of Boys.[18] they took Everything they could get. they Hens left there Roost and went Into the woods. the Rooster would Say Sherman. they would call the Roll and leave and In fact all feather tribes would cry Sherman. they Say they are not goin to leave A House In S.C. they commence Fighting the Same Dey they went on Main land.[19] one of His Main officers got kill. our Rid Has not come In from the front yet. the Lieutenant told me when they come we would go to Savannah Ga to Do Provost Duty again. our Head Quarters would Be there. I Hope we will go there. last Sunday we ~~cant~~ caught A Reb Spy all most In camp. He Said He Belonge to the Gun Boat Wabash.[20] we took Him Down to Beaufort to Head Quarters and Put Him In Jail and now our Boys are after another one. He was was at the Edge of our camp. Johnnys are get very troublesome. we will Have to Use them Rough again then will Stay at Home. If we Do go away I will write to you so you must not Stope writing. Som-

---

17. The Seventeenth Corps crossed the Coosa River the night of January 14. Nelson Diary, January 14, 1865; Report No. 3, Itinerary of the Union Forces, November 1–December 21, 1864, *OR*, ser. 1, vol. 44, 25–55.

18. This was a common observation of Sherman's hardened troops. Alonzo Reed wrote to his mother that "there is abought 17000 men of Sherman at Beaufort they look very rough." Capt. Nelson described Sherman's troops as a "rough set of men, but good fighters." Expecting stately, martial soldiers in both appearance and bearing, Chaplain Waring expressed surprise, if not disappointment, in Sherman's men in a letter to the *Weekly Anglo-African*, stating that "taken altogether, Sherman's army certainly does not come up to the common idea of a well-appointed body of troops." Alonzo Reed to Mother, Coosa, S.C., January 11, 1865, Alonzo Reed letters; Nelson Diary, January 13, 1865; William Waring to editor, Beaufort, S.C., February 15, 1865, *Weekly Anglo-African*, March 4, 1865.

19. No battle of note occurred between Sherman's forces and Confederates around this time; however, Capt. Nelson mentioned hearing cannon in the direction of Pocotaligo the morning after Sherman's army crossed over the river. Nelson Diary, January 14, 1865.

20. The *Wabash* was a frigate built at the Philadelphia Navy Yard in 1856. It served as flagship of the South Atlantic Blockading Squadron and was an active force in the blockade of Charleston between 1862 and 1864. The *Wabash* also participated in the December 1864–January 1865 assault on Fort Fisher, N.C. Osbon, *Handbook of the United States Navy*, 265.

thing abought the weather you would not Bleave me If I would tell you. the Frogs Peeps Evry knight and musketo and Gnat are So Bad that you cant go to Sleep. on Picket they allmost Eat you Up A live. Everything look as green as Ever the Did in Sumer. no more at Presant.

City of Charleston SC   March 3th 65

Dear Mother   It Is with Pleasure I Set Down to write A few lines to you. It Been two month Sence I written A letter to Enny Body. I Receive your letter Regular and Paper one from Lue one from Rhuma[21] and was glad to Hear from them. we Been out on A Raid over two month. It Rain most of the time. we marched over 200 miles to get to Charleston. we Had three Fight on our Raid.[22] the Reb would leave there Houses and Everything In It. we would Burn them Up. Looking glass worth $500. we Had four Brigade. our was the Second. It Is the Largest Rid In this Department. I Have not Been well for over three Month. I Am at Presant In the Hospital. Some Say I got the Dropsy. I Am Bloted all Up. one or two Day my face Swollen So I Could not Se But I Am getting Some Better.[23] I am goin to Stay till I Do get Better. most likely we will Stay Hear most of the Summer Doing Provo Duty. the Reb are not tame. Abought Every Day they Shoot Some of our men so the Genral Shoot them with out Court Marshall. the woods Is full of them. we Hunt them like wolf. the City Is A Dirty Place. the Best Part of It Is Burnt Up or Destroyed By Shells.[24] the City Is 10 miles Squar It

---

21. Rheumah Crain Hawley, referred to in an earlier letter as Mrs. Hawley.

22. The raid Murray talked about here was the regiment's movement from Beaufort toward Charleston in January and February 1865.

23. Murray was admitted to the Hospital in Charleston on February 26, 1865. Medical records indicate various, but similar, diagnoses of dropsy, anasarca, and chronic pericarditis. Anasarca is generalized massive edema (swelling) while dropsy is edema often caused by kidney or heart disease, and pericarditis is inflammation of the heart. John Murray, Carded Medical Files, CMSR.

24. The Union bombardment of Charleston that began in mid-1863 and lasted on and off for almost six hundred days destroyed much of the city. Gen. Beauregard ordered the last of the Confederate forces to evacuate the city on February 15, 1865. Before they left, Confederate soldiers set ablaze piles of cotton, rice, and other supplies to keep them from falling into Union hands. The city was still smoldering when Union soldiers entered. Alonzo Reed had a similar observation, commenting that Charlestown "looks horiable knocked all to pieces by the shells from our gun boats." Alonzo Reed to Dear Mother, Savanah, Georgia, March 2, 1865, Alonzo Reed letters.

~~the~~ Is the ownley Place look like Hom Sence we left Mayrland. we had two men Shoot Comming through the Quarterment on the Road goin After Rat[25]. one man got Shoot In our Company.[26] It Been Raining Hear for three Days Steady. we Have no tents But tore Down Houses and fence and make Shantys to sleep under. we are Soldering In good Earnest. It will take Some to the Grave But this Summer we my Be Home.[27] that Is the talk In this Department. you must Excuse this Short letter and Excuse the lenght of time. Sence we Started I Have Receive seven letters and two Papers. that make five. ~~So good~~ Give My love to Father and Grandmother.

Be Careful not Direct to Charleston Because It not All Quite Yet.

Lockport   March the 13 1865[28]

My Dear son   to whrite a few lines to This morning to let you know that I am not verry well nor have not Bin for the year past But that thanks to god that i amonst with the living. My Dear son i wish to here from you Wonse more this side of the grave whrite And let me

---

25. The rest of this word is cut off at the edge of the page. Murray might have written "ration," perhaps implying that the men were stealing food.

26. William Mason, Company E, died in a field hospital on February 10. Mason received a gunshot in his right thigh while on picket near Heyward, S.C. He died shortly after the amputation of his leg. William Mason, CMSR.

27. This statement indicated an awareness that the war was in its final stages and that the Confederates were all but defeated.

28. Civil War letters often can be read as an ongoing conversation between soldiers in the field and family and friends on the home front. Families at home had chests and trunks to stow away letters. Sarah likely kept John's letters safely stored near her so that she could read them over and over in perhaps a desperate attempt to maintain the tenuous link with her son as he marched and fought hundreds of miles away. Except for the few letters returned to Sarah after John's death, the other half of this conversation has been lost to us. Murray had little room for unessential items, even those as precious as letters and, like most of his comrades, was unable to keep stacks of letters from home. If he was able to keep a few particularly meaningful letters, they apparently did not accompany him to the hospital and were not part of his personal effects when he died. Thus, the only extant letters from Sarah are those included in this collection, returned to her in a bundle following the death of her son. Those dated March 13 and March 25 might have reached Murray as he lay in the hospital. If so, perhaps his mother's words comforted him. The last two letters, written April 11 and April 18, arrived after his death. Someone at the hospital or in his regiment was compassionate enough to ensure these, and perhaps other personal items, were sent to his mother, either directly or via his regiment.

know where you are. i have Not had Enny letters for 4 weeks or more.[29] I dont know Whether your sick or in the hospitle or taken prisoner or not. I want to here from you so bad. do whrite soon And let me know where you are. Dont for git your Mother. can wait to prepare for death while you have time And Opportunity if you are alive you stand on slipery ground any.[30] Dear son if I never see you Enny do strive to meet me in heaven. Excuse my short letter for i am in A hurray to Mail. this is from your Affectionate Father And Mother and gran Mother who send our love to you. whe all send our love to you our Dear son. dont send Enny more letters to your Aunt Jane. she is fals as she can live. let me know if your on the Croo Soo Island or not. if you have Orders to go some where else. let me know you Captain name. i have sent you 3 letter And have not received Enny. 4 And 5 weeks whe have bin to the Post Office And received no letters from you. this is from your Dear Mother who loves your Dear Soul.[31]

Mrs. Asher Wells   Lockport Niagara C.O.   N.Y.[32]

Lockport   March the 25th 1865

Dear son   It was with pleasure that I have the opertunity to whrite to you wonse more This side of the grave for I have whriten This make 4 letters that I have whriten to you And received no Answer till now.[33] I made up my mind that you was dead. I have bin greatly troubled in mind A Bought you. I did not know wether you Was taken pris-

---

29. After writing fairly consistently throughout his service, Murray did not, according to his mother, pen any correspondence between January 17 and March 3, when he wrote his last known letter.

30. Sarah's entreaty to her son to prepare for death while he had the time and opportunity, especially if he stood on "slippery" ground, embodies the idea of the "Good Death" characteristic of mid-nineteenth-century Americans. Preparation of one's spiritual condition was part of the centrality of readiness to the "Good Death." Sarah perhaps feared that his time in the army had tested her son's spirituality. See Faust, *This Republic of Suffering*.

31. There is a three-cent stamp in the folds of this letter, indicating that Sarah periodically sent stamps to her son, as he so often requested.

32. Written on the back of this letter is the following: "From the seat of War   Washington   All to gether in one Envelope   these letters come last after Death returned letter."

33. Presumably, the letter referred to here was Murray's letter dated March 3.

oner or not or bin kiled on the Battle field or sick as it prove To be. you say you have the Dropsy. if so This is your second sickness. it may be your last sickness. as i have given council And Always wish to strive to tell you through much sickness. Dear son i say to you seek god with all your Heart for god turns none A way that comes with A humble Heart. I have told you my Health is poor. I never Expect to feel much Better while I live. My prear to god is if I never should see you in this wourld My Dear son promise to meet me in Heaven. I must tell you when I received your letter March the 20 I have bin sick A Bed And Could not Answer before. I want you to whrite As often as you can to me And let me know wether you are geting Better or not. And if you dont git Better I want know it. if you cant whrite some kind friend would Whrite And let me know By your Asking them.[34] in this last letter you sent your Father Went to Cambria And took the letter with him And Lucinda[35] Broke It open. she said it was Love Joy whriting And she must look in that letter so he told her she might so Lucinda And Emma they would whrite that knight to you. if you git Emma letter wish her much Joy And husband.[36] Excuse my short letter for My Eyes is bad. this is from your Father And Mother And Grandmother that Ever remembers you A round our firesides But i shall put All in the hands of god to the future.

Yours in love My Dear from a Mother that love your soul. I must now bid you good By till the Next time.

A letter from Rich Hollenbeck in the Army. Sargon Major. Company E 127 Ridgment U.S.C.T. Well Done for Dick Hollensbeck[37] Esq.

---

34. If Murray was too weak to write in the hospital, he could have asked for assistance as his mother indicated, if just to ease her mind. Nurses, comrades, and others often wrote letters for wounded and sick soldiers as they lay in hospitals. Amid a predominantly illiterate community, African American soldiers and civilians often depended on others to write letters to, and read letters for, them. Alonzo Reed, whose letters have been referenced throughout this collection, was barely literate when he entered the army. Many of the wartime letters to his mother were penned by fellow soldiers, possibly even John Murray, as they belonged to the same company.

35. Cambria, Niagara County, near Lockport.

36. Presumed to be Emily, Lucinda Crain's niece. According to an affidavit she gave in Sarah Wells's pension claim, Emily came to live with her aunt Lucinda in the summer of 1857. U.S. Federal Census, 1860; New York State Census, 1865; John Murray, CWPF.

37. Richard Hollenbeck, Company E, 127th USCT. Richard enlisted as a substitute for Samuel McKane on August 11, 1864, at Seneca, Ontario County, N.Y. Beginning in early

Richard wanted to know where you was so he could whrite to you.

your Aunt and her Boy is going A the first of April and i am glad.

My Dear son dont be weary with your Mother. whrite to me wonse more your General name And Captain Name. do whrite it plain. I have mis laid those letters And cant find them. I dont no that it will do me Enny good.

My Dear son   dont be weary with your Mother complaints. i dond wish to weary your patience not while your are sick But your Father have not paid his tax yet. i am a fraid he will have some trouble a bought it. it has bin so cold this winter it frose his hogs. the snow has bin so deep he has not hauled Wood this Winter.[38] snow has bin so deep times is. Lue dont whrite to you Enny more. she has not paid me as she said she would for keeping her Child. she is not true to Mother nor me.[39] so good By til next time. Whrite soon And let me know how

---

February 1865, he operated as a sharpshooter. Richard Hollenbeck, CMSR; U.S. Federal Census, 1850; New York Census, 1855, 1865; 127th USCT, Record of Events (reel 217).

38. A fall from a horse in 1832 seriously injured Asher Wells in the head, chest, and wrist. These injuries disabled him for the remainder of his life and hindered the family's economic stability. With money borrowed from Washington Hunt, former governor of New York for whom he at one time drove carriage, Wells purchased two and a half acres of land. Asher worked this small plot of land on which the family lived. As did many African Americans, the family struggled. Until his enlistment, some of the money John earned working for Chester Shelley (Lucinda Crain's uncle) and on Albert Adams's farm went to help pay the mortgage on the land. The family faced increasingly difficult times after John enlisted, even supplemented with whatever meager amounts he sent home in his letters. This poverty was largely what prompted Sarah to request a pension. John Murray, CWPF; U.S. Federal Census, 1860, 1870; New York State Census, 1855.

39. The Lue in this letter does not appear to be Lucinda Crain. There were two women named Lucinda in the same extended family. Lucinda Crain was the daughter of Josiah and Ruth Crain. Lucinda Hawley was the daughter of Lyman and Rheuma Hawley. Lucinda Crain married Henry Singer between 1870 and 1875 but did not have any children before her death in May 1881. In 1855, Lyman Hawley and his wife, Rheuma, lived with their daughter, Lucinda. According to the federal census five years later, Amos Albert, a seven-month-old whose parentage is not identified, lived in Lyman Hawley's household along with Rheuma and Lucinda. Despite the seemingly disconnected names, Amos might have been Lucinda Hawley's son. A notation in the census shows that Lucinda, aged nineteen, had married within the year. Amos would have been around five when Sarah wrote this letter, and it could be that she had taken the child in or otherwise provided for his care. Further complicating the matter is that in a later letter of April 18, 1865, Sarah mentioned Aunt Jane in reference to an unnamed child's care and schooling with a

you are. Love Joy do let me know your Commanding General name And your Doctor Name who waits a pon you And the Chaplain Name your minister name. I hope you will let us know in your next letter you send us. your father request dont forg it it in your Next letter. whrite it plain so i can read it. good by till next time.[40]

Lockport   April the 11th 1865

My dear son   It is with pleasure that I sit down to whrite A few lines to you hoping these few lines will find you Better then you was in your last letter of March the third. whe was All glad to here from you Wonse more. whe did feel quite troubled for you. that long spell where I received no letters from you my sole was troubled to know wether you was living or not. whe thought the Reb had taken you prisoner or you was dead. whe could not tell. But i thank the Lord you are still a live. you say you are in the Hospitle. i think you had Better stay there till you are better so the Rebs wont shoot you. I suppose you have heard how Richmond Is fallen. is fallen I hope to rise no more for Ever. whe Heard that Jef Davis was in the santuary hearing the word of god when General Lee went And told him he could Hold out no more. the Minister give him A Note. he started wright away in his Carridge to the Depot for Dansvill.[41] General Lee surrendered And All his Army. Abraham Lincon Walking over the ruines of fallen Richmond.[42] My Dear

---

rather vague reference to some problems between the two women. U.S. Federal Census, 1860, 1870, 1880; New York State Census, 1855, 1865, 1875.

40. Written at the top of this page is "these letters come last death."

41. On April 1, 1865, after a ten-month siege, Gen. Grant's forces struck all along the Petersburg line. The Confederate army collapsed. The next morning, Sunday, April 2, Gen. Lee sent a telegram stating that he could not long hold his position and advised government officials to prepare to leave Richmond. Confederate president Jefferson Davis received Lee's message while attending service at St. Paul's Episcopal Church. Davis and his cabinet abandoned the capital and fled south on the only remaining open rail line, the Richmond and Danville. Later that day Confederate forces evacuated Richmond. The following morning Union troops began to enter the Confederate capital. See Lankford, *Richmond Burning*.

42. President Lincoln visited Richmond on April 4, 1865, just two days after Confederate forces evacuated. His arrival had none of the trappings of a victorious leader. As the USS *Malvern* ferried the president's entourage up the James River toward the Richmond docks, sunken ships, dead horses, and floating ordnance blocked its way. Lincoln and his

son when you receive these few lines from a Mother who Love you be not dismayed be of good cheer. This cruel War is Almost to a close whe think. Love Joy do tell me in your next letter if you are gitting better or not. i hope the time may come when this Cruel War will End when whe can see our sons our friends round our fire sides wonse more in this Wourld. so that whe can say this peace is like a river to my sole both temporal And spiritual. tell me All the News you can tell me. if you have good treatment where you bee or not. i dont know Wether you can tell or not. dont do Enny thing of the kind if your not permitted to do so to injure your self not by Enny means. Jane Ann Van Buren[43] Went a way April the 5. she treated me shameful. she never thanked me nor paid me nor said Enny thing a Bought It. but i was glad she took her Boy and left. i wanted the Monney verry Bad to pay a deat. i Expected she would Leave her Boy on my Hands. Dont never answer her letters no Never. Excuse me for not whriting to you before. My Health is so verry poor this last year And my Eyes trouble me so bad that i feel thankful that i can whrite. what if I could not whrite to you would have to go to the Neighbour for them to whrite. there would not be much whriting you. I have whriten more to you My Dear son then i have in all my life time. dont feel As though your Mother had slited you. your Gran Mother send her love to her grand son. she hopes that she will live to see you wonse more. she seems to mean that she was Deprived of your company so quick. This is from your Father And Mother your Ever all of us well Wicher to Our Onley son. My Dear son if i should Never see you this side of the do strive to meet me in heaven where the parting hand is no more for ever. my head ake so bad. good Night My son. Write soon let me know how you are getting a long. A few more lines from Dick Hollenbeck. He is promoted Srgon Major Company E 127th Ridgment U.S.C.T.[44] He said there was 200 Hunred Thousand

---

landing party boarded a barge towed by a small tug, but the tugboat ran aground. In the end, the president of the United States made his entry into the fallen enemy capital in a humble rowboat manned by a dozen sailors. The president and his party then made their way on foot through the streets amid the still-smoldering fires lit by the Confederates when they evacuated. After an informal meeting with local Confederate leaders, Lincoln took a tour of the city. See Gorman, "Conqueror or a Peacemaker?"

43. Presumably this is the same Jane whom Murray mentioned in his letters.

44. Hollenbeck's military service records indicate his rank as sergeant, not sergeant major. Richard Hollenbeck, CMSR.

Niggroes waiting like so Many hungry Wolfs for the Rebs. I suppose Dick is in this fight at Richmond.[45] Dick wanted to know what Ridgment you was in. Look out for a letter from Dick I have bin whriting to him.[46]

Lockport[47]   *April the 18th 1865*

I received your letter the same day I Mail One to you. i was glad to here from you that you was gitting better of your sickness. I hope My Dear son that the lord will Heal Boath sole And Body to Do his Will While you live. If i never should see you In this wourld that I might be so happy As to meet you In heaven where the parting Hand can never come. this greate Union the greate victory that has bin Acheved that Richmond is fallen I hope To Rise no more. But menny A Mother heart must Ake for Husband or son in this Cruel War. but keep good Courage. No Nation can be free with out sheding Blood. so if this be true the Collerd soldiers will have a name in History I hope if Justus is done them. there is no Collerd Men in Lockport. they All gone to War. the Old men are here. those to young to fight Are her. I received your letter April the 11th And Mail one the same day to Beaufort. I Mail one to Dick Hollenbreck. He wanted to know where you was so I told him to Direct to Beaufort. if he is not killed At Richmond I presume you Will her from him. Directon to Dick Richard Hollenbreck srgon Major Company E 127 Ridgment U.S.C.T. He said in his letter In Front of Richmond there was 200 Hundred Thousand Niggroes Waiting like so Menny Wolfs for the Rebs. poor fellow I dont know wether he is a live or not.[48]

---

45. The 127th USCT was involved in the siege operations against Petersburg and Richmond from September 1864 to April 1865. It was on duty in the trenches north of the James River until March 1865 and on the Appomattox Campaign from March 28 to April 9. 127th USCT, Record of Events.

46. "These letters come last After John Love Joy Murray Death" is written at the end of this letter.

47. Written at the top of the letter were the words "the last Day April 19 i recd the last letter from LoveJoy Murray After his 1865 Death april 19 some time ago." Written on the side of the letter was "Hospitle."

48. Richard Hollenbeck survived the war, though at the muster out of his regiment he was sick in a New Orleans hospital. Richard Hollenbeck, CMSR.

the reason why i whrite to you so much is because your Aunt Jane[49] has treated me verry mean. i did not know wether you received All my letter or not. she never said I thank you or kiss my foot for taking care of her Boy. she was to pay me one Dollar a week for His Board. i sent him to school 2 Terms. I wanted the Money verry bad but she is gone And i am glad. i sent the Boy to school And he staid at home. he was with me 51 Weeks. Now i must close my letter. Excuse all mistakes for i am sick most of the time. i feel that i cant hold out Much longer. this last year has Over come me. i have kept my Washing til now. i cant Do no more. i make out to do my work And that is all. my health is verry poor this spring. from your Affectionate Father And Mother And Gran Mother. I must stop i feel sick. good By Dear Son. i sent you 2 letter stamps in other letter. your Father has verry Bad luck. it has bin a verry hard whinter. his hogs frose foze to Death. the snow was so deep. he burnt his fence to keep warm. his colt is sick. i gess it will Dye. if it does he will have no team this spring to go to work with. you spoke of not receiving Enny Money. I am a fraid you never will. they have give you good promises from the first your bounty Money And your wages. My Dear dont feel hard Toward me. you are afflicted And so am I. cant work hard Enny more. your Gran Mother is failing sloly. If it was in your power to help me a little Without Distressing you self I should be glad. Dont feel hard my Dear son to me for letting my wants knowing to you. may god Bless you And restor you Health Again. Is my prayer rite whrite soon. good By Till the Next time.

this is from A Mother to her only son Mrs. Asher Wells Lockport Niagara CC

I Mail one letter the same day I received this April the 11th And one 3 weeks Before and I shall Mail this just as quick as i can send it to Lockport. I Envy neither the Head nor the Heart. you have plenty of green sauce vegitable where you are but here is cold raines A gloom prospect Before us. Wrigte soon. A great Day April the 14 the flag on fort Sumter will be raised.[50] there will be a shout in the Camp.

---

49. There is some confusion as to exactly whom Sarah wrote of here. In her letter of March 21, 1865, Sarah complained that Lue (Lucinda) had not paid her or her mother, Catharine, for the care of a child. Here she referred to "Aunt Jane" in the same manner.

50. Four years to the day after Maj. Robert Anderson surrendered Fort Sumter, he once again raised the Union flag over the battered remains of the fort.

Bibliography

Abbreviations

AGO   Adjutant General's Office
CMSR   Compiled Military Service Records
CWPF   Civil War Pension Files
NARA   National Archives and Record Administration
OR   *Official Records of the Union and Confederate Armies*
ORN   *Official Records of the Union and Confederate Navies*
USCI   United States Colored Infantry
USCT   United States Colored Troops

Published Sources

Adams, Virginia M., ed. *On the Altar of Freedom: A Black Soldier's Civil War Letters from the Front.* Amherst: University of Massachusetts Press, 1991.

Ash, Stephen V. *Firebrand of Liberty: The Story of Two Black Regiments That Changed the Course of the Civil War.* New York: Norton, 2008.

Barton, David, and Nigel Halls, eds. *Letter Writing as a Social Practice.* Philadelphia: John Benjamin Publishing, 1999.

Belz, Herman. "Law, Politics, and Race in the Struggle for Equal Pay during the Civil War." *Civil War History* 22, no. 3 (1976): 197–213.

Berlin, Ira, Barbara J. Fields, Joseph P. Reidy, and Leslie S. Rowland. "Writing Freedom's History." *Prologue: Journal of the National Archives* 14 (Fall 1982): 129–39.

Berlin, Ira, Joseph P. Reidy, and Leslie S. Rowland, eds. *Free at Last: A Documentary History of Slavery, Freedom, and the Civil War.* New York: New Press, 1992.

———, eds. *Freedom: A Documentary History of Emancipation 1861–1867.* Vol 1., ser. 2, *The Black Military Experience.* Cambridge: Cambridge University Press, 2010.

Bilbly, Joseph. *Civil War Firearms: Their Historical Background and Tactical Use.* Boston: De Capo Press, 1997.

Black, Andrew K. "In the Service of the United States: Comparative Mortality among African American and White Troops in the Union Army." *Journal of Negro History* 79, no. 4 (Autumn 1994): 317–33.

Bollet, Alfred Jay. *Civil War Medicine: Challenges and Triumphs.* Tucson, Ariz.: Galen Press, 2002.

Bonner, Robert. *The Soldier's Pen: Firsthand Impressions of the Civil War.* New York: Hill & Wang, 2007.

Brimmer, Brandi C. "'Her Claim for Pension Is Lawful and Just': Representing Black Union Widows in Late-Nineteenth Century North Carolina." *Journal of the Civil War Era* 1, no. 2 (2011): 207–36.

Bross, John A., and Justine Bross Yildiz. *Letters to Belle: Civil War Letters and Life of Chicago Lawyer and Volunteer Colonel John A. Bross, 29th U.S. Colored Infantry*. Independently Published, 2018.

Browning, Robert M. *Success Is All That Was Expected: The South Atlantic Blockading Squadron*. Washington, D.C.: Potomac Books, 2002.

Bryant, James K. *The 36th Infantry United States Colored Troops in the Civil War: A History and Roster*. Jefferson, N.C.: McFarland, 2012.

Carmichael, Peter S. *The War for the Common Soldier: How Men Thought, Fought, and Survived in Civil War Armies*. Chapel Hill: University of North Carolina Press, 2018.

Cetina, Judith Gladys. "A History of Veterans' Homes in the United States, 1811–1930." PhD diss., Case Western Reserve University, 1977.

Churchman, John W. "The Use of Quinine during the Civil War." *Johns Hopkins Hospital Bullet* 17 (June 1906): 12–13.

Cimprich, John. *Fort Pillow: A Civil War Massacre, and Public Memory*. Baton Rouge: Louisiana State University Press, 2011.

Davies, Wallace E. "The Problem of Race Segregation in the Grand Army of the Republic." *Journal of Southern History* 13, no. 3 (August 1947): 354–72.

Dearing, Mary R. *Veterans in Politics: The Story of the G.A.R.* Baton Rouge: Louisiana State University Press, 1952.

Denison, Frederic. *Shot and Shell: The Third Rhode Island Heavy Artillery Regiment*. Providence, R.I.: For the Third R.I.H. art. vet. Association, by J.A. & R.A. Reid, 1879.

Devine, Shauna. *Learning from the Wounded: The Civil War and the Rise of American Medical Science*. Chapel Hill: University of North Carolina Press, 2014.

Dobak, William A. *Freedom by the Sword: The U.S. Colored Troops 1862–1867*. Army Historical Series. Washington, D.C.: Center of Military History, United States Army, 2011.

Downs, Jim. *Sick From Freedom: African-American Illness and Suffering during the Civil War and Reconstruction*. New York: Oxford University Press, 2012.

Dyer, Frederick H. *A Compendium of the War of the Rebellion*. 3 vols. New York: Thomas Yoseloff, 1959.

Faust, Drew Gilpin. *The Republic of Suffering: Death and the American Civil War*. New York: Knopf, 2008.

Fields, Barbara J. *Slavery and Freedom on the Middle Ground: Maryland during the Nineteenth Century*. Yale Historical Publication Series. New Haven, Conn.: Yale University Press, 1987.

Fleche, Andre M. "'Shoulder to Shoulder as Comrades Tried': Black and White Union Veterans and Civil War Memory." *Civil War History* 51, no. 2 (June 2005): 175–201.

Gallagher, Gary W. *The Confederate War: How Popular Will, Nationalism, and Military Strategy Could Not Stave off Defeat*. Cambridge, Mass.: Harvard University Press, 1997.

Gannon, Barbara A. *The Won Cause: Black and White Comradeship in the Grand Army of the Republic*. Chapel Hill: University of North Carolina Press, 2011.

Glatthaar, Joseph T. *Forged in Battle: The Civil War Alliance of Black Soldiers and White Officers*. New York: Free Press, 1990.

Glover, L.H., ed. *A Twentieth Century History of Cass County, Michigan*. Chicago: Lewis Publishing, 1906.

Gorman, Michael D. "A Conqueror or a Peacemaker? Abraham Lincoln in Richmond." *Virginia Magazine of History and Biography* 123, no. 1 (2015): 2–88.

Gourdin, J. Raymond, ed. *Voices from the Past: 104th Infantry Regiment, USCT, Colored Civil War Soldiers from South Carolina*. Westminster, Md.: Heritage Books, 2007.

Hargrove, Hondon. "Their Greatest Battle was Getting into the Fight: The 1st Michigan Colored Infantry." *Michigan History Magazine* 75, no. 1 (January/February 1991): 24–30.

Hicks, Robert D. "'The Popular Dose with Doctors': Quinine and the American Civil War." *Distillation Magazine*. Fall 2013/Winter 2014. https://www.sciencehistory.org/distillations/magazine/.

Hill, Norman N., comp. *History of Knox County Ohio Its Past and Present* . . . Mt. Vernon, Ohio: A. A. Graham, 1881.

Hudson, Leonne M. "A Confederate Victory at Grahamville: Fighting at Honey Hill." *South Carolina Historical Magazine* 94, no. 1 (January 1993): 19–33.

Humphreys, Margaret. *Intensely Human: The Health of the Black Soldier in the American Civil War*. Baltimore, Md.: Johns Hopkins University Press, 2008.

Jenkins, Wilbert L. *Climbing Up to Glory: A Short History of African Americans during the Civil War and Reconstruction*. Wilmington, Del.: Scholarly Resources, 2002.

Johnson, Edward C., Gail R. Johnson, and Melissa Johnson Williams. *All Were Not Heroes: A Study of the "List of U.S. Soldiers Executed by U.S. Military Authorities during the Late War."* Chicago: E. C. Johnson, 1997.

Kelly, Patrick J. *Creating a National Home: Building the Veterans' Welfare State: 1860–1900*. Cambridge, Mass.: Harvard University Press, 1997.

Lamm, Alan K. "Men of God, Men of War: African American Chaplains in the Civil War." *Curtana Sword of Mercy: A Journal for the Study of the Military Chaplaincy* 3, no. 1 (Fall–Winter 2011): 5–17.

Lankford, Nelson. *Richmond Burning: The Last Days of the Confederate Capital*. New York: Penguin, 2002.

Levine, Bruce. *Confederate Emancipation: Southern Plans to Free and Arm Slaves during the Civil War*. New York: Oxford University Press, 2006.

Logue, Larry M. "Union Veterans and Their Government: The Effects of Public Policies on Private Lives." *Journal of Interdisciplinary History* 22, no. 3 (Winter 1992): 411–34.

Logue, Larry M., and Peter Blanck. "'Benefit of Doubt': African-American Civil War Veterans and Pensions." *Journal of Interdisciplinary History* 38, no. 3 (Winter 2008): 377–99.

Long, Gretchen. *Doctoring Freedom: The Politics of African American Medical Care in Slavery and Emancipation*. Chapel Hill: University of North Carolina Press, 2008.

McRae, Norman. *Negroes in Michigan during the Civil War.* Lansing: Michigan Civil War Centennial Observance Commission, 1966.

Manning, Chandra. *What This Cruel War Was Over: Soldiers, Slavery, and the Civil War.* New York: Knopf, 2007.

McSpadden, Jennifer, ed. *A Leaf of Voices: Stories of the American Civil War in the Words of Those Who Lived and Died, 1861–1865.* Indianapolis: Indiana Historical Society Press, 2014.

Metzer, Jacob. "The Records of the U.S. Colored Troops as a Historical Source: An Exploratory Examination." *Historical Methods* 14, no. 3 (Summer 1981): 123–33.

Miller, Edward A. *Gullah Statesman: Robert Smalls from Slavery to Congress, 1829–1915.* Columbia: University of South Carolina Press, 1995.

—. *The Black Civil War Soldiers of Illinois: The Story of the Twenty-Ninth U.S. Colored Infantry.* Columbia: University of South Carolina Press, 1998.

Mitchell, Robert E. "The Organizational Performance of Michigan's Adjutant General and the Federal Provost Marshal General in Recruiting Michigan's Boys in Blue." *Michigan Historical Review* 28, no. 2 (Fall 2002): 115–62.

Murdock, Eugene C. "New York's Civil War Bounty Brokers." *Journal of American History* 52, no. 2 (September 1966): 259–78.

———. *Patriotism Limited, 1862–1865: The Civil War Draft and the Bounty System.* Kent, Ohio: Kent State University Press, 1967.

Norris, David A. "Forty-Rod, Blue Ruin & Oh Be Joyful: Civil War Alcohol Abuse," Warfare History, September 20, 2015. http://warfarehistorynetwork.com.

Osbon, B. S., comp. *Handbook of the United States Navy: Being a Compilation of All the Principal Events in the History of Every Vessel of the United States Navy from April 1861 to May 1864.* New York: Van Nostrand, 1864.

Paradis, James M. *Strike the Blow for Freedom: The 6th United States Colored Infantry in the Civil War.* Shippensburg, Pa.: White Mane Books, 1998.

Prechtel-Kluskens, Claire. "'A Reasonable Degree of Promptitude': Civil War Pension Application Processing, 1861–1885." *Prologue: Journal of the National Archives* 42, no. 1 (2010): 26–35.

Prince, Bryan. *My Brother's Keeper: African Canadians and the American Civil War.* Toronto: Dundurn, 2015.

Redkey, Edwin S., ed. *A Grand Army of Black Men: Letters from African-American Soldiers in the Union Army, 1861–1865.* New York: Cambridge University Press, 1992.

Regosin, Elizabeth A., and Donald R. Shaffer. *Voices of Emancipation: Understanding Slavery, the Civil War and Reconstruction through the U.S. Pension Bureau Files.* New York: New York University Press, 2008.

Reid, Richard M. *African Canadians in Union Blue: Volunteering for the Cause in the Civil War.* Kent, Ohio: Kent State University Press, 2014.

———. *Freedom for Themselves: North Carolina's Black Soldiers in the Civil War Era.* Chapel Hill: University of North Carolina Press, 2008.

———. "Government Policy, Prejudice, and the Experience of Black Civil War Soldiers and their Families." *Journal of Family History* 27, no. 4 (2002): 374–98.

———, ed. *Practicing Medicine in a Black Regiment: The Civil War Diary of Burt G. Wilder, 55th Massachusetts*. Amherst: University of Massachusetts Press, 2010.

Robertson, John, comp. *Michigan in the War*. Michigan Adjutant General's Office. Rev. ed. Lansing, Mich.: W. S. George, 1882.

Samito, Christian G. "The Intersection between Military Justice and Equal Rights: Mutinies, Courts-martial, and Black Civil War Soldiers." *Civil War History* 53, no. 2 (June 2007): 170–202.

Shaffer, Donald R. *After the Glory: The Struggles of Black Civil War Veterans*. Lawrence: University Press of Kansas, 2004.

———. "Marching On: African-American Civil War Veterans in Postbellum America, 1865–1951." PhD diss., University of Maryland at College Park, 1996.

Skocpol, Theda. "America's First Social Security System: The Expansion of Benefits for Civil War Veterans." *Political Science Quarterly* 108, no. 1 (Spring 1993): 85–116.

Smith, John David, ed. *Black Soldiers in Blue: African American Troops in the Civil War Era*. Chapel Hill: University of North Carolina Press, 2003.

Smith, John Thomas. *A History of the Thirty-First Regiment of Indiana Volunteer Infantry in the War of the Rebellion*. Cincinnati: Published by the Author, 1900.

Smith, Michael O. "Raising a Black Regiment in Michigan: Adversity and Triumph." *Michigan Historical Review* 16, no. 2 (Fall 1990): 23–41.

Smith, Michael Thomas. "The Most Desperate Scoundrels Unhung: Bounty Jumpers and Recruitment Fraud in the Civil War North." *American Nineteenth Century History* 6, no. 2 (June 2005): 149–72.

Spurgeon, Ian Michael. *Soldiers in the Army of Freedom: The 1st Kansas Colored, the Civil War's First African American Combat Unit*. Norman: University of Oklahoma Press, 2014.

Taylor, Paul. *"Old Slow Town": Detroit during the Civil War*. Detroit: Wayne State University Press, 2013.

Trudeau, Noah Andre, ed. *Voices of the 55th: Letters from the 55th Massachusetts Volunteers, 1861–1865*. Dayton, Ohio: Morningside House, 1996.

United States Department of Agriculture. *Usual Planting and Harvesting Dates for U. S. Field Crops*. Agricultural Handbook Number 628. National Agricultural Statistics Service, December 1997.

Warner, Ezra J. *Generals in Blue: Lives of the Union Commanders*. Baton Rouge: Louisiana State University Press, 1964.

———. *Generals in Gray: Lives of the Confederate Commanders*. Baton Rouge: Louisiana State University Press, 1959.

Washington, Versalle F. *Eagles on Their Buttons: A Black Infantry Regiment in the Civil War*. Columbia: University of Missouri Press, 1999.

Wiley, Bell Irvin. *The Life of Billy Yank: The Common Soldier of the Union*. 2nd ed. Baton Rouge: Louisiana State University Press, 1978.

Willis, Deborah. *The Black Civil War Soldier: A Visual History of Conflict and Citizenship*. New York: New York University Press, 2021.

Wilson, Keith P. *Campfires of Freedom: The Camp Life of Black Soldiers during the Civil War*. Kent, Ohio: Kent State University Press, 2002.

Wilson, Sven E. "Prejudice and Policy: Racial Discrimination in the Union Army

Disability Pension System, 1865–1906." *American Journal of Public Health* 100, no. s1, Supplement 1 (September 1, 2010): s59–s65.

Newspapers

Brooklyn Daily Eagle, New York City, New York
Cass County Republican, Dowagiac, Michigan
Christian Recorder, Philadelphia, Pennsylvania
Detroit Advertiser and Tribune, Detroit, Michigan
Detroit Free Press, Detroit, Michigan
Douglass' Monthly, Rochester, New York
Free South, Beaufort, South Carolina
New York Times, New York City, New York
New South, Hilton Head, South Carolina
Palmetto Herald, Port Royal, South Carolina
Weekly Anglo-African, New York City, New York

Archival Sources

Alonzo Reed Letters, David M. Rubenstein Rare Book & Manuscript Library, Duke University.
Book Records of Volunteer Union Organizations, 102nd USCT Infantry, 5 vols., E112–15, RG 94, NARA.
Captain Wilbur Nelson, Company I, 102nd USCT, Diary, 1864–1865, Wilbur Nelson Papers, Michigan State University Archives & Historical Collections.
Civil War Carded Medical Records, boxes 3712–3713, RG 94, NARA.
Civil War Pension Files, RG 15, NARA.
Civil War Regimental Casualty Lists, 102nd USCT, E 652, box 75, RG 94, NARA.
Compiled Military Service Records, RG 94, NARA.
Consolidated Correspondence, Records of the Office of the Quartermaster General, 1774–1985, RG 92, NARA.
Court-Martial Case Files, Records of the Office of the Judge Advocate General (Army), RG 153, NARA.
First Michigan Colored Infantry: History of Officers, Records of the Michigan Military Establishment, RG 59-14, folder 12, oversize box (ovs) 80, Archives of Michigan, Lansing.
First Michigan Colored Infantry: Monthly Returns, 1864–1865, Records of the Michigan Military Establishment, RG 59-14, folders 4–5, ovs 80, Archives of Michigan, Lansing.
First Michigan Colored Infantry: Muster-In Rolls, Records of the Michigan Military Establishment, RG 59-14, folders 1–3, ovs 80, Archives of Michigan, Lansing.
First Michigan Colored Infantry: Muster-Out Rolls, Records of the Michigan Military Establishment, RG 59-14, folders 6–11, ovs 80, Archives of Michigan, Lansing.

Letters Received. Ser. 360, Records of the Adjutant General's Office, 1780s–1917. Colored Troops Division, RG 94, NARA.

Letters Received by the Adjutant General, Main Series, 1861–1870, m619, Roll 0321, RG 94, NARA.

Private William P. Woodlin, Co. G, 8th USCT, Diary, The Gilder Lehrman Institute of American History.

New York State Census, 1845–1875.

Record of Events, Records of the Adjutant General's Office, 1780s–1917, RG 94, m594, 225 reels, NARA.

United States Federal Census, 1860–1940.

U.S. War Department. *Official Records of the Union and Confederate Navies in the War of the Rebellion*. 30 vols. Washington, D.C.: Government Printing Office, 1894–1922.

———. *The War of the Rebellion: A Compilation of the Official Records of the Union and Confederate Armies*. 128 vols. Washington, D.C.: Government Printing Office, 1880–1902.

Index

Page numbers in italics refer to images.

abolition and abolitionists, 6, 8, 58n70; newspapers, 11–12
Adams, Albert G., 6–7, 29, 46, 50n41, 129n38; birth and death, 46n23, 52
Albert, Amos, 129n39
alcohol, 54, 79–80, 83
Allen family (George and Mahetable), 123n14
Alvord, Henry H., 97, 109n33
Ames, William, 96, 107n27
Anderson, John, 9
Anderson, Robert, 133n50
Andrew, John, 8, 22n47
Annapolis, Md., 22, 41–42; Murray's letters from, 46–51; Ninth Army Corps at, 47nn27–28
Appleton, George, 112n43, 114n45
Appomattox Campaign, 1, 57n66, 132n45
artillery ammunition, 95n51, 96–97, 97n3, 118. *See also* Canister and Grapeshot; gun boats; rifles
artillery units. *See* Third Rhode Island Heavy Artillery
Ashepoo River, 57n67, 118
Atlanta, Ga., 84n18, 86, 102n15, 111n41

Baker, Wallace, 59n75
Balding Station (Fla.), 74, 75–76, 84
Baldwin, Fla., 1, 63, 76n51, 76n53
Baltimore, Md., 41, 46, 50, 51
Barnes, Henry, 41, 49, 54n58, 85n19; battalion drills, 49n37; Murray's comments on, 30, 53, 56, 99n10; recruitment efforts, 8–9, 22, 26–27
barracks, 9–10
Battery Burnside, S.C., 62, 67n20, 68, 86n24
Battery Taylor, S.C., 67n20, 68, 86n24
Batts, Andrew, 112n43, 120n7

Baza, James, 112n43
Beaufort, S.C., 10, 102, 107n27, 111, 124; gun batteries, 67n20; hospital, 110n40, 113, 116, 120, 121; Murray's letters from, 58–61, 64–73, 89, 98; 102nd USCT deployment to, 18, 30, 42–43, 78, 79, 81n8, 103n19, 118; regiments stationed at, 58n71, 59n72, 60, 62, 86n24
Beauregard, P. G. T., 119, 125n24
Benham, H. D., 69n25
Bennett, Orson W., 32n86, 97
Bennett, William True, 27, 44n14, 46, 49, 51, 54, 66n13; background, 46n21; at Hilton Head, 70
Birney, William, 57
Blackman, Wesley, 81n8
Black soldiers, 15–16, 36, 49n35, 58n70, 71n35, 132; bounties and bonds, 26–29; emancipation and, 8, 11; health and illness, 18, 20, 92n41; literacy and letter writing, 11–12, 15, 128n34; mistreatment of, 64n9, 74n46; Murray's comments on, 112–13; pay inequality, 21–25; relations with White soldiers, 29–31, 54, 85n20, 103; state regiments, 42n5, 71n35; stationed at Beaufort, 58n71, 59; voting rights, 102n16
Blair, Austin, 8, 21, 53n55, 72n37, 85n19, 87, 88
Blake, William, 81
boats. *See* gun boats; steamers
bonds, 26–27
boredom, 79, 80
bounty money, 8, 25–29, 53, 67, 85, 133; deserters and, 46
Bradbury, Sherrard, 46n20
bridges, destruction of, 60, 76, 99–100, 116; between Charleston and Savannah, 57n67, 61, 64–65, 67n17, 70, 109, 113–14
Broadhead (Brodhead), Jane, 122n11
Bromley, William, 73, 90

Brown, John, 10
Buffalo Express, 98n5, 101, 113
Bullard, Augustus, 80
Burnside, Ambrose, 41, 47, 50, 51, 64n8
Butler, Benjamin, 112

Calloway, Creed, 79–80
Campbell, William, 28
Camp Chandler, Md., 42, 48, 49n37
Camp Ward, Mich., 9–10, 22, 27, 28, 45n16, 49n35; deserters, 46n20; flag presentation ceremony, 44n14
Canister and Grapeshot, 55, 65, 75, 109n33, 122
Charleston, S.C., 66, 70; burning of, 72, 94, 125; fall to Union forces, 42n4, 95n51, 117n48, 119, 125n24; Murray's hospitalization and death in, 1, 3, 34, 125n23; Murray's letter from, 125–26; 102nd USCT advancement to, 87, 118–19; Sherman's advancement to, 96, 102, 117
Charleston and Savannah Railroad, 65n10, 120n6; expedition objective, 57n67, 67n17, 97, 107n28
Charleston Neck, S.C., 35, 119
Chipman, Henry L., 30, 34, 70, 87, 88, 99n10, 107n27; arrest, 59; background, 54n58; concerns about rifles, 68n23; Honey Hill expedition, 96, 97n3, 109n33; leave of absence, 83n14; Savannah expedition, 119
citizenship rights, 24–25, 36, 58n70, 85. *See also* voting rights
Clark, Nelson, 83n14, 118, 119
class discrimination, 2
Coastal Division, 107n28, 118
Colcock, Charles, 109n34, 109n36
Confederates, 36, 49n36, 92n42, 96, 105n25, 109n36; capture of Fort Pillow, 74n46; casualties, 110n39; Charleston and Savannah sieges, 94n47, 95n51, 106, 109, 118–19, 125n24; evacuation of Atlanta, 84n18, 111n41; evacuation of Milledgeville, 102n15; fall of Richmond, 33, 56n62, 130, 132; at Ladies Island, 80–81, 87n26; prisoners, 60, 74, 81, 89; skirmish at Cuckhold Creek, 118; skirmishes in Florida, 62–63, 62n2, 76n51, 87n29; soldiers, 31, 35, 57n67; treatment of Union soldiers, 65n9, 74n46; unofficial truces, 90n40. *See also* names of battles
"contrabands," 32–33, 66–67, 76n53, 78, 86, 92–93; right to vote, 102; term usage, 32n84, 52n48
Coosa (Coosaw, Coo Saw) Island, S.C., 79, 82n11, 118; Murray's letters from (September–October, 1864), 81–90, *91*, 92–95; Murray's letters from (November–December, 1864), 99–110, 112–14, *115*, 116–17; Murray's letters from (January–March, 1865), 120–25
courts-martial, 23, 79–80, 92n41
Crain, Lucinda ("Lue"), 6–7, 43–44, 56, 60, 88, 129; family, 123n13, 128n36, 129n39; Murray's letters to, 43n12, 50, 58, 85n22, 114, 121
Curtis, James B. F., 19n41

Dahlgren, J. A., 105n23
Davis, Charles, 27
Davis, Jefferson, 105, 130
Davis, Nathan, 112n43
Davis, O. A., 87n27
Degraff (Degroff, Degraugh), Elias, 7, 73n42, 90n39, 104n21, 116
deserters, 28, 33, 45n16, 46, 86n25, 92; execution of, 52
Detroit, Mich., 8, 9, 36, 48–49; Murray's letters from, 43–46; population (1860), 49n35; Wayne and Lenawee counties, 26, 27, 28
Detroit Advertiser and Tribune, 8, 13, 27, 36, 68n23
Detroit Colored Ladies' Soldiers' Aid Society, 44n14
Detroit Free Press, 26–27, 36, 56n63
Deveaux Neck, battle of, 10, 20, 118, 120n5; wounds and casualties, 97–98, 98n4, 112n43, 114, 114n45, 120n7
Dickinson, John Jackson, 77, 82, 87n29
disease. *See* illness
Dockhrity, Charles, 73
Douglass, Frederick, 58n70
dress parade, 48
drills, 16, 49, 53, 58n71, 59, 79, 96; at Beaufort, 62, 64; daily schedules, 49n37

earthworks, 96
Edinburgh, N.Y., 5
Edisto River, 57n67, 67n17, 118

Eighth USCT, 76n52
election (1864), 33, 101, 102–3
emancipation, 6, 8, 11, 12–13, 104
Emancipation Proclamation, 76n53, 104n22
enlistment, 48n29, 69n24; of Black soldiers, 16, 21, 42nn5–6, 58n70, 77n53, 105; bounty money and, 25–28, 46; from Canada, 46n20; of enslaved persons, 105n25; literacy and, 17; Murray's, 7–8; pay and, 21–23, 25; terms, 89n34, 93
Enrollment Act (1863), 25
enslaved refugees, 32–33, 52n48, 67n21, 76n53, 93n43, 118
enslavement, 16, 20, 104n22, 105n25
Ester, James, 27
executions, 23, 52n50, 59n75, 65n9, 89n33

Fifty-Fifth Massachusetts Colored Infantry Regiment, 7, 59n75, 60, 107n28, 119; casualties, 109n35; letters from, 11, 65n9, 71n35; protest over pay inequity, 23n49
Fifty-Fourth Massachusetts Colored Infantry Regiment, 7, 23, 61n80, 107n28, 111, 112; attack on Fort Wagner, 64n9; battle of Olustee, 62n2; casualties, 109n35
Fifty-Sixth New York Infantry, 59, 60, 64n7, 97
financial difficulties, 14, 21, 24, 26, 95n50, 129, 133
fires, 57n67, 109n34, 113, 117, 131n42; Charleston, 94n47, 125n24
First Michigan Colored Infantry, 47n26, 48n34, 49n36, 53n53; at Camp Ward, 9–10, 49n35; enlistment and recruitment, 7–9, 26, 48n29, 69n24, 89n34; flag presentation ceremony, 44n14; redesignation, 1n1, 42, 58, 67; unequal pay and, 21–25. *See also* 102nd United States Colored Troops
First South Carolina Colored Regiment, 74n44. *See also* Thirty-Third USCT
Florida, 84, 87n29, 100; Murray's letters from, 74–78; 102nd USCT deployment to, 62–63, 86n24; rattle snakes, 82
Floyd, London, 77n3
food, 20, 47, 50, 54, 73; fresh produce, 60, 61, 65, 78, 101; hunting, 76; prices, 99; rations, 73n43, 100, 120
Forrest, Nathan Bedford, 65n9, 74n46

Fort Burnside, S.C., 62, 67n20, 68, 86n24
Fort Pillow, Tenn., 65n9, 74
Fort Sumter, S.C., 133
Fort Taylor, S.C., 67n20, 68, 86n24
Fort Wayne, Mich., 9n20, 10n23
Foster, John Gray, 58n71, 64, 82n10, 87–88, 110n39; background, 64n8; Savannah and Charleston expedition, 67n17, 96–98, 106n27, 107n30, 109n36, 120n5
Fourth Massachusetts Cavalry, 77n55
Frank Leslie's Illustrated Newspaper, 54
freedom, 15–16, 76n53, 93n43, 104
Freeman, George G., 24
furloughs, 44n13

Gainesville, Fla., 77n55
Georgetown, S.C., 119
German population, 49n35
Gilmore, Quincy Adams, 42, 47n26
Gooding, James Henry, 11
grand rounds, 69
Grant, Ulysses S., 51, 56n62, 130n41
Grapeshot. *See* Canister and Grapeshot
Gray, John, 110n40
guard duty, 20, 35, 51, 57, 60, 89; at Beaufort, 62, 69–70, 72; on Coosa Island, 79, 84; falling asleep on, 79, 92n41
gun boats, 61, 86, 87, 90, 105, 109; at Hilton Head, 52, 53, 56, 57; *John Adams*, 92, 94, 103, 105n24; *Pawnee*, 105n24, 114n44; *Thomas Walker*, 89; *Wabash*, 124n20
guns. *See* rifles

Hall, James, 61
Hardee, Nelson, 80
Hartwell, Alfred, 107n27
Hatch, John P., 57n67, 76n53, 77nn54–55, 107n28, 110n39
Hawley, Lucinda (daughter), 123n13, 129n39, 133n49
Hawley, Lyman and Rheuma, 123n13, 125, 129n39
Hell Gate, S.C., 100
Henson, James, 79, 92n41
Hilton Head, S.C., 42, 58n71, 67n17, 70; marching orders to, 48n33, 73n41; Murray's letters from, 31, 52–54, 55–58
Hollenbauch (Hollenbeck, Hollenback), Lanson, 122n11

146

INDEX

Hollenbeck, Richard, 128–29, 131–32
Hollenbeck, Rosana, 123n14
Honey Hill, battle of, 10, 20, 30, 90n38, 109n34; medals awarded, 97n3; objective and commanding officers, 96–97; wounds and casualties, 97, 109n33, 110nn38–40, 120n7
Hood, John B., 84n18
horses, 48, 76n53, 77, 78; killed in battle, 57n67, 61, 96, 130n42
hospitals: Beaufort, 18, 110n40, 113, 116, 120, 121; Charleston, 1, 34; DeCamp (New York Harbor), 121n9, 123; duty, 19, 51; letter writing from, 128n34; Murray's resistance and admission to, 1, 20, 34, 101, 123n16, 126n28; New Orleans, 132n48
Howard, Oliver O., 120n6
Humphreys, Margaret, 19, 20
Hunt, Washington, 29, 129n38

illness: common treatments for, 108n32; dropsy and anasarca, 34, 125n23, 128; from exposure, 9–10; feigning, 92n41; malaria, 17n36, 34, 83n15; Murray's recurring, 21, 52, 88, 89, 93, 100–101, 106–8; in 102nd USCT, 18, 59, 65, 82n10, 88n31, 90n37; Sarah Wells's, 14, 126, 128, 133; typhoid pneumonia, 120n7
income. *See* pay inequality
insects, 125
inspections, 53, 68n23, 72, 79, 87, 102
Irish population, 49n35
Isham, Festus, 123n13

Jacksonville, Fla., 62n2, 63, 75, 75n47, 77n55
James River, 130n42, 132n45
Jennings, Edward, 18n4, 19n44
Jewett, Edward, 81n8
Johnson, Alexander, 120n7
Johnson, Isaac, 110n40
Johnson, Thomas, 80
Johnson's Island, Ohio, 89
Johnston, Joseph, 35

laborers, 16, 23, 24, 32, 79
Lady (Ladies, Lady's) Island, S.C., 80–81, 83, 87n26, 111
Lake Shore and Michigan Southern Railway, 50n38
landownership, 8, 29, 105, 129n38

Lee, Robert E., 1, 105n25, 130
letter writing, significance of, 4–5, 10–12, 15, 17n35, 126n28, 128n34
Leverton, Chancy, 73
Lincoln, Abraham, 1, 130n42
Lindsay, A. E., 96–97, 110n40
literacy, 7, 11, 17, 128n34
Lockport, N.Y., 1, 6, 7, 12, 29, 90; Sarah Wells's letters from, 126–33
Lockport Journal, 98n5, 101, 113
Loveland, Emily, 50n40, 56, 128

Madry, Jesse, 80, 97
Magnolia, Fla., 63, 75n47, 76n53, 77n54, 78, 81n7
malaria, 17n36, 34; quinine and, 83n15
Marshall, Joseph, 110n40, 120n7
Maryland, 104; Baltimore, 41, 46, 50, 51. *See also* Annapolis, Md.
Mason, William, 126n6
McClellan, George B., 102–3
McKendrie, Edward, 24, 34, 53n51, 87–88, 87n27; background, 54n58; Murray's opinion of, 30, 99n10; reports of illness, 90n37, 92n41
McPherson, James, 11
medical care, 18–20, 110n40. *See also* hospitals
mercury poisoning, 108n32
Merrill, A. S., 70n28
Michigan, 7, 26, 53n55, 68, 71, 84; voting rights, 72n37, 85n19
Militia Act (1862), 22–23
Milledgeville, Ga., 102n15
Miller, Thomas, 77n53
money: bounty, 8, 25–29, 49, 85n21, 133; sending home, 15, 21, 43–44, 51, 59, 61, 82, 85, 95, 102, 123
Montague, C. S., 96, 107n28
Morgan, Joseph, 110n38
Morgan Island, S.C., 82
Morris Island, S.C., 61, 84n17, 92n42
Murray, Alonzo (birth father), 6, 123n15. *See also* Wells, Asher
Murray, Catharine (no relation), 3
Murray, John Lovejoy: arrest for desertion, 45n16; attitude toward southerners, 16–17, 31–33, 67n18, 67n21, 74n44, 99; birth date, 5–6; bounty concerns, 27–29, 85; at Charleston city, 125–26; comments on race relations, 29–31, 54, 55, 85, 99; Crain family connection, 6–7,

43n12; criticism of enslaved refugees, 32–33, 92–93; death, 1, 10, 17–18, 34–35, 126n28, 127n30; enlistment and training, 7–10, 27, 43–46, 58n68, 129n38; extant images, 85n22; hope for promotion, 43; hospital duty, 51; interest in politics, 33–34, 101, 102; pay concerns, 21–25, 48, 52–53, 67, 68–70, 81–82, 84, 95, 123; penmanship and grammar, 17, 38, 48n32; recurring illnesses, 21, 52, 88, 89, 93, 100–101, 106–8, 125n23; resentment of pacifists, 122; scope of correspondence, 12–16, 20–21, 37, 126–27nn28–29

National Archives and Records Administration (NARA), 1
Nelson, Wilbur, 24, 51n44, 76n53, 90n40, 106n27, 118n1, 124n19; comments about weather, 66n12, 75n49; concerns about rifles, 68n23, 73n40; description of Sherman's troops, 124n18; Grant's victory and, 56n62; notes on Seventeen Corps, 120n6, 123n12, 124n17; payroll duties, 95n49
New England states, 42n5, 85n19
newspapers, 8, 11, 13, 33, 49n35, 98n5, 101
New York, 6, 35–36, 41, 68; DeCamp hospital (David's Island), 121n9
Niagara County, N.Y., 6, 29, 128n35
Ninth Army Corps, 41, 47nn26–28, 48n34
Ninth USCT ("Mayrland 9"), 59, 60n79, 64n7, 66, 70, 73n41, 76n52; at Camp Stanton, 59n72; overview of, 57n67
Noble, William, 76n53

occupation duties, 10, 119
Ohio, 41, 89n35
Olustee, battle of, 62, 65n9
102nd United States Colored Troops (102nd USCT), 13, 37, 40, 73n41, 85n19, 105n26; backgrounds of soldiers, 16; at Beaufort, 18, 41–43, 58–59, 58n71, 62, 86; Charleston and Savannah expeditions, 57n67, 67n17, 97, 107n28, 113–14, 116–17, 118–19; commanders, 54n58, 69n25, 76n53, 83n14, 87nn28–29, 96; deployment to Florida, 62–63, 77n55; duties, 33, 35, 96–98, 118–19; enlistment papers, 17; homecoming and disbandment, 35–36; incident at Ladies Island, 80–81; new recruits, 84n16,

93, 94–95, 103; original designation and renaming, 1n1, 58, 59, 67; pension applications and files, 2n4, 3nn7–8; physicians, 18–19; race relations, 30–31; sickness and deaths, 17–18, 65, 82n10, 88n31, 89–90, 90n37; wounds and casualties, 65n9, 110n38, 110n40, 112n43, 120n7, 126. *See also* First Michigan Colored Infantry
127th USCT, 131, 132n45
opium, 108n32

pay inequality, 12, 21–25, 48–49, 67n19, 69–70
payroll muster, 24, 45, 95, 117n47, 123n16; refusal to sign, 52–53
Peace Democrats or Copperheads, 122n10
pensions: applications and success rates, 2n4, 3n5; files and contents, 3nn7–8, 13; Sarah Wells's claim, 1–3, 4, 45n16, 129n38
Philadelphia Navy Yard, 114n44, 124n20
photographs, 11, 85n22
physicians, 18–20, 110n40
picket duty, 10, 20, 42, 63, 67n18, 74, 98; at Beaufort, 59, 60, 66; at Charleston Neck, 119; at Coosa Island, 79, 81–82, 86, 87, 90, 103, 117; deserters and, 86n25; exchange of goods during, 90n40; at Hilton Head, 52, 53, 55; at Ladies Island, 80–81, 83, 87n26, 111; at Savannah, 119, 124
Pocotaligo (Pocotaliga), S.C., 96, 106n27, 107n28, 111, 116, 124n19
Porter, William, 83n13
Port Royal Island, S.C., 79, 92n42, 96, 98, 118
postal services, 4–5, 72, 84, 116, 122; stamps, 71, 81, 86, 93, 101, 114, 127n31, 133
Potter, Edward E., 35, 107n28, 109n34
Powers, Volney, 96
prisoners of war, 83n13, 124, 130; camps, 89n35; Confederate (rebels), 60, 74, 81, 89; executions, 57, 65n9, 74n46, 89n33
protests, 21, 23, 25
punishment, 121

quinine, 83–84, 93, 108; side effects, 93n45

race relations, 2, 29–31, 54, 55, 60, 66n13, 85; health and illness and, 20, 92n41. *See also* voting rights

railroads. *See* Charleston and Savannah Railroad; train travel
rations, 73n43, 75, 83, 100, 120
recruitment, 17n36, 84; Barnes's efforts at, 8–9, 26–27; bounties and, 25–28, 46n22; of enslaved refugees, 33, 67n21; pay equity and, 21–22; of physicians, 19
Redkey, Edwin, 11
Reed, Alonzo, 3n8, 102n16, 124n18, 125n24, 128n34
refugee soldiers. *See* enslaved refugees
Richmond, Va., 33, 48, 56, 56n62, 130, 132; Lincoln's tour of, 130n42
rifles, 49, 55n61, 63, 64, 68, 72; cleaning, 88; inspections, 68n23; models, 49n36; poor quality of, 73nn39–40
rumors, 53, 56nn62–63, 89n34, 94n47, 100n11, 107n30; prevalence of, 33, 44n15, 71n35, 93n44

Sasser, Robert, 16
Savannah, Ga., 100n12, 107, 111, 121; 102nd USCT deployment to, 107n30, 119, 124; Sherman's army in, 111n41, 113, 116–17, 119n2. *See also* Charleston and Savannah Railroad
Saxton, Rufus, 42, 64n7, 96, 107n28
Schumaker, Henry, 52n50
scouting parties, 33, 76n53, 77n54, 86, 111n41
Second South Carolina Colored Infantry Regiment, 60n79, 66, 70, 74n44. *See also* Thirty-Fourth USCT
Seventeen Corps, 120n6, 123n12, 124n17
Seventy-Fifth Ohio, 77n55
Shelley, Chester F., 6, 29, 129n38
Sherman, William T., 35, 96, 97, 100n11, 105, 110, 121; advance to Charleston, 102, 106, 119; capture of Atlanta, 84n18; capture of Savannah, 111n41, 113, 116–17, 119n2; at Coosa River, 24n19, 123n12, 124n17; troops, 124n18
Simons, James, 10
Sixteenth Michigan Volunteer Infantry, 87n27
Smalls, Robert, 119n2
Smith, Gustavus, 96
soldierly misconduct, 79–80, 121n8
Southworth, George, 96
Spence, Ambrose, 10
Spiers, William, 18n40, 19
spirituality, 14, 127n30

Spotsylvania Court House, 56n62
Stanton, Edwin, 8, 21, 22n47, 26
Stark, Henry, 52n50
steamers, 47, 118; *Boston*, 57n67; *Cannonicus*, 63; *Cleveland City*, 36; *Cosmopolitan*, 110n40; *General J. K. Barnes*, 121n9; *Georgia*, 41; *Malvern*, 130n42; *Planter*, 119n2; *Wyoming*, 63. *See also* gun boats
St. Johns River, 63, 75, 77n54, 82
Stoneburner, George, 69n25
Strother, David, 110n40
Sullivan, W. H., 45n16
surgeons, 18–20, 110n40

theft, 81
Theuston, John, 112n43
Third New York Artillery, 96, 107n28
Third Rhode Island Heavy Artillery, 55n60, 76n53, 77n55, 96, 107n28
Third South Carolina Volunteer Infantry Regiment, 23
Thirty-Fifth USCT, 62n2, 63, 76n53, 107n28
Thirty-Fourth USCT, 64n7, 66n13, 73n41, 76n51, 76n53, 107n27; deployment to Florida, 62, 63
Thirty-Third USCT, 46n21, 66n13, 70n31, 74n44, 119
Thompson, Catharine (Murray's grandmother), 45n17, 46, 60, 133n49
Thompson, Ezekiel, 110n40
trade, items of, 90
train travel, 35–36, 41, 50, 130n41
Trudeau, Noah, 11
Tuttle, Johnathan B., 50
Twenty-Ninth Connecticut Colored Infantry, 47n25, 48n33, 59n72, 60n79, 62; Elias Degraff of, 7, 73n42, 90n39, 104n21
Twenty-Sixth USCT, 47n25, 48n33, 60n79, 73n41, 107n28; at Beaufort, 59n72, 60, 62, 64n7, 86n24

Uncle Sam, 24, 43, 58, 60, 73, 82, 84, 103; "Iron Rod," 95; "Packet Peices," 52; "Pills," 64, 81
uniforms, 34, 48n30, 48n32, 49n35, 83; hats, 58n70, 59; knapsacks, 74n45
Union army, 21, 32n84, 35, 57n66, 62n2, 65n9; Black enlistment, 8, 11, 16, 46n20; bombardment of Charleston city, 42n4, 94, 95n51, 119, 125n24; DeCamp

hospital, 121n9; Dickinson's cavalry and, 77nn54–55, 87n29; gun batteries, 67n20; occupation of Richmond, 33, 56n62, 130, 132; rifles, 49n36; unofficial truces, 90n40. *See also names of battles*

U.S. Congress, 25, 52, 69, 85n20; Act of 1866, 29, 69

U.S. Pension Bureau, 1, 2, 3n5, 3n7, 4n9. *See also* pensions

U.S. War Department, 9n20, 23, 42n5

Van Buren, Jane Ann ("Aunt Jane"), 122n11, 123n15, 127, 129n39, 131, 133

veterans, 2, 3n7

Vincent, Wesley, 17, 18n40, 19, 34

voting rights, 8, 72n37, 85n19, 102

Wade, John, 110n40

Walker, William, 23

Waring, William, 13, 28, 44n14, 63, 90n37, 124n18

Washington, William H., 79–80

Wattson, Martha, 50, 52, 56, 61n80, 112, 114

weather, 41–42, 43, 53, 126; cold at Camp Ward, 9–10, 10n23; on Coosa Island, 88, 94, 99, 103, 104, 109–10, 113, 120, 121, 122; Florida heat, 75, 76, 84; rain at Camp Chandler, 46–48, 50, 51; South Carolina heat, 17, 65–66; winter in Lockport, 129, 133

Weekly Anglo-African, 11, 71n35, 124n18

Wells, Asher (Murray's stepfather), 6, 21, 29, 123n15, 129n38; letters from son, 45–46, 56–58, 60, 64

Wells, Sarah (Murray's mother), 122n11; birth and marriage, 6; bounty money, 29; letters to son, 13–15, 20, 123n15, 126–33; pension claim, 1–3, 4, 45n16; work, 29, 56

West Point, 42n4, 42n6, 54n58, 64n8

wheat harvest, 57–58, 58n68, 65

White, Philip, 110n40

White soldiers, 16, 18, 59n72, 60, 92n41, 99; health care and physicians, 19–20; letters written by, 11, 15; pay, 21, 22, 25; relations with Black soldiers, 29–31, 54, 85n20, 103

Wiley, Bell Irvin, 10

Willis, Deborah, 11

Willis, John, 70n28

Windsor, Ont., 28, 46

Winslow, Oliver, 79, 92n41

winter huts or shanties, 82, 120, 126

Woodlin, William P., 56n62, 93n45

wounds, 13, 35, 36, 67n17, 111; deaths from, 65n9, 74n46, 120n7; Deveaux Neck battle and, 98n4, 112n43, 114, 114n45, 116, 120n7; Honey Hill battle and, 97, 109n33, 110nn38–40; treatment for, 108n32, 110n38, 110n40

Wright Sound, S.C., 98, 100n12, 105

Yeager, T. D., 1, 3, 4, 4n9

NEW PERSPECTIVES ON THE CIVIL WAR ERA

*Practical Strangers: The Courtship Correspondence of
Nathaniel Dawson and Elodie Todd, Sister of Mary Todd Lincoln*
EDITED BY STEPHEN BERRY AND ANGELA ESCO ELDER

*The Greatest Trials I Ever Had:
The Civil War Letters of Margaret and Thomas Cahill*
EDITED BY RYAN W. KEATING

*Prison Pens: Gender, Memory, and Imprisonment in the
Writings of Mollie Scollay and Wash Nelson, 1863–1866*
EDITED BY TIMOTHY J. WILLIAMS AND EVAN A. KUTZLER

*William Gregg's Civil War: The Battle to
Shape the History of Guerrilla Warfare*
EDITED AND ANNOTATED BY JOSEPH M. BEILEIN JR.

*Seen/Unseen: Hidden Lives in a
Community of Enslaved Georgians*
EDITED BY CHRISTOPHER R. LAWTON,
LAURA E. NELSON, RANDY L. REID

*Radical Relationships: The Civil War–Era
Correspondence of Mathilde Franziska Anneke*
TRANSLATED BY VICTORIJA BILIC
EDITED BY ALISON CLARK EFFORD AND VIKTORIJA BILIC

*Private No More: The Civil War Letters of
John Lovejoy Murray, 102nd United States Colored Infantry*
EDITED BY SHARON A. ROGER HEPBURN

Heartsick and Astonished: Divorce in Civil War–Era West Virginia
EDITED BY ALLISON DOROTHY FREDETTE

www.ingramcontent.com/pod-product-compliance
Lightning Source LLC
Chambersburg PA
CBHW011232160426
43202CB00021B/2983